Van's Memories

Volume 1 of 2

D1709706

By

Urbanes Van Bemden

Van's Memories — ...... from work and play
Volume 1 of 2
Author: Urbanes Van Bemden

The best things in life are the people we love,

the places we've been,

and the memories we've made along the way. -Anon

Dedicated to

my son Jeff, and daughter-in-law Karen,

for always being there for me,

my grandkids and great grandkids for bringing me much joy,

my brothers and sisters—all 12 of them,

my friends I've made along the way,

and my wife, Brenda, the love of my life.

Acknowledgments

Many people have influenced my life—family, friends, co-workers—and I wish I could thank each one here. I will name a few, hoping they will understand my gratitude.

- My Dad and Mother for immigrating to America
- Dr. Foley at Letourneau for suggesting that I write a paper on Numerical Control which I didn't know anything about
- Dick Fisher at Sundstrand Machine Tool in Belvidere, IL for offering me a position in the NC Programming Department upon graduation
- Chuck Hutchins for offering me a job as an Application Engineer at Comshare in Ann Arbor, MI
- Ken Stephanz for inviting me to become a founding member of MDSI
- Steve Imredy, VP of the International Division, for asking me to become part of his team
- Jack Clausnitzer at Brighton NC for hiring me when I was terminated at MDSI/Applicon
- Gary Zimmerman from LIAIM for allowing me to design his orphanage in Bolivia
- Jeff Sannes for supplying me with a free copy of Autodesk Architectural Desktop 2007 (a $5K software package) that I used to design the orphanages for various non-profit organizations
- Sara Hill for helping me install Architectural Desktop on my computer and countless hours helping me learn this new software package (the support manuals are 2100+ pages)
- Ted Locke for donating an HP Designjet 800 42 inch Roll Printer to print my blueprints for the various non-profit mission organizations that I volunteered to do design work for
- Lars Dunberg for asking me to help him in designing "The India Hope Center" Orphanage in Motipur, India. It was a great experience
- Lee Horsman for helping me tremendously in the formatting of my book and guidance as to what is involved in writing and publishing a book
- Rod Porter for inviting me to ski in Aspen and introducing me to Paul Wagner and John Kwiatkowski (Big John) and for inviting me to become part of the Aspen Ski team
- Chuck Ferrari, Ray Butler, Jerry Funk and John Reynolds for hiking the Colorado 14ers with me
- My wife Brenda for putting up with me when I was down in my office and she was wondering when I would come up to eat, watch the news and be sociable

Thank you all for your unwavering support, encouragement and friendship. Your contributions have been invaluable to me and have helped me achieve my goals.

FOREWORD

To share Van's personal experiences from boyhood escapades in the Netherlands, to his antics aboard the ship to America, to his family's arrival and life-changing experiences as dad, mom, Van and twelve siblings adapted to American culture, to his amazing educational journey at LeTourneau, to his key participation in successfully building a company enjoying the worldwide premier position in numeric control applications, reading and digesting Van's memories will take you on a global trek that will surprise and inspire you.

Imagining the experience of Nazi occupation of his hometown with its enforcement of forced labor (including Van's father's compulsory engagement in the construction of Nazi coastal bunkers), followed by real-life experiences of his family's immigration from post-WWII Netherlands to be immersed in a new culture, succeeding at miraculous levels articulated in *Van's Memories*, is as educational and informative as it is incomparably fascinating.

Vicariously visiting, enjoying, and being entranced by this chronicle of adventure, romance, and historically significant intersections to which we all owe so much, is a pleasure difficult to adequately describe. Example? Identifying errors in program codes by watching the application in action, writing corrective code and physically delivering it for installation! This responsibility often required midnight oil followed by lengthy auto trips to manually install new programs in factories far removed from mainframe access. Remote file sharing we take for granted today was ignited by these primitive CAM methods and it is not an exaggeration to recognize them as the driving force from which modern technologies emerged. Van's pioneering efforts in this field are recorded in this story!

Eschewing the rigors of proper grammar, the flavor of Van's written narrative expressed in colorful, albeit less than grammatically correct prose, delivers an easily imagined sense of "being there"—seeing, hearing, touching and yes, even smelling, the story of the moment. Pungency in different forms laces the boyhood antics, highs and lows of family events, hobbies from hot "muscle" cars to water sports, snow skiing (at this writing Van still challenges the slopes of Colorado's highest ski resorts), and impressively articulates the value of faith-based friendships and extended relationships.

In candid (occasionally disturbing) descriptions, Van has recorded his memories for his descendants; however, this writer, genetically unrelated, attests to the book as a wondrously entertaining, educational and inspiring autobiography of an unusually talented and marvelously enlightening friend, Urbanes Van Bemden ... we just call him Van.

Lee Horsman

Table of Contents

Preface

As I reflect back on my life, I find God has blessed me more than I could have ever dreamed. I would like to share my memories with my family and friends, since I feel it has been an amazing and interesting journey. I actually started writing **Van's Memories** more than 20 years ago and got all the way through my high school days (some 45 pages). Then I laid it to rest for about 15-20 years and only picked it up a few years ago and really started working on it about 1 year ago. It is now documented with over 3200 photos and over 800 pages, taking me thru the year 2023. One of the biggest regrets I have is not spending more time with my parents gathering family history before they passed on. Upon the death of my Mother, I was handed a couple of shoe boxes full of family photos and most had no information as to who, what, when, and where on the back. This was especially true regarding my Dad's side of the family.

My journey began in war torn Europe, and thankfully our family survived and left The Netherlands, with its tulip-strewn fields and windmills.

Grand Rapids, Michigan welcomed us. We were legal immigrants fortunate to be sponsored by an uncle.

LeTourneau University in Texas became my salvation, providing me with an education I had not thought possible. There, among the hum of machines as I worked my way thru school, I discovered my passion: **Computer Aided Design and Computer Aided Manufacturing (CAD/CAM)**.

In the university town of **Ann Arbor, Michigan**, I helped birth a software company. The **International Division** became my playground, and I, an international traveler, thoroughly enjoyed it. My business travels took me to Europe, Scandinavia, Asia, and Australia.

At age **58**, unplanned, I stepped into retirement. Family and Colorado's rugged peaks called, and I answered. I am forever grateful for the privilege of watching our grandchildren grow up.

Woodmen Valley Chapel became our church home. Through a couple of mission organizations, I was privileged to be involved in designing orphanages with the help of donated software. I traveled to Bolivia 6 times and to India 3 times to review blueprints and participate in the actual construction of these orphanages. Through God's favor, I am blessed with a legacy etched in bricks and concrete and compassion.

Brenda, my partner in adventure, held my hand as we traveled across the west. While visiting national parks, my camera became an extension of my soul, capturing beautiful moments. Over **100,000 digital photographs** now exist in my library, each photograph a testament to my enjoyment of nature's beauty.

And then there was snow—the soft hush of powder beneath skis. Colorado's slopes embraced me. At **85**, I still love skiing and am grateful to still do so.

As I write these memories, I am humbled, for I have lived a blessed life. This is my story—**Van's Memories**—waiting to be shared with you.

With gratitude, **Van** (and a little help from AI)

In the beginning...

Grandpa and Grandma Boot

My Grandfather Izaak Boot married Lena De Vos, Feb 18, 1897, in the village of Kortgene, a small, picturesque village on the island of Noord Beveland in the Zeeland province of the Netherlands. Noord-Beveland, an island with no bridges connecting it to any other island or the mainland, was populated mostly by farms where, for the most part, people were born, raised, married, died and were buried. This describes my grandparents, Izaak and Lena Boot.

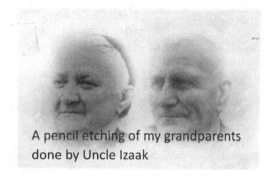

A pencil etching of my grandparents done by Uncle Izaak

Only known photo of my mother as a youngster (about 9 yrs. old)

This is the only known picture of them at this age in their lives.

My mother was born to Izaak Boot and Lena (DeVos) Boot on Nov 7, 1914. She was number eleven in a family of twelve children. Grandma Boot birthed fourteen children but two died before their first birthdays.

Most of my mother's 5 brothers and 6 sisters married and raised their families in and around Kortgene.

Noord-Beveland was one of many islands in the Zeeland province in the southern part of Holland just north of the Belgium border. The only real exception to brothers and sisters staying in the Noord Beveland area was my Uncle Gerard who, as a young man, immigrated to America and lived in the Grand Rapids, MI area.

Mom's entire family

This is a photo of the Boot family with all the grown kids— Grandma and Grandpa Boot in front. My mother is the 2nd from the right. I believe they are positioned from the oldest ladies starting on the left to the youngest ladies, and the same for the men.

My mother never knew any of her grandparents on either side of the family. They had all passed away before she was born.

Mom with all but one sibling. Mom is second from right

where the police came to the house and the nanny climbed into the attic and pulled up the stairway to escape.

My dad was born April 14, 1910 in a village called Tholen. He lived there for about a year before his family moved to Zuid-Beveland. He too came from a large family. They had 3 boys and 4 girls. Dad was the middle boy. My dad lost his mother when he was 10 years old. She apparently had a bad infection in her leg and one thing led to another. The doctor tried to help her but she eventually died of the infection. After his mother died, Grandpa Van Bemden had lots of different nannies to help raise the family. My mother told me he had lots of problems with the various nannies who stole various things like blankets and household items from him. My mom told of one instance

Dad with his 2 brothers and 4 sisters

2

My dad dropped out of school when he was 12 years old to begin working on a farm as a handy man. Thus, at the age of 12, his formal education ended abruptly. That was not uncommon for the average working-class Dutch family at that time. Obviously, he was to learn a lot more over the years in the school of hard knocks. Being a handy man at the age of 12 really meant doing anything and everything, like what we jokingly would call a "gofer" today, do this, do that.

House in the middle is dad's house

My dad met my mother thru my Uncle Izaak (the painter) who invited my dad and another one of his buddies who was working on the island of Noord-Beveland to come over to his house for a vlslt. The story goes that, later in the day, Uncle Izaak invited my dad and his buddy to join him at my Grandpa Boot's house which was, I guess, quite a normal thing to do Saturday evenings. That is where he first saw my mother. They apparently hit it off right from the start. He came over every so often to visit my mother during their courtship. Since my dad was still living at home on a different island, he had to make sure he left Mom's place in time to catch the last ferry from her island to get to his island. That meant he had to leave by 8:30 pm, then he still had more than a 2-hour ride on his bicycle to get home. Sometimes he stayed over for the weekend at Mom's house to attend her church, the Nederlands Reformed Congregation, which also had a church in the village of Kortgene. When he stayed over for the weekend, he would have to leave exceedingly early Monday morning to get to work on time.

Grandpa and Grandma Van Bemden

A year or two before my dad got married his father, Grandpa Van Bemden whom I never met, got remarried. To hear my mother tell the story, Grandpa Van Bemden's new bride was a stern hard lady to live with.

My dad was engaged to my mother for 2 ½ years before they got married. The wedding took place in Kortgene on March 17, 1935. Dad was 24 years old, and Mother was 20. My dad was not feeling well the day of the wedding because he had a throat infection which a doctor lanced for draining accumulated pus. Bucking tradition, he rode in a car to the church; however, my mother insists nobody noticed he wasn't in the traditional crowd marching to the church.

A "farm helper" didn't make as much money as a seasoned veteran, so my dad and mother didn't have a whole lot of money when they got married. He worked for 12 guilder/wk. and 2 of those guilders went to pay for the rent in the little house (actually a shed they had redone to make it livable) they rented from the farmer he was working for at that time. This is the same little house that Joe, Ike, and I were born in. Sometime later, the farmer turned it back into a shed to store farm wagons, etc. Years later, when some of my brothers and sisters visited Holland, they noticed this little house had been turned into a barn spawning a family joke we heard at family gatherings— "some of us were actually born in a barn."

There weren't many tractors in the Netherlands and most of the farming, i.e. plowing, etc., was done with big Belgian draft horses. My mother tells me dad could really plow straight. I guess that was important. I have several photos of him plowing with a team of four big Belgian horses. I guess that's a trait he carried with him to America because, years later when we lived on the farm in Ravenna, MI when we put in all

new barbed wire fences, they were as straight as an arrow—even the rows of corn had to be perfectly straight.

Dad plowing with 4 horses in heavy Zeeland clay

Grandpa Boot

My mother also worked in the fields in the summer performing various tasks like thinning sugar beets, cutting hay with a sickle, stacking wheat into sheaves piling them up to wait for the threshing machine to separate the grain from the chaff. In the wintertime she, being one of the younger sisters, would help clean the house and take care of her brother's and sister's kids. Most of her family lived in and around the village where they were born. When my mother was still at home, my Grandpa Boot became mayor of the town but she doesn't know how long he held the post.

As Hitler was beginning his political rise to power in the late 1930s, my parents' desire to immigrate to America was denied by the Nazis. When the war ended, reinstituting his earlier invitation, Uncle Gerard once again began working on our behalf to facilitate our family's immigration to the United States. However, I learned much later, it wasn't my Uncle Gerard and Aunt Connie, but Dan Van Ree, an elder in our church and Aunt Connie's uncle, who succeeded in securing the necessary documentation.

The first 9 years

The House I Was Born In

I was born at home in Kortgene, Oct 27, 1938. Kortgene, a small city in the southwest Netherlands, in the municipality of Noord-Beveland, Zeeland, is about 15 km northeast of Middelburg. It received city rights in 1431 but was flooded in 1530 and 1532. The new settlement received city rights in 1684. Kortgene, elevation about three feet above sea level, is the largest village on the Island of Noord-Beeveland in the Zeeland province of the Nederlands.

Because Kortgene had no hospital or obstetric clinic, everyone was born at home with only a midwife present. I was born in a small house on the "damweg" (Dam Road) just off the main street in the village. My brothers, Joe and Ike, were also born there.

Mom describes her memories of my birth as a dark night with no light and all the windows covered to prevent aircraft from dropping bombs on us. She says the small house was nice enough but, because it was eventually converted into a shed for storing wagons and farming equipment, my grandkids tease about "Grandpa being born in a barn." The house originally belonged to a Boer (Dutch for farmer) not far from my grandparent's house and an early employer of my father. All the Van Bemden's oldest kids were born in this little house.

Our last house in the Nederlands

I do not know exactly when we moved to the house that we lived in when we immigrated to America, but it was sometime between the time Lena and I were born because Mom said that Lena was born in the new house. Thus, it must have been sometime in 1939. This was a new house but it did not have inside plumbing. What it had was a basin to catch the rainwater

and a one-hole outhouse attached to the house. Once in a great while, the water tank got kind of low. We drank the water as it came out of the storage tank. It was not boiled or anything like that. I guess one builds up immunities to fight off the bacteria.

Some have mistakenly thought this is a photo of Johannis and me in a pre-kindergarten group of

Mom, Johannis, Izaak, Urbanus and Lena

kids in the little Dutch book titled: <u>Kortgene In Oude Ausichten</u>, However, it is really a picture of Johannis and Izaak with five or six cousins.

Johannis & Izaak in pre-school – Johannis & Izaak are sitting on the

52. De kleuterschool van Kortgene in 1939. We kennen ze deze keer allemaal nog. Bovenste rij van links naar rechts: juffrouw A. Barendse, Leen Goulooze, Wim de Looff, Bram Koets, Gerard Kramer, Ko Welleman, Piet Smallegange, Leen van der Maas, Lieven Boot en juffrouw J. Welleman. Op de tweede rij: Corrie van Schaik, Gerard Boot, Pietje Boot, Jenneke Klop, Jo v.d. Linde, To v.d. Linde, Koos Boot, Ko Boot en Izaak Boot. De vijf kleuters in stoeltjes: Janneke van den Bos, Corrie van Halst, Sjaan van der Maas, Jan Clement en Kaatje de Fouw. Zittend op de voorgrond: Jo van Bendem en Banie van Bendem.

I have scattered memories of public school experiences. While Mom's descriptions of Miss Baranus, our kindergarten teacher, are of a genuinely nice lady, this is a sharp contrast with my memories of Mrs. Poerastamper, my 3rd and 4th grade teacher, who I remember as mean. I think I was in her class sitting at my desk dipping a pen into an ink well when my knuckles were cracked with a ruler. This could have been my punishment for hanging cherry stems from my ears as earrings or perhaps an attempt to make sure I used my right hand rather than my left. This was a common practice at that time when being lefthanded was undesirable. They also often made natural left-handers wear mittens on their left hands to force them to use their right hands for writing.

A family as large as ours had more than its share of injuries requiring medical attention. On one occasion, Dad had to take me to the doctor on Sunday afternoon to remove a pea I had stuck up my nose. Another memorable injury left me permanently scarred when a kid from across town threw a rock hitting me in the mouth. All my teeth at that time were permanent and the impact of the rock broke off a piece of my front incisor which I sported for years till I eventually had it capped.

Our Dutch heritage played out in appetites a bit different from normal American cuisine. I think most Americans are aware of the European appetite for horse meat and I have memories as a young boy during the war standing in line for our family's share of a horse killed in the war, butchered to be shared by the villagers. My sister, Lena, and I stood in line with my older brothers holding pots to get pieces of the horse meat. Even though my dad had a big pig in the building in the back of the garden, it was reserved for the Germans. However, occasionally, the villagers would kill a pig and butcher it hoping and praying they would not get caught. On these rare occasions, kids would beg for "Speck Koshees" (pork rind). We kids thought this was certainly one of the finer things in life. My Grandpa Boot's appetite for swine brains motivated him to be first in line anytime a hog was slaughtered. Cooked properly, it is considered a delicacy and Grandpa was very fond of it. Dad used to dry various fruits (apples, peaches and a few others) upstairs in our new house and we occasionally snitched a few.

I remember running behind farmers' wagons as they passed through the village on the way to unload their wagons full of sugar beets. We would sneak up behind them and hop on to steal (throw off) some sugar beets to take home to mother for boiling into sugar.

During the war our family experienced firsthand the effort required to duplicate the Bible story of Ruth describing how the poor were allowed to "glean" the fields of the wealthier farmers whose harvests left behind grain. Anything edible was welcome and we found enough wheat to justify our gleaning efforts. (See Ruth 2:2-3)

Johannis' wife, Carol, recites a story about Johannis helping dad bring electricity into a chicken coop in the backyard. She says Joe was about 8 years old when he and dad were working together and dad would instruct Joe to plug the cord into the wall socket when the time was right. Apparently, dad, standing in a puddle of water when Joe plugged in the cord before dad instructed him too, was almost electrocuted. In Europe, household electricity is 220-240 volts delivering twice the shock electricity produces in the states.

Windmill In Our Village

We had a windmill in our village where everyone went to get their grain ground into flour. I remember the man who worked in the windmill was always as white as a ghost from all the flour dust.

My dad kept his axe honed to a razor's edge. He had been chopping wood for our stove when he left the axe untended. The axe almost cut off my thumb when I was being pulled on an old wooden sled behind dad's bicycle on a dike where he was rooting out a tree stump. I slid forward on the sled and, in the process, hit the axe with my wrist just above my thumb requiring several stitches.

1945

Here is a photo of mom with most of her sisters. Mom is next to her youngest sister, Lena, who is standing on the left.

Our island was surrounded by brackish water (diluted salt water) requiring temperatures well below freezing to freeze deep enough for safely transporting anything heavy across it. However, one winter it did freeze deeply enough to allow

Mom's Sisters: Maria, Kotie, Joe, Lena and Mom

pedestrian traffic to cross the bay to another island. Using the ice as a supply bridge, we enjoyed faster, cheaper and more convenient personal delivery of household supplies.

Men carrying supplies across the frozen channel – winter of 1946-47

While the oft referenced image of ice skating in Holland has merit, my time on the ice was limited to sledding simply because I had no skates. Our wooden sled with steel runners was propelled by poles with a nail stuck in the end much like today's ski poles. Holland's flatness, broken only by dikes, required muscle power – we were either pushed or we pushed ourselves with poles.

I was four or five years old when, staying overnight with my cousin, Izaak Boot, I wet the bed. That was unforgivable. Many years later, as an adult visiting Kortgene on business trips, I was invited to

Typical winter scene around Kinder Dijk

stay with my cousin, Izaak (apparently all memories of my childhood accident had been forgotten).

In the winter when there was not a whole lot to do on a farm, my dad worked at various odd jobs. Before the introduction of cranes, longshoremen with strong backs loaded and unloaded ships. With large sacks weighing 100KG (that's a couple of hundred pounds) on their backs, they trudged up and down the plank of the ship to the warehouses.

One-time Johannis ran his bicycle into the harbor and dad had to get it out of the mud. I don't know whether the brakes didn't work or whether he simply lost control, but it was quite a sight. Luckily, it was low tide.

Johannis, Izaak and I were hunting bird eggs on some of the smaller outlying islands failing to watch the tide. Our only

Kortgene Harbor at low tide

way home was to swim across the isthmus we had walked across before the tide came in. On this day, I learned to swim (really dog paddled); it was the only way back to shore and safety.

8

As far as I'm concerned, few meals exceed delectable steamed mussels. Zeeland, the heart of mussel production, provided many sumptuous feasts. Anytime I'm in Holland, I make every effort to enjoy a meal of steamed mussels. As kids, my brothers and I often scavenged eels and snails from their sanctuaries behind pilings in the harbor. While the snails weren't as large as their counterparts in France where restaurants get as much as $1 apiece or more for them as escargot, when mom boiled them, they were delicious.

Lena, Izaak, Johannis and Urbanus

Christmas in the Netherlands

For most children in the Netherlands, the most important day during December is the fifth, when Sinterklaas (St. Nicholas) brings them their presents. St. Nicholas Day is on the 6th of December, but in the Netherlands, the major celebrations are held on December 5th, St Nicholas Eve. The name Santa Claus comes from the name Sinterklaas.

It all starts on the second Saturday of November (the first Saturday after 11th November) when Sinterklaas travels to a city or town in the Netherlands. Dutch tradition says St. Nicholas lives in Madrid, Spain, and every year he chooses a different harbor to arrive in the Netherlands, so as many children as possible get a chance to see him.

Sinterklaas travels with his servants called "Zwart Pieten' (Black Peters). When Sinterklaas and the Black Peters come ashore from the steamboat, all the local church bells ring in celebration. Sinterklaas, dressed in his red robes, riding a white horse, leads a procession through the town.

Sinterklaas and Zwart Pieten

On New Year's Day we traveled around to our relatives to wish them a "happy new year" and beg for a nickel.

During the war, we put cork underneath the windows so when the bombs dropped, the explosions would not break the windows so easily. When the air raid sirens wailed, Mom would have us lie down in the hallway in case the house was blown away. Occasionally we were not allowed to go outside and lots of times a curfew from 7PM to 7AM was enforced. At night, we had to cover our windows and could not have any lights on.

Watching documentaries of World War II on the History Channel evokes memories of skies filled with squadrons of bombers flying over our village on their way to attack Germany. As a young boy, the skies seemed almost black because of all the airplanes during these allied air raids.

Despite the abuses of German occupation during which they forcefully evicted our neighbors (the Case Moreman family) from their home to set up area headquarters in their house, the German soldiers did not treat us kids unkindly.

Except for China, the Netherlands boast more bicycles per capita than any other country. This was no less prevalent during the war than it is today and the occupying Germans confiscated large numbers of them to prevent their use by resistance fighters. Because the Dutch people depended on their bikes, we found clever ways to hide them from the Germans. Dad hid his under one of our beds and he told stories of neighbors hiding theirs in manure piles and between rows of vegetables in their gardens. Even today, bikes are a popular means of getting around in a small flat country like Holland with its many narrow streets. No small contributor to the popularity of bicycles is the cost of gasoline. Consider the implications of gas pricing during the war and think about gas prices today (2005). In Holland, $5 is the equivalent of $2.50 and a gallon of gas is $5—we complain when we pay $2.50-3.00 at the pump.

My dad had to work in a forced labor camp building bunkers along the North Sea coastline for the Germans. He and my Uncle Adrian lived in a barracks along with many others in the camps. Dad never talked much about those days but he told one story of a night when he and Uncle Adrian were grilling a piece of sausage over a potbellied stove in the middle of the barracks when a German guard emphasized his authority by firing a bullet through the floor accompanied by his threat: "The next one's for you!"

On rare occasions dad was allowed to come home but he did not attempt to conceal his contempt for the Germans. I understand and appreciate his feelings; however, I think it is ironic that, as my business travels took me into Germany, I developed great friendships with my German business acquaintances.

German WWII Bunker

Recently, when I was discussing this period in the life of the Van Bemden family with my mother, she did not remember a lot of the details. As a matter of fact, she was simply happy and thankful to be able to forget that period of her life.

I have an unforgettable memory of German soldiers marching in front of a tank, surrendering with their hands in the air to the Canadian soldiers liberating our island. Their first stop was a makeshift compound surrounded by barbed wire fencing in the middle of our town square. Their internment there was temporary and I've never known where thy eventually lived out their imprisonment.

We thought the American and Canadian soldiers were crazy when we learned they ate frog legs. We never heard of such a thing. They were in luck because there were lots of frogs in the ditches around the village.

A successful hunt – 13 rabbits and 1 pheasant

Unaware of the danger, my brothers and I had great fun finding unspent bullets we sank into fence posts then, using a nail as a firing pin, with a hammer we "fired" the bullet. We are very fortunate nobody was ever seriously injured.

A group of farmers formed a hunting party forming a line across a "polder" (field) driving wildlife before it. As they worked their way the length of the field shooting any animal that moved, they accumulated an impressive quantity of edible game – mostly rabbits and pheasants. An old farm wagon retrofitted with wire hooks was festooned with dead trophies destined for the butcher shop.

Izaak and Urbanus – notice Van's wooden shoes

My mother says I fell down a lot and it seemed as though I always had a skinned-up nose and knees. I have an old picture to prove the point where Ike and I are seen in clothes that my mother made from old soldiers' uniforms, and I am wearing wooden shoes. Ike had shoes that should have been thrown away years earlier. In this shot, I have homemade bandages wrapped around a finger on each hand.

Like most houses, ours had no central heating; thus, spent ammunition casings filled with hot water and placed at the foot of our bed helped ward off the cold on frigid winter nights.

Church buildings rarely featured any kind of heating other than the familiar potbellied stoves like those in our houses. The Van Bemdens carried small wooden boxes containing embers from our home stove to church where they served as foot warmers.

The Nederlands Reformed Church (Gereformeerde Gemeente) we attended featured a raised pulpit in the sanctuary. This was a common design carried to the US by Europeans conditioned to hearing their sermons dispensed by the minister from a lofty perch. While our raised sanctuary pulpit was more centrally located, many raised pulpits were off to one side overlooking the congregation at an angle. Another common practice was for the men and boys to sit on one side of the church and the women and girls to sit on the other side. I vaguely remember sitting with my mother from time to time, thus I suspect young children were allowed to sit with either parent.

The Church we attended in Kortgene

Despite the small population of the Village of Kortgene, there were two churches in it:1) our Dutch Reformed Church in this photo and 2) "Nicolaaskert Protest ante Gemente" or "De Grote Kirk" (the big church as we referred to it), was a protestant church we did not attend.

During the war when no one had any money, bartering facilitated the exchanging of survival goods. This practice resulted in an eye injury my mother suffered. It occurred when my dad's efforts to tightly fasten a belt around a packet of trade goods he intended to transport on his bicycle to Uncle Ike, a professional painter in Goes, broke a small piece off the buckle which flew into my mom's eye. I believe my mom was wearing glasses which may have prevented a more serious injury.

1946

This is a picture of Piet and Hendrika taken in the Netherlands. I think Piet is probably 3 yrs. old and Hendrika 2 yrs. old.

Some of us kids who were hanging out of the upstairs window saw dad carrying a small casket where our still born sibling, named Willem (child #9), was placed. My parents never talked about Willem. Quite frankly, I do not really know whether he was still born or whether he lived an hour or a day. Years later when I was in Kortgene, my Uncle Adrian pointed out Willem's grave when we were visiting the village cemetery. One of his sons who was in his early twenties was killed in an automobile accident and buried there. I do not recall his name, but he apparently had a romantic crush on my sister, Jeni.

Piet and Hendrika in the Netherlands – Hendrika is wearing wooden shoes

On the way to America

On our way to Amsterdam to board the ship that would carry us to America, I rode in a motor vehicle (a flatbed truck) for the very first time. On this trip I also experienced my first thrilling underground experience as the road to the ship took us through a tunnel under one of the canals. Because none of us had ever been to a big city, Amsterdam's tall buildings and the wharf with its huge ships added to the thrill of our journey.

The new Veendam

The ship that would take us to America was the Veendam. To us it was a big ship, but it was nowhere near the size of the Queen Mary, Titanic or any of today's cruise ships—in later years we referred to it as a banana boat. I believe the name of that boat is still being used because I saw it years later docked in Vancouver, BC, when Brenda and I were on vacation there. The photo above is a much newer and larger Veendam than the one we took across the Atlantic. The photo below is of the Veendam we took to America.

Veendam ship that brought us to America

The Veendam was hit several times during WWII requiring it to be towed to a shipyard, repaired, and bombed again, and again.

The Veendam featured two passenger accommodation classes: 1) 195 first class cabins and 2) 357 tourist and crew staterooms. She commenced her first post war sailing on 21 February, 1947, from Rotterdam to New York. The ship was extensively used by Dutch immigrants moving to North America in the period 1948 to 1952. On 30th October, 1953, the last voyage carrying 600 passengers arrived in New York whereupon it was sold for scrap to the Bethlehem Steel Company of Baltimore. Demolition started in November, 1953.

First class was officially off limits but my siblings and I viewed the entire boat as our playground. Crossing the North Atlantic in the winter was a thirteen-day journey. Often the seas were rough causing sea sickness among the passengers; however, only Johannis and mom suffered and their bouts only lasted one day.

Every once in a while, when the waves in the North Atlantic were high, the propeller of the ship would be out of the water and then it would momentarily gain some rpms and you could feel the whole boat vibrating – this is common on boats with propellors and it is called cavitation. We also saw some flying fish—or at least that is what we thought. Now I know they were fish with huge fins, and they were gliding.

Our family did not have enough money to fund the crossing; thus, mom told me one of my uncles loaned us enough to buy our tickets.

HOLLAND AMERICA LINE

LIST OR MANIFEST OF ALIEN PASSENGERS FOR THE UNITED

TOURIST CLASS
S.S. VEENDAM — Passengers sailing from ROTTERDAM — DECEMBER 2 ND., 19 47

Copy of manifest recording all the Van Bemdens that boarded the Veendam on Dec 2, 1947

Van and Uncle Urbanus

Years later, a cousin told me my dad had inquired about immigrating to Russia as an alternative to America. However, when our minister explained there were no Nederlands Reformed Congregation churches in Russia, he abandoned the idea entirely.

My Uncle Adrian's interest in leaving Holland to relocate to Russia has been embellished by years of storytelling. Eventually, however, my parents got tired of hearing it.

I have no memory of ever meeting any of dad's side of the family when we lived in the old country. Years later, on a business trip to Holland, I met my namesake, Uncle Urbanus, and a couple of my aunts from dad's side of the family. Uncle Urbanus lived in the village of Goes and made his living delivering fruit and vegetables there.

14

In 2005, my brother Cornelis sent this photo of my mother and seven of the kids sitting on a couch. 1949 is written on the back of it. We were in America and that would put us in our cement block house in Dutton.

Piet, Adriaan, Mom, Cornelis, Lena, Urbanus & Hendrika

The North Sea flood of 1953. One of the worst disasters ever suffered by Kortgene was the North Sea flood of 1953 when forty-nine people, including our relatives, Marien Nijsse and two of her children perished.

Lower and improperly maintained dikes at Kruiningen, Kortgene and Oude Tonge were first to fail before the domino effect took out St. Philipsland, large parts of Tholen. Zuid-Beveland, Noord-Beveland, Walcheren, and Zeeuws-Vlaanderen. Additionally, some areas on Noord-Brabant and Zuid-Holland, especially the peninsulas of Zuid-Holland, were submerged as well.

Marien Nijsse and the two children

**In America 9-18yrs
Dutton, MI (Grand Rapids)**

Statue of Liberty

After thirteen days at sea during the winter of 1947, we had our first sighting of the Statue of Liberty. To me, the thrill of seeing the grand old lady was tempered by fear of our boat tipping over from the weight of all the passengers lined up on one side!

The Statue of Liberty, an icon, a national treasure, and one of the most recognizable figures in the world is a cherished symbol of millions who make the journey to experience her history and grandeur in person. She is the statue of Liberty, a symbol of freedom, inspiration, and hope. It is written on the Statue of Liberty: "Give me your tired, your poor, your huddled masses yearning to breathe free, the wretched refuse of your teeming shores."

We were finally in America realizing my dad's dream! His efforts to follow Uncle Gerard's immigration had been thwarted by Hitler's rise to power during which immigration was prevented.

Uncle Gerard had made the successful transition in his early twenties, establishing his family on a small farm near Dutton (Grand Rapids), Michigan. His generosity and commitment to seeing our family join him was exercised when he prepared for our arrival by building a cement block house for us on the corner of M37 and 76th street prior to our arrival.

Like millions of others, we were processed through Ellis Island. Following our officially sanctioned acceptance, we were met by a member of the Nederlands Reformed Congregation in Paterson, New Jersey. None of our family spoke English; thus, Uncle Gerard's selfless act of setting us up for our first few days in America with a Dutch speaking host, made our entry much more pleasant than it otherwise would have been.

Our arrival on a weekend began with dividing our family into four groups to be placed with four different families from the Paterson, NJ Nederlands Reformed Congregation. Their religious practice preventing a broad spectrum of weekend entertainment duplicated ours we had left in Holland—however, it did not prevent me from creating a bit of excitement during an innocent Sunday afternoon walk. On that auspicious Sunday afternoon, Joe, Ike and I went for a walk around the block. Discovering a peculiar red box, I had never seen before, in my polished Dutch, I queried a lineman working on a pole as to the nature of the device. He ignored my curiosity prompting me to turn the crank on the box a few times. A few minutes later, a firetruck arrived and my arrival in America began with the same disciplinary exercises I had suffered in the homeland!

Family of 10 immigrants welcomed on arrival by relatives and a house

The following Monday, my dad and mother, along with eight kids and a greatly appreciated translator, a member of the church hosting us, boarded a train for Grand Rapids, MI. As night fell, our kind travelling companion secured pullman bunks for all eight kids. This welcome accommodation was a fitting end to the first weekday of adventure in our new homeland.

No Housing Worries for Them

The following afternoon we were met in Grand Rapids by my uncle with some deacons from the church destined to be our first church family. We all piled into the cars and drove to Uncle Gerard's farm. Because our house wasn't finished, we were Uncle Gerald's guests for several months.

In 2005, I was back in Grand Rapids, MI visiting my mother, where I had the opportunity to sift through all her old family photos and I ran across an original copy of an article that appeared on Page 1, **Dec 17, 1947,** in the Grand Rapids Press the day we arrived in Grand Rapids, MI. It included a photo of our family with my uncle and aunt who were at the train station to meet us. It read as follows:

> Not for the Cornelius Van Bemdens and their eight children are the housing worries that confront most immigrant families of that size when they reach this land of shelter shortage.
> Arriving from The Netherlands Tuesday to make their home near Dutton, they found awaiting them a neat new concrete block house which Mrs. Van Bemden's

brother and sister-in-law, Mr. and Mrs. Gerard Boot, 3028 Seventy-Sixth St, SE, have built and furnished for them. Sacrificing leisure and recreation, neighbors, friends and relatives of Mr. and Mrs. Boot organized "bees" to assist in the project and get the new house ready in time. The house, located in a corner of the Boot's 80-arcre farm, which Van Bemden, a farmer in the old world, will help run. It is ready for occupancy except for a few "finishing touches," Mrs. Boot said, and the Van Bemdens will move into it soon.

Unanimous: Finest Present.
When they got their first glimpse of their new home Tuesday afternoon, they agreed unanimously it is the finest Christmas present they ever had. Accustomed to closer quarters in The Netherlands, they found their new home's three bedrooms, living room, kitchen, and basement unimaginably spacious.

Arrival of the Van Bemdens is the culmination of many months of effort on the part of Boot to bring his sister and her family to this country. Because he started proceedings before the war, consular officials gave his application priority when immigration restrictions were lifted. The Van Bemdens could have come last May, Mrs. Boot explained, if their family had been smaller, but travelling with eight children and two grownups presented a problem that was not hurdled immediately.

Spend Holidays with Boots
"But anyway, they're here in time for Christmas," their hostess said happily.
Before moving into the new home, the Van Bemdens will spend the holidays with the Boots, who have arranged a celebration that will make up to the newcomers for having missed their own St. Nicholas day Dec 5. By that time, they were well on their way across the Atlantic. They embarked from Rotterdam, Dec 2.

Despite a stormy voyage, none of the large family suffered even momentary seasickness, they reported. Arriving in New York on schedule Saturday morning, they spent the weekend with friends in Paterson, NJ.

Mrs. Van Bemden is the first member of her family to come to America to join her brother, who has been here 17 years. Left behind in their hometown of Kortgene, Zeeland, were 10 brothers and sisters and their father, Isaac Boot, now 78. The mother died during the war. A Red Cross message about the death was the only word Boot had from his relatives in The Nederland's in the war years.

Fared Well in War.
The Van Bemdens fared better in the German occupation than many of their countrymen, they said on arrival here. Although there was fighting all around them, their town fortunately escaped destruction except for a few sporadic bombings that left their house undamaged. Clothing was scarce but, because of the Van Bemdens occupation, their food problems were not as acute as they otherwise might have been.

Although never actively identified with the Dutch underground, the Van Bemdens had their "own ways" of resisting the Nazis, the father reported grimly. Occasionally during the long occupation, they were forced to house Nazi soldiers.

The Van Bemden children are a comely set of "steps" ranging from Johannes 12, down to Adriaan 2. In between are Izaak 10; Urbanus, 9; Lena 7; Cornelius 6; Piet, 4; and Hendrika, 3. The newcomers spent Tuesday afternoon exploring the Boot's spacious farmyard and getting acquainted with the four Boot children, Gerard, 11; Robert, 8; James, 5; and Tommy, 2. Other American relatives include an aunt, Mrs. Nellie Meulenberg, 529 Hall St., SE, and several cousins.

Shortly upon our arrival some of the deacons from our church (Mr. Mieras is one I remember) took us to the Salvation Army and some other stores and bought us some shoes and clothing. What I did not know until 2005, was that my dad sent most of our clothes we brought to America back to Holland because the clothes that we had taken to America (knicker pants, etc.) were not the style worn in America and they were new since they were bought for our trip to America.

Dad and Uncle Gerald worked on the farm in the daytime and at Nash-Kelvinator at night. How long they worked there I do not recall.

Grandpa Boot hoeing his garden

Shortly after we arrived in America, my mother's dad (Grandpa Boot) died. He was 78 years old. I remember Grandpa Boot as a gentle man who was very much at peace with himself. I can still picture him hoeing in his "hofje" (garden).

One of the questions that invariably comes up whenever someone finds out that I came from the old country is: "Why did you or your dad come to this country?" Obviously, there wasn't a whole lot that I could do about it, I had no input in the decision; however, my dad, like most people back in Europe, viewed "America as the land of opportunity" and "the streets were imagined to be paved with gold." Certainly, being in America one has

more opportunities, but I found out that one must work just as hard, if not harder, to make it big. Most countries in Europe have a socialistic leaning government and the government "takes care of you lots better than they do here." Of course, what they do not tell you or want to admit is that all the socialism costs them lots more in taxes.

1948.

Below is a photo of my Uncle Gerard's family Uncle Gerard and Aunt Connie, Gerard, 11; Robert, 8; James, 5; and Tommy, 2.

Uncle Gerard Boot's Family

In the summertime we helped haul hay into the barn with my uncle's old Chevrolet truck. Uncle Gerard always backed this old Chevy truck on the ramp of the barn that led up to the hay loft. Because he ran it so few times, it always had a dead battery; and so, he would use the slope of the ramp to start it. In the fall and winter, we also helped pick the field corn by hand. Husking corn by hand when the corn is all dried is rough on your hands. This was in the days before they had mechanical corn pickers.

Uncle Gerard and Dad making a haystack

Uncle Gerard had an old Farmall tractor with steel wheels and huge lugs. These types of wheels were popular years ago. Goodyear and other tire makers had not figured out how to make "big" tractor tires.

1949

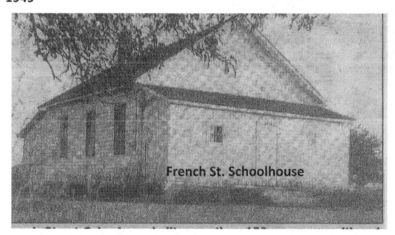

French St. Schoolhouse

Since my uncle lived out in the country, the nearest school was a one room country schoolhouse named "The French Street School." The first farmers in the area were French, hence the name French Street. It was about 1/2 to 3/4 mile down 76th street. This schoolhouse was built around the mid-1850s. Four or five of us attended classes there and none of us spoke a word of English. Mrs. Crumback, a very dedicated schoolteacher, just did not know what to do with us.

I believe we all started out connecting dots, the old 1, to 2, to 3, etc. We did not do this long, however, and as soon as we started to say a few words in English, it was obvious we weren't educationally behind the American students. Because the curriculum in Holland was more advanced than in America most of us were ahead of our fellow students in our grade.
Mrs. Crumback who eventually became a dear friend of our family, should have been given the teacher of the year award for tolerating all those little Hollanders. Her technique of having older kids read stories to us was very effective. Our language barrier required the first books to be elementary but, when we reached the point where we could read them, we read them back to our mentors. This technique allowed Mrs. Crumback to work with other students during the time we were reading. Teaching grades K-8 had to be a serious challenge and, if Liz Finkbeiner's comment years later saying my brothers, Joe and Ike, were mean to the other kids is true, this had to add to the difficulty Mrs. Crumback faced daily. Mrs. Crumback's stress was increased when she suffered severe injuries in an auto accident.

One of Mrs. Crumback's policies in her dedicated attempts to make education as pleasant as possible was her sensitivity to the weather's effects. During the winter when that one room schoolhouse (I suspect devoid of any insulation) was too cold to foster concentration, this dedicated teacher gathered older students to arrive early for building a fire in the potbellied stove before the other students arrived. Indoor plumbing was not an amenity of our schoolhouse. For a drink of water, we had to go outside and use a hand pump. The pump required priming for each use; thus, we shared a dipper and we all drank from the same bucket.

Mandatory weekly church service attendance spawned many new experiences for our family. Uncle Gerard's family transportation wasn't adequate; thus, my dad learned to drive and he purchased a 1938 Hudson Terraplane from a member of the church we attended. From the photo, you can imagine eight pairs of eyes peeking out the windows as our family plied the streets. This was a fancy car featuring a fold down table similar to today's airplane trays in the rear hatch. As we were returning home from church one Sunday, the car threw a rod. Repairs were costly.

While we lived in the house in Dutton, I stepped on a rusty nail resulting in blood poisoning. Evidence included a red streak crawling up my arm on its way to my heart. My mother soaked my arm in hot Epsom salts. Convinced I was about to die, I begged her to pray really hard for me and my presence here today is evidence of the power of her prayers.

We were a family of pickers – when strawberries were in season, we harvested them for my uncle. He also enlisted our aid in harvesting cantaloupe and watermelons from a rented field somewhere around Middleville to be sold in the Farmers' Market on Fulton St. in Grand Rapids.

We older boys also picked some beans and other vegetables at Dan Van Ree's and Uncle Dan Winn's truck farms at various times in the summertime.

We were taking a break from picking strawberries when we observed Uncle Gerard stuffing his cheek with Copenhagen. Responding to their request, Uncle Gerard generously shared a plug resulting in two young boys regretting it—they were both sicker than dogs.

While I escaped the embarrassment of chewing tobacco, I suffered my own humiliating event when Rob cajoled me into urinating on an electric fence. Further imagery is left to the reader's imagination but, needless to say, it was a shocking learning experience!

My dad was a man of few words; thus, when I asked him what was under a horse's tail, he lifted me up and stuck my face as close as possible to our nag's rear end. I've never forgotten exactly what resides under a horse's tail.

My dad left his job at Keller Brass to accept a position with Standard Supply Lumber. He apparently found it necessary to remind his boss of his past history in Holland as a farmer and he intended to return to that way of life.

1950

A View of Our Barn

Dick Rottschaffer, owner of several Standard Supply Lumber companies in the greater Grand Rapids area, invited us to live on his farm near Sullivan, MI. Both house and barn required extensive remodeling. The final results were remarkable enough to garner attention as the largest dairy farm in Muskegon County after which an article appeared about it in the Farm Journal magazine.

Again, all the kids who were of school age attended a one-room country schoolhouse in the little town of Sullivan. I was the only student in my class for two years running, then a neighbor moved in next door, and they had a girl, Linda Stark, who was in the same grade as I was. I learned many years later that Linda Stark became a missionary. Linda had a brother named Joseph who was Casey's age.

Sometimes dad would take us to school in our 1938 Pontiac that Dick Rottschaffer gave to us. Sometimes some of the older boys would grab the rear bumper of the car and try to hold my dad's car back. The dirt was very loose in front of the school where he dropped us off and it was not all that hard to hold back a car if there were enough strong farm boys trying. All the Pontiac cars back then had stripes on the hood as well as on the trunk. They also had an Indian head as the hood ornament. In 1926, GM introduced a companion Marque to GM's Oakland line: Pontiac.

Google has this to say about the Indian hood ornament. The brand was named after Pontiac, Grand Chief of the Ottawa Native Americans. Because of this, Native American imagery was used in marketing throughout the early life of the brand. In 1956, the Native American head design was retired.

My mother tried learning how to drive the Pontiac with a floor mounted straight stick. It seems she was always missing the gears. She never mastered it and subsequently she always depended on someone else to drive her around.

My dad never had much of a formal education and I think he dropped out of school when he was about 10-12 years old. He always wanted us to get a good education and used to say that being educated was not like carrying a 100 lb. bag of potatoes on your back.

We all helped on the farm. Every one of the kids had a chore or two to do each day. Joe and Ike helped dad milk the cows, feed the pigs, etc. I remember my dad really getting upset because I

22

got to sleep in until 6 o'clock in the morning and he, Joe and Ike were busy feeding and milking the cows. He called me lazy. That really cut to the bone. I made a vow to myself that he would never say that again. From that day forward I too got up at the crack of dawn.

Dad with a young Friesian Holstein

Ike with one of the young cows

We three oldest boys all helped doing the various chores on the farm. We drove tractors, the pickup truck, the new 1951 Chevrolet station wagon, etc. Lena, being the oldest girl, helped mom raise the younger brothers and sisters and helped with various household chores. Lena had a clever nickname for each one of us. I had several—one was Bani, and another was Kriel Haan (Bantam Rooster--small fry).

With our animals, garden and indigenous fruit trees and berry bushes, Mom's canning and cooking skills kept us well fed year round. My memories of canned tomatoes, peaches, pears, pickles, carrots, peas, beans, corn plus sauerkraut aged in huge ceramic crocks make me yearn for earlier times. We took advantage of a cellar where perishable foodstuffs were kept during summer heat. Mom baked all our bread and by husbanding our cows, pigs and chickens, we rarely bought any eggs, milk or meat from a grocery store (supermarkets were not popular in our area of Michigan.)

Mom's skills with sewing and knitting produced dresses and blouses from printed flour sacks and feed sacks for my sisters; her knitting kept us warm with sweaters and mittens. Often with stitches over stitches, she mended socks by the hour.

Flour Bag Dresses Common in 1930's – 40's - & early '50's

The Van Bemden family on the farm

This is a photo of the Van Bemden family taken on the farm in Ravenna. I believe mom is holding Wilma, the first of the Van Bemdens born in the U.S. Four more kids came later.

Dad would generally buy the groceries on Tuesday night when he would make his 30–35 mile one way journey to take us older children to catechism.

Catechism was a big deal in our culture. However, teenagers didn't take it seriously as evidenced by Tuesday night classes during which Rev. Lamain would make his way up and down each row of pews testing every one of the kids attending by asking one of the Heidelberg Catechism questions from the memory work assigned for that week. We quickly made a joke of his efforts by accurately predicting which question each of us would get by simply counting down the numbers ahead of us. During these classes, boys sat on one side of the room, girls on the other.

Our Sundays were devoted to church with services in the morning, afternoon, and evening. In our mid-teens, we were allowed to go downstairs in the afternoon and listen to an English reading service delivered by one of the elders. In the afternoon, in the main sanctuary, Rev. Lamain delivered the sermon in Dutch. For these services, our parents invested in a roll of Lifesavers for each one of us in an attempt to keep us occupied and quiet during the extended sermons. Dutch was our family's primary language. It was the dominant communication in our house unless non-Dutch-speaking visitors were in our home.

My middle school years in Ravenna allowed me to make new friends. Gary Blackmere and Leonard Crawford became close buddies. The Crawford family also had a dozen or more kids. Strength in numbers provided a layer of protection against any misguided bully who considered victimizing any of the Van Bemdens. Early school reputations established by Joe, Ike and me added to the protective umbrellas we enjoyed.

We had a highly active shop class and the instructor had us do lots of projects. I still have several of them. I made a couple of wooden nightstand lamps my parents had for years and, a few years ago, my mother gave them back to me. She used a galvanized metal scoop that I made in shop class in her flour and sugar jars for years.

Van in Coveralls and Hand-knit Sweater

Most of my school clothes were hand me downs from either friends of the family and/or from Joe and Ike. I remember wearing overalls to school. I even have one of my school pictures of me in overalls. I should have worn my sweater over the top of my overalls; so it would not have been so obvious. Notice also the sweater I have on was hand knit by my mother. I guess I was not very conscious of how I dressed.

Mrs. Gaylord, one of my favorite teachers, had been a missionary in Africa. On Fridays, leaving me to lead the class in spelling bees or geography lessons, she had speaking engagements prompting her to have her hair done. I think she was comfortable with this arrangement because, most of the time I was one of the last people standing when there was a spelling bee. I credit my technique of using my fingers as a pencil to spell out the word behind my back made me one of the better spelling students in the class. My grades were good enough that Joe and Ike teased me anytime my report card came out with a C on it.

During recess and lunch hour, we would choose up sides to play baseball or "pom-pom-pull away" or "I'll fetch you away." You knew well who the good players were and obviously they would get chosen first.

Shep, our dog, provided hours of fun with his ferocious attacks on anything we found – sticks, boards, rags—to tease him with. Sitting on the old pumphouse playing with Shep entertained us for hours and he knew when the game was over when we climbed down from our perch and turned our attention to something else. Often "something else" translates into a call to come in for some homemade bread. At these times, timing was critical. We raced to the kitchen arriving just as Mom was pulling a loaf out of the oven. There is nothing better than hot bread with butter and sugar. It does not get any better than that.

A lice infestation at school prompted all the parents to find remedies. Moms was to run a fine-tooth comb through our hair extracting the tiny little buggers.

One-year, bumper crops of potatoes prompted the US Agriculture Department to sell surplus spuds for cattle feed at very low prices. When my dad found out about this, we started getting a truck load a week to feed to the cows. When the truck driver would deliver these potatoes, he would dump them in the barnyard and when he was through dumping his load, he would take out a bag of blue powder and sprinkle it all over the potatoes so they would not be used for human consumption. Well, it rained one time after we received a load and all the blue powder washed off. From that day forward, and until we stopped getting them, we never bought any potatoes. I vaguely remember that we had a cow choke on a potato motivating us to cut them into smaller pieces with our shovels.

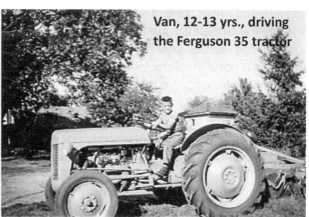

Van, 12-13 yrs., driving the Ferguson 35 tractor

I remember one time when I was driving the Ferguson tractor cultivating a field of corn, a squirrel ran across the open field and I took off after it and finally caught it with my bare hands, it bit me and part of its tooth broke off and lodged between one of my finger joints. It was years before I could straighten out my finger. I believe it finally dissolved.

Although we had some trees that served as wind breakers on each side of the large garden area, and we had a rather good-sized orchard, there weren't a whole lot of trees around so seeing a squirrel was somewhat unique. Years later, when relatives came over from the old country, they would get excited about seeing a squirrel. I guess there weren't a whole lot of squirrels in the Nederlands and on the island of Noord Beveland in particular.

Putting up hay at our farm meant stacking hundreds of bales in the barn. Since most of our machinery on the farm was new, we had the latest and best implements around. When our new elevator for lifting hay bales into the loft arrived, farmers from miles around came by to see it in action. This elevator allowed us to replace twine with wire creating more efficient storage because the bales could be more compressed making them considerably heavier; but, without the elevator, lifting them into the hay loft was too difficult. This same elevator was pressed into service for storing corn in the cribs which were often filled to overflowing.

After a busy day stacking hay, sometimes dad would take us swimming in Crockery Creek, not too far from the house. This creek had a nice deep swimming hole directly under the bridge. Some of us with a daredevil streak would dive or jump off the bridge into this hole without worrying about hitting the bottom and breaking our necks. The windbreak trees surrounding our property were ideal for daredevil playtime with my brothers. We climbed as close to the top as we could, then like orangutans featured these days on Animal Planet, or more like Tarzan in the movies from our childhood, we swung from tree to tree.

Our farm neighbors, the Albrights, had a son who rigged up a basketball hoop by cutting the bottom out of an old bushel basket and mounting it in their barn. Occasionally, Ike and I would go there to play basketball. To get to their barn, we cut across the fields often catching one of Elmer's horses to ride bareback up to the barn. The lure of basketball often took precedence over family chores. On Sunday afternoons, when it was Ike's turn to babysit younger siblings, milk the cows, slop the hogs and perform other chores as ordered by our folks while they were attending church, Ike abandoned our farm to sneak over to Albrights for a pick-up basketball game. Like most kids, we looked for easier faster ways to finish chores. When dad wasn't around, and we were milking all the cows by ourselves, we cranked up the pulsing action on the milk machines. We ignored warnings about the stress this puts on a cow as our priorities always seemed more important.

If I was lucky and Joe or Ike had not beaten me to it, I would get to drive the 1951 Chevy station wagon up to the Sinclair gas station which was a couple of miles down the road and get a newspaper. I had learned how to manually shift driving the tractors, thus driving a straight stick automobile was not a problem. I was only about 12-13 years old at this time and could barely see above the dashboard. We never bought any gas there because we would always fill the car up with farm gas. We were not supposed to do this, but we did; and I suspect that most other farmers did likewise. The reason you were not supposed to do this was because no road taxes were assessed on farm gas. I learned years later the gas company started to put a dye in the farm gas to prevent farmers from doing what we did years earlier.

Sun tans in my teen years were as popular as they are today. However, my dad did not appreciate our interest in them (probably because of growing up in Holland where the sun was considerably less worshipped than in America). Thus, to avoid confrontations, we waited till our folks went to church before lying outside in our swimsuits. Anticipating their return from church, we were always dressed and waiting inside; however, I doubt they were fooled since the effects of the sun on our skin were impossible to ignore. Commercial sunscreen was unheard of but baby oil mixed with iodine worked well.

I remember Joe used to plaster his hair down with Brylcreem hair dressing. He always had a big curl in his hair. Brylcreem was oily, sticky, Vaseline-like gel that was used for the slicked back look.

In the early 1950s a polio vaccine was developed by US physician Jonas Salk. The Salk vaccine was in wide use by the late 1950s. There was another polio vaccine, namely the Sabin's live virus oral polio vaccine administered in drops or on a sugar cube. All the Van Bemden kids received the Sabin polio vaccine.

I remember both Dad and Ike loved pickled herring and I can still picture them holding a pickled herring by the tail and letting it slide down their throat. I personally never developed a liking for them, although I enjoy most fish.

One of the rules at the Van Bemden household was that, unless you were in your mid-teens, bedtime was 7:00 PM. Obviously, in the middle of the summer, there were still several hours of daylight left; but for my mother and dad to get some peace and quiet, 7:00 PM was bedtime for the younger kids. Of course, we would all hang out the windows, etc. Sometimes when we got a little rowdy and too noisy, dad would sneak upstairs with his belt off and beat the living tar out of us. Mom would be at the bottom of the stairs hollering: "Case, don't beat them to death!" in Dutch.

One unusually rainy spring, the commercial dairy truck we depended on to pick up milk we sold to them was unable to get through the mud to our house creating a surplus of milk we had no way of preserving. To prevent it from souring, mom portioned it out so the pigs received a special treat of fresh milk before she shocked all of us by using the washing machine to churn the remainder into butter! Any time the electricity power grid failed; we were pressed into service to milk thirty to forty cows. This took quite some time prompting us to be looking for a different solution; thus, when Johnny Kase showed us how to use the vacuum outlet on our tractors to drive a generator that could power one Surge milking machine, we were ecstatic.

We only had one large galvanized stock tank in the barnyard to satisfy the thirst of our entire herd of milk cows. On a few occasions, we captured wild turtles and threw them into the tank.

The telephone service out in the boonies was strictly a party line and there was always an operator involved. We would have one ring, the next party down the line would have two rings, etc. I don't remember how many rings ours was. Occasionally, we probably listened in on somebody else's call.

One spring day we had a real surprise visitor to our farm. Because of the severe winter in Canada, the snow owls were coming farther south than normal and one of them stayed on our farm for several days. It was a confident raptor allowing us to get close enough to convince us we might successfully capture it; alas, it was also smart enough to fly away anytime our approach threatened its freedom.

An early to mid-1950s Schwinn bike

When Joe and Ike were in their early teens, dad bought-new Schwinn bicycles for them. These bikes had everything: lights, a horn, basket in the front, white-wall tires, etc. Once the newness wore off, Joe and Ike allowed the rest of us to ride them. Sometimes when we were playing, we camouflaged the bikes with twigs. We also fastened playing cards to the frame with clothes pins through the spokes creating the sound of a roaring car as the wheels turned.

Dick Rottschafer also had a farm in Drenthe, MI which provided summer jobs for us baling and stacking hay. Compared to the flatlands of the greater Grand Rapids area, this farm's fields were rolling hills making tractor operation dangerous. The threat of rolling over trapping us under it prompted us to stand on the running board on the uphill side ready to abandon the machine if it tipped over on its side. Another time when we were transferring cattle from one farm to the other, the cows were rounded up and put loose in a stake truck dad had borrowed from a friend. When we got to a steep but short hill to get over the railroad tracks, all the cows moved to the back of the truck lifting the front wheels off the ground. Thus, dad had no control over where he was going because he could not steer the truck. Luckily, this was a very short distance and there was no oncoming traffic.

In my Ravenna middle school shop class, I designed a contraption to shake fruit out of their trees when they were ripe. My design featured a wide belt wrapped around the trunk of the tree and then, in a figure eight, it looped over the power takeoff of the tractor. By creating an eccentric loop, the belt shook the tree powerfully enough to dislodge ripe fruit without damaging the tree allowing fruit to fall into a foam-lined canvas lying on the ground strategically placed to catch free falling fruit. Years later, this idea was patented by someone else and much of today's commercially marketed fruit and nuts are harvested by this invention. I should have followed through with my idea and today I would be a multi-millionaire.

We installed new barbed wire fences around the entire perimeter of the farm. We used the tractor to pull the wire tight and hold it in place while staples to hold it in place were pounded into the fence posts. The tension on the wire fencing was extreme and Ike's hand was seriously injured when the barb-wire snapped allowing the wire to inflict a deep laceration on Ike's thumb.

Bluebirds, very scarce today despite the Audubon Society's attempts to restore them by installing copious nesting boxes, were plentiful in my youthful days on the farm. Old hollowed out fence posts made ideal nesting places for the birds; but metal fencing has reduced their natural habitat. Lots of times when we were cutting hay, wild animals like pheasants and skunks ran in front of the hay mower and literally lost their heads and/or legs. An injured skunk releases its defensive odor which no amount of washing, even with bleach or camphor, can effectively eliminate.

A dog my dad rescued from the Muskegon County Humane Society was so mean he had to be tied up all the time. Even though his tether was a chain, he circled the pole so many times the chain wore through the pole and he broke loose. His first act of freedom was to jump into the pig pen where he ate a piglet sealing his fate. Dad found a new home for him.

Raiding turtle dove nests provided opportunities for us to try raising young squabs into adults but we were never successful. I think our failure was due to enzymes parent doves have assisting digestion of corn in their offspring. Unaware of this deficiency, our attempts to force feed the little birds had little positive effect and they died. Starlings are the true "dirty birds." Nesting in barns produces bales of hay covered with bird dung. Attempting to clear our barn of the birds, we stationed ourselves at the open windows of the barn to catch and kill them as another of our siblings ran back and forth on the threshing floor scaring the birds into flying toward the open windows. We were effective exterminators without the benefit of chemicals and poisons.

Disobeying dad's rule, Pete and Cora were caught playing in the hay loft. While dad proceeded to punish Pete by kicking his rear end, Cora, hoping to avoid equal punishment, in her haste to exit the loft, fell. Apparently, dad felt this was enough punishment for her and she escaped further corporal correction.

Farm life in Ravenna included butchering pigs and chickens for our own dining pleasures. From a butchered pig, mom created 'head cheese,' one of my favorite culinary delights. Head cheese is a mixture of everything a pig's head can deliver: ears, tongue, brains, eyeballs, etc. Ground into puree and cooked in a pot, I always looked forward to enjoying this delicacy. Chitterlings, a deep south staple the folks reduce to "chitlins," are made from swine intestines thoroughly cleaned and fried into crisp strips. As tasty as they can be, thorough cleaning is absolutely necessary.

Silage Is animal feed created by chopping and mixing alfalfa or other grass with corn stalks and leaves or sorghum, bush bean vines like pintos or soybeans, with grain –mostly corn but often other grains like cracked sorghum, millet, etc. When it is thoroughly mixed, spontaneous combustion creates enough heat to literally cook the mix producing liquor. When this liquor-soaked mixture is contained in a pit or silo, the weight compresses it and the liquor sometimes ferments. This fermented liquor collects and runs out into small pools. On our farm, these pools were accessible to our pigs. Imagine the fun we had watching adult pigs wobbling around after sucking up this "farmers' moonshine!"

Bantam roosters have a well-earned reputation for being feisty. We had an old mirror in the barn where our rooster could see himself in it. He saw what he thought was a competing counterpart and went on the attack. He fought that interloper's reflection so viciously he bloodied himself. Years later, I saw a similar thing at my brother Adrian's house in Florida where a red cardinal saw himself in the reflection of a window and was covered in blood beating himself up banging the window attacking its own reflection.

In the summers when Joe and Ike were working at the Black Dirt farm, Casey, about ten years old and I, about twelve to thirteen, had to pick up the slack. At that early age, we drove the tractor to cultivate the corn, mow the hay and do whatever had to be done. After a day in the fields, we were covered from head to toe with dirt and caked on mud from our sweat. I don't recollect having a shower in our Ravenna house; thus, I suspect we used an open garden hose to clear the dirt before we entered the house.

Snapping Turtle

One day when some of us were mucking around in one of the ponds on Sanders Black Dirt farm, I was feeling around in the mud, and I almost lost a finger to a large snapping turtle. We ran over to be where Joe and Ike were working, and they drove one of the tractors with a front-end loader over to where we had been playing and dug it out of the mud. Mr. Sanders killed it and butchered it. That was the first time I ever knew of anyone eating a turtle. I guess they have about a half dozen different types of meat in them and supposedly it's quite good. As you can see, they look like they could be quite mean, and they are!

When Joe and Ike were in their early to mid-teens, in the summertime, they worked at Sanders Black Dirt farm which was just a mile or so down the road from where we lived. They scraped, stockpiled and loaded dump trucks with black dirt. One day while they were working, Joe accidentally ran over Ike's legs. Joe was driving the dump truck moving some dirt into piles and Ike had just finished loading the truck with the front-end loader on the Ford tractor when he ran to the truck, jumped on the running board which was somewhat loose, slipped off and fell under the rear wheels of the truck. Both of his legs were broken in two places. Later, Ike told the story of how he tried to get up and his legs just buckled under. The broken bones were bad enough but one of them was a compound fracture allowing him to see the broken end piercing his leg and trousers. I was cultivating corn on our farm when I saw the ambulance go by, unaware of the fact that they were going to pick up my brother, Ike, who was badly hurt. Shortly after Ike's accident, my dad quit the farm and we moved to a 10 acre farm in Cascade, MI.

My sister, Wilma, was the first of our family to be born in the United States. She was born at Aunt Lena and Uncle Dan's house with a doctor in attendance. **
**Side Note: Uncle Dan and Aunt Lena Wynn were not blood relatives but, because they were close friends of the family, that is how we referred to them.
Mom was at Uncle Dan and Aunt Lena's delivering Wilma but dad was home with the rest of us when a thunderstorm generated a ball of fire that erupted from an electrical outlet in our living room and rolled across the floor exiting through another outlet on the opposite wall. We were sitting on the couch and this phenomenon profoundly frightened us.

When mom was delivering babies, all the kids stayed with friends. On the occasion of Jaci's birth, mom delivered her in the back seat of our 1938 Pontiac. The back seat, comfortable for passengers, was less than ideal for a delivery room but, despite a police escort, dad didn't get to Butterworth Hospital in time for Jaci to be delivered there. My sisters, Jaci and Maria, are about 11 months apart.

When we lived in Ravenna, we all kissed Jaci goodbye as dad and mom took her to the hospital in Grand Rapids. She was very sick and we did not know what her illness was. We feared she might not return. Mom could not explain beyond saying the doctors gave her a lot of vitamins, she mentioned B12, which makes me suspect Jaci had pneumonia from which she recovered.

We lived out in the boonies (aka: boondocks as people would say) and that was back in the days when travelling salesmen came by ever so often to sell you things like Fuller brushes and Watkins drugs. I remember playing cowboys and Indians and the cowboys had cap guns that had a roll of caps that produce a loud sound and a puff of smoke when a small explosive charge is ignited. I believe in this day and age it would be strictly prohibited. I also remember that for a while we got a truck load of spent grain (malted barley and/or other grains) delivered once in a while to feed to the cows and pigs.

Before television commercials and the internet, printed materials like the newspaper, magazines and comic books were the domain of advertising. Yes, radio spawned soap operas and we were deluged with commercials when we listened to radio programs but my interests were targeted by ads published in magazines and comic books. When we lived in Ravenna, I sent away for information regarding "How to Become an Airplane Mechanic," "Mathematics Made Easy," and a "Charles Atlas Body Building" course. The Charles Atlas course had an interesting ad that featured him and then a cartoon of a skinny guy with a girl at the beach. This ad ran forever! The following paragraph and ad were lifted off the internet.

Charles Atlas Ad

Here a comic strip depicts a beach scene featuring a bully kicking sand in a weakling's face - this is the catalyst for taking action to improve to a far more 'manly' physique. The advertising campaign featuring his name and body was possibly one of the longest lasting campaigns of all time. Atlas trained himself to develop his body from that of a scrawny weakling to eventually becoming the most popular bodybuilder of his day.

About the time we moved off the farm in Ravenna, pickles were starting to be grown on many of the farms around the neighborhood. In 1949, Don Swanson built a huge pickle factory in Ravenna. Vic, our neighbor across the road from us, a bachelor, lived with his Polish mother. She could not speak a word of English and Vic leased their farm to grow cucumbers for Swanson's pickles. Soon

there were lots of Mexicans working the fields during cucumber harvesting time. Let it be known that Michigan is the number one producer of pickles in the US. Below is a photo taken in 2004 of the Swanson Pickling Co. with more than 1,300 fiberglass tanks, each able to hold 905 bushels of cucumbers, with fermentation taking from four to six weeks.

Don Swanson Pickle Factory in Ravenna, MI

Another thing I remember about Vic, our neighbor, was that while we were harvesting wheat, oats and rye with a brand-new combine, he was using an old-fashioned threshing machine. Threshing with an old fashioned machine was quite an operation and fun, as well as interesting, to watch—very labor intensive! It took lots of helping hands to do threshing the old-fashioned way.

An old Threshing Machine

We lived on the farm in Ravenna for 3 ½ years. Years later my mother told me my mom and dad did not really like it there because there were so many Catholics in the neighborhood. Thus, in September of whatever year (I believe it must have been 1952), we moved to Cascade, MI.

Cascade, MI, 1952

When I was in middle school, we moved from Ravenna, MI to a small farm (I think it was about ten acres) in Cascade, Michigan, with a full-size barn and silo. Initially we had a few milk cows, some ducks and geese, also quite a few chickens.

Our house on Cascade Road was a huge house built around the turn of the century. We bought it from the Mast family that went to the same church as we did. It had five bedrooms, a half bath upstairs and two bedrooms downstairs. None of us had our own bedroom and we all doubled (or more) up. Joe and Ike were in one bedroom and Casey and I in another. I think Lena and Cora, and perhaps Wilma, shared another bedroom.

Van and Wilma in front of our house on Cascade Rd. 1956

I can still see Ike lying in a bed in front of the window in the family room after we moved to Cascade, listening to the radio that Mr. Sanders bought for him at the beginning of his recovery period. It was at that time that Ike dropped out of school. I can also picture him sliding from chair to chair to go to the bathroom. I guess they did not have any walkers in those days. He only had crutches.

I did not remember that dad worked as a janitor at the church for a year or two when we first moved to Cascade until my mother reminded me of it years later. He also did work around Rev. Lamain's house now and then—things like cutting the grass and trimming bushes, etc. I guess some of the kids were mean to him in that they would dump paper towels on the floor etc. Knowing my dad, who was very much a no-nonsense kind of a guy, this had to irritate him and he could not do a whole lot about it. After a certain amount of time, my dad asked for a raise. Mr. Weststrass, who was on the consistory and somewhat assertive, did not think that he needed one; so, dad quit and went to work at Imperial Metal Products in Grand Rapids.

When we first moved to our small farm on Cascade Rd., we had a couple of cows and a few chickens and some ducks and geese. The geese were almost like watch dogs and they were

32

never inside the barnyard. They pretty much had the run of the place and it seemed they would always stick around the house. Anytime someone would drive into the driveway, they would start honking. My mother even tried to pawn off cooked goose eggs for us to eat but nobody liked them. We dug a shallow pond next to the barn for the ducks and geese, but we could not keep water in it because it didn't have a clay liner. Sometime after that we tried digging a shallow pond down in the hollow by the old hickory tree in the back forties but that too did not retain water very well. Eventually we gave up on having a pond for the ducks and geese.

One time dad brought home an Isetta, which was a small Italian car. The whole front end of it opened to let one sit down. This was basically a two-person car. This was in the days of the Nash

1958 Nash Metropolitan

Metropolitan and the Crosley cars. These cars were real sub-compact by today's standards.

Dad had most of his minor car repairs done by Marty, who ran the Shell station in Eastmont, MI. This fellow was a real Jew hater. I remember one time Walt gave dad a newspaper sized pamphlet containing a list of influential Jews in positions of power. According to the pamphlet, somehow these Jews controlled all the money in the US—perhaps the world.

Gary DeArmond became a good buddy, and he was a real nature lover. He set traps to catch muskrats and other animals. I think he got $1 for each fur. He lived on Laraway Lake, and he raised a lot of ducks. He also fished a lot. Sometimes he would go fishing during lunch for trout in the stream on the edge of Cascade Elementary School playground. He was the one that told us about going to Michigan bakeries and getting a barrel full of day-old bread, cup cakes, pies, etc. for $1 to feed his ducks. We started doing this and sometimes, when we got there, the clerk who ran the day-old store, did not have a full barrel and they would simply go to the rack and pull off loaves of bread and break the wrapping and throw it in the barrel. When we got home, we would go through the barrel and eat what we knew was good since they tore into the packages in front of our eyes.

Chuck Dykhuizen was a classmate who, in the 7th grade, contracted rheumatic fever and was gone for most of the school year. Other classmates with whom I went through middle school as well as high school, were: Perry Vanderveen, Adrian Gilder, Pete Van Stee, Danny Koetsier, and Fred Koetsier. Danny Koetsier had a 1939 Ford he drove around in the fields behind his house.

One day while some of us, and I do not remember who, were playing (probably horsing around is more likely) around the house, we must have gotten mad at each other, and we were throwing stones trying to hit each other. I hit my sister Jaci in the head. It made a huge gash and required several stitches to close it leaving a scar. Luckily, when she wears bangs, her hair covers it up well. I really got a verbal thrashing (I do not remember whether I got a physical beating) that evening when my dad got home from work.

In the wintertime we made a pile of snowballs and threw them at semi-trucks as they went by the house. We also had homemade sling shots we used occasionally. These homemade slingshots were better than the "Whamo" ones you could buy in the stores. On one occasion, Pete threw a snowball and hit a pipe the trucker was smoking.

There was a relatively large pond not too far from the house that froze over in the winter and we usually got to it before the ice was very solid. We would walk over it and it was really rubbery. I don't think any of us kids ever fell thru and I believe it was simply pure luck that we didn't. In the summertime we would skip rocks across it. The one that got the most skips was the winner.

Before the interstate highway system was built, we lived on Cascade Road, also known as US 16, the main highway connecting Detroit with Grand Rapids. There was a lot of truck traffic on this highway. When we first moved there, we could literally feel the ground shake when a truck with a heavy load rumbled by.

Shortly after we moved to Cascade, we discovered hundreds of goldfish in an old abandoned gravel pit so we transferred a bucket full of them to our stock tank where they thrived. We had them for quite some time and, one winter, when the water was quite a bit lower than normal, it froze solid (or awfully close to it). We were pleasantly surprised when the frozen water thawed and the goldfish had survived.

During an overnight at Rob Boot's house, we went for a walk to Dutton, which was about 1½ mile from his house. On the way back, we found the remains of a burned-out flare stuck in the dirt. We pulled it out and placed it on the road with the sharp point up. Lo and behold, not five minutes later a car ran over the flare puncturing one of his tires. This was in the days when all car tires had inner tubes. Convinced the driver saw us put it on the road, we were so scared we ran and hid in the corn field.

Farmall Cub Tractor

When we first moved to Cascade, we had a Farmall Cub tractor we used to plow our garden. Eventually, we put a Model "T" engine in it delivering a lot more horsepower and speed. At faster speeds, the front wheels wobbled. That was not a problem with the factory engine, but it was never designed to go as fast as with the Model "T" engine in it.

Dad bought a Silver

Silver King Tractor like ours

King tractor with a single front wheel designed to be the "fastest road tractor ever made." We used this tractor to haul manure from the Vander Boon slaughterhouse which was in the Ada, MI area and was quite a few miles down the road. It also allowed us to retrieve fertilizer from the Beltline Turkey Farm which was only a few miles from where we lived.

Whom ever went with dad to load the manure would ride home on top of the manure spreader. I guess we probably had a rug or something that we would sit on. I really do not remember that part of it.

Memories of dad hanging hams in the old smokehouse after salting them in an old tin bathtub add to the nostalgia of my childhood days on the farm.

One time we found an old pistol in the rafters in the barn and dad made us throw it into the old marrow pit. When Mr. Lucas, our next-door neighbor, found out about our discovery, he wanted it. We tried digging it up out of the old marrow pit, but it had been corroded beyond recovery by the minerals in the pit.

We cleared 10 acres of woods and hauled the logs back to Cascade on a 4-wheel hay trailer pulled with the International pickup truck my dad bought while we still lived on the farm. It was quite a task and took us weeks to clear this plot of land.

Case Gebuist, a good friend of the family, preferred working with a pair of horses rather than a tractor for farm work—particularly pulling a hay wagon. He just loved horses. He only had one arm. I do not recall how he lost his arm.

Playboy magazine centerfold photos adorned the interior walls of our neighbor's outhouse. I remember one time sneaking over there and stealing a few. I do not remember what we did with them or how long we boys might have kept them and I'm sure we successfully hid them because I have no memory of ever being held responsible for them. I am sure our parents never discovered them. We probably hid them in the barn—I really do not remember.

Gary DeArmond and I were both volunteers in Civil Air Patrol which involved watching the sky for airplanes from a ground observation station/tower located next to the Cascade Middle School (which is like a tower in the national forest where they have people looking for wildfires) and determining the plane's position and time of sighting and then reporting to the authorities. This was at the time when people in the US were very much afraid of the big bear (USSR) coming over to the US and bombing us. Gary gave me a half dozen parakeets and a large cage. I do not remember how long I had these birds, but I really enjoyed them. I even raised some chicks (young parakeets). Gary DeArmond, Danny Koetsier and I were crossing a pasture and a young bull came running after us. I picked up a good-sized branch, hid behind a tree and, when the young bull came close enough to where I was hiding, I hit it in the head with the club and dropped it to its knees.

One of our distant neighbors maintained an apiary (honey bee hives). Gary, Danny and I raided it but realized we had been observed in the act by the owners. We escaped by running to our barn and climbing up into the cupola. From this elevated vantage point, we watched our frustrated beekeeping neighbors driving up and down the road unsuccessfully searching for us. Shimmying across the railing at the top of the barn, roughly 20-25 feet above the floor, was dangerous but I guess we were not afraid. Today there is a familiar saying: "have no fear" for someone who dares to do anything and everything. It was simply a matter of hanging on and not letting go.

Howard Clark, a buddy I haven't mentioned yet, lived with his dad in a small mobile home along Cascade Road. His older brother was in the Army stationed in Germany. Howard walked miles up and down Cascade Rd visiting his buddies. His dad worked at Cascade Lumber Yard and spent most of his nights at the local pub. Thus, Howard had no home life to speak of prompting me to conclude he was lonely just looking for a friend. On warm spring or fall days, the lure of skinny dipping with Howard in one of the lakes near our house was irresistible. Of course, my parents didn't know about it and, since I wrote my own school absentee excuses forging my mother's name, I was never caught in the act.

One Halloween night, Howard and I filled a burlap bag with straw attaching a long string to it and laying it down in the middle of US 16 (Cascade Rd) waiting for someone to go by. When a good Samaritan stopped to get it out of the road, we yanked it away. Howard joined the Navy

Howard Clark, Van and Gary DeArmond at our 25th

when he turned 18. I had not seen or heard from Howard since I left home for college. At our twenty-fifth wedding anniversary party at Lena's house, Howard showed up. A few years later I was told that Howard Clark had died. He could not have been much more than in his early 50s.

Another Halloween, a couple of my high school buddies and I pinched what we thought to be the gas line on the school bus. We got into real trouble when it was discovered we had pinched the brake line. In retrospect, this was a stupid thing to do. We could have been charged with a felony if the principal had really wanted to stick it to us.

All the kids had to take Saturday evening baths and be ready to go to church the next morning all cleaned up. Now my mother did not run new/fresh water for every kid. The way I remember it was that we older ones would take an individual bath first and then a couple of younger ones would use that same water. Then the next oldest one, ...

When I turned sixteen, I went to the East Grand Rapids police department to get my driver's license. I had been driving for some time, so it really was not anything new. I sat down and took a written test and then we went to the car to take my driving test. I asked the policemen, "Should I drive around the block?" He said: "I'll tell you where I want you to go." Anyway, I passed it with flying colors, and I was on my way. I went to Lowell High School and rode the school bus for 4 years. Hardly anyone going to high school back then had their own car and even fewer had parents who would allow their kids to drive a car to school; thus, high school parking lots were much smaller and emptier of students' vehicles than those today.

One night when my parents were not home, I took the Nash Statesman out for a short spin along Spalding Ave., famous for its "S" curves, and I wound up in the ditch. I really panicked. I ran to Fred Koetsier house, which was only a short distance away, and knocked on the door. When his dad came to the door, I explained what had happened and he was kind enough to get his Farmall tractor out and pull me out of the ditch. I parked the car back in the garage and never told my parents about it. To this day, I do not think they ever knew.

My farm chores prevented me from participating in high school athletics. We had a huge garden my dad expected to be husbanded well enough to earn the distinction of being the biggest and most weed free garden in the county. Keeping it that way was my responsibility. My younger brother, Casey, told me years later dad had relaxed his obsession about this allowing Casey to participate in several sports.

Farm chores took precedence over all other activities. We simply were not allowed any extracurriculars until all the chores were properly completed. Many times my buddies helped finish chores like hoeing the garden to spring me in time to pursue other endeavors.

For my size, I excelled at throwing the shot-put. I never really was very competitive because I did not take it seriously enough. Despite my toughness which was distinctly superior to my competitors, it wasn't enough to encourage me to invest the level of time required to become a champion. Our track coach recruited me to run the mile. I had not trained for it, and the first time I ran it, I took off like gang busters and tried to stay with the guys who always placed. Well, I burned out and ran out of steam about ¾ of the way through the event and I think I came in next to last. That was my one and only running of the mile event. Before the advent of flexible fiberglass poles, the track coach loaned me a bamboo practice pole. Practicing in our yard did not produce competitive results and my track and field experiences were well defined by the lack of skills, training and results I've described.

My younger brother Casey and I peeled enough potatoes to last a lifetime. I can still picture us sitting on a couple of overturned pails peeling potatoes. To put some fun into it, we would try to see if we could peel the entire potato without the peel breaking in two. Another one of our morning chores was for us to make all the beds. That was not necessarily a "girls" job. In the wintertime when we had the furnace on, we would also have to clean and dump the ashes. I do not ever remember dad or mom assigning chores by gender.

Our basement was a real Michigan basement. The furnace, installed in the basement, was fueled from a dirty coal bin where a ton or so of coal was stored. In the wintertime, we always had to clean the ashes out of the coal burning furnace before we left to go to school. Each evening, dad would go downstairs, fill the firebox with coal and then shut off the air supply as much as possible so the furnace would burn all night and he would not have to ignite a fire in the morning. In other words, he tried to keep the fire going all night long. In the morning on more than one occasion, he had the fire so hot it would burn your feet if you stood on the grate. Responding to a radio ad, dad bought 100 starter chicks. The space behind the furnace was an ideal temperature for raising baby chicks until they were mature enough to be transferred to the chicken coop. We had to calculate profit and loss by keeping track of those who died or were killed by invaders like mink and weasel.

Mom canned hundreds of jars of tomatoes, pickles, beets, peaches etc. The large fruit cellar in the basement was where all our canned foodstuffs were kept. Occasionally, we would sneak downstairs, open a jar of canned peaches and eat them. In the summertime, mom canned fruit and vegetables and she made pies—oh, the pies! So good! In addition to the produce we raised in our garden we also picked wild blackberries. Wild boysenberries proliferated all around us but we never did anything with them. I guess no one ever told us these were edible.

Mom depended on a small gas stove in the basement to boil her canning jars and launder white sheets. Mold we sometimes discovered inside the canned foodstuffs suggested perhaps mom's efforts to produce vacuums in the jars were less than completely successful. I think she reused some of the canning lids and rubber seals and they did not seal correctly.

Often, in the summertime, we went to the dam on the Thornapple River to go swimming. One of the more daring things to do was to shimmy up the column on the Cascade Dam building, climb to the top, and jump down into the river. Shimmying to the top of the building was tricky and dangerous, but being young, oblivious to the dangers, we had no fear.

One of my science projects was a water wheel. It was crudely put together and the science teacher used it for years as an example of how not to make a project. I didn't have the money required to purchase the pieces to make the waterwheel; however, no way was I going to hit dad up for money to properly complete my project. It truly was the worst project I ever did.

Van – 15-16 yrs. old

Encouraged by the prowess of Harry Mast, one of my brother Ike's buddies who excelled in body building and demonstrations of muscle power, I developed an interest in weight lifting. Harry could do chin-ups by simply gripping the 2 x 10 floor joists in our basement and I saw him raise the front wheel of a heavy 1938 Packard off the ground by lifting the front bumper.

Beginning with heavy objects of one type or another in our basement, I eventually secured a set of real weights and, from time to time, a buddy or two from school would work out with me.

On two occasions during my high school days, my strength and muscle exploits created memorable events. One of them occurred when Mr. White, study hall monitor, confronted me regarding what he considered to be excessive trips to the library. I was wearing a skin tight shirt I particularly liked and, in his attempt to assist me in returning to the study hall room from the library, he grabbed my shirt. I reacted with: "Don't stretch the merchandise!" Recognizing his error and the potential for my response, he responded by releasing his grip on my shirt inviting me to exact my revenge by pulling on his shirt! Because this all occurred in front of a study hall full of impressionable students, I was more than a little smug.

On another occasion, during an all-school assembly where we were treated to a demonstration of weightlifting by a physical fitness professional, I accepted the challenge to join the man on stage for a contest of comparing strength. Limiting the contest to a series of "clean and jerk" exercises, we gradually increased the weights till we had 250 lbs. on the barbell. To my astonishment (and pride), I successfully cleaned and jerked the 250 lbs. but the instructor failed!

I heard later he told our PE teacher, Mr. Perry, he would never again invite a volunteer for his demonstration. He was a good sport, however. At Caledonia High School where my cousin, Robert Boot attended, he presented his program but recounted my successful challenge.

During my high school years, when my classmates (and my brother, Casey, with whom I shared a bedroom) were reading comic books, I was immersed in muscle magazines. Because I felt comic books failed to deal with reality, e.g., what the real world was all about, I refused to waste my time reading them. I've never seen any comic strip or book presenting a hero doing anything productive, have you? Thus, to this day, I don't read the comic strips in the daily newspaper.

Long hot summer work days often ended with sessions around the dinner table with all the kids suffering the boredom of Dad's reading from the Bible. I provided a bit of relief during these sessions by attending without wearing a shirt. While Dad was reading, I was demonstrating my ability to flex my pectoral muscles, making them bounce up and down.

My US history teacher, an elderly lady named Mrs. Dole, whose naturally white hair was more blue than white, had an annoying habit of adjusting her bra and slip straps during class. She had been teaching this course forever and it was no secret her tests were the same year after year making it relatively easy for students to cheat. However, on one occasion, a cheater was off one number making all his answers wrong and he flunked the course. Mr. Avery, the business math teacher, was a very stern fellow who rarely smiled. His sense of humor was very dry, very British one might say.

The Lowell Showboat was docked along the Flat River easily boarded from the path connecting the high school to downtown Lowell. The vessel, a barge powered by a concealed outboard motor, was made to look like a paddle wheel steamer with a paddle wheel like a Mississippi riverboat. Every year the town of Lowell presented a show on this stage. It was also a great place for kids to play tag.

Lloyd Miller and I earned free lunches by setting up the cafeteria tables in our high school gym. We enjoyed this concession for a year or so and, not only did it allow us to earn our lunches, we were also allowed to leave class earlier than the rest of the students. Another high school buddy, Gary DeArmond, and I were throwing rocks at ducks in the river and I happened to hit a mallard in the head killing it. We fished the dead duck out of the river and, with no regard whatever for the implications of it being out of duck hunting season, Gary stuffed it under his coat to take home for dinner. Only later did we consider the ramifications and were glad we had escaped the potential consequences. One time Ike and Harry Mast borrowed a truck which was used to carry beer kegs. They drained the kegs and got quite a bit of beer which, unbeknownst to my parents, they kept in some of mom's glass canning jars down in the basement.

Joe and Ike were both employed by the Nash Body Shop, which resulted in our family developing a preference for this brand of automobile. We owned a Nash Statesman but, unfortunately, Ike rolled it on his way home from work.

Unlike the general American population, Europeans enjoy eating horsemeat. A pet store on 28th Street sold it as dog food but, occasionally, when Joe and Ike were coming home from work, they would stop and get a large supply of it. The store owner assumed we had a bunch of hungry dogs to feed but mom would fry it up for us. It is quite good and tasty. I just recently read in the local newspaper that the U.S. Government was trying to reduce the number of wild mustangs out west and one of the primary countries where lots of them were being sold was France.

On one occasion Mom bet Joe and Ike that if they could eat a ½ gallon of ice cream they could have it free. They could not and wound up paying for it themselves.

In the summer of my fourteenth year, I worked for Harry Mast's brothers, John and Gerald, who were brick layers. I mixed mud, kept them in a good supply of bricks and moved the scaffolding around as necessary for the jobs. It was hard work, but I was fit as an ox and enjoyed it. Plus, it allowed me to earn a little bit of money. They paid me $1.50/hr. The summer of my 15th year, I was working at Durrant Nursery for $1/hr. when I was offered $1.50 to work for some brick layers. Not sure of the prudence of accepting the offer, I called in sick as a way of returning to the nursery if I didn't want the brick layer job. After a couple days, Cal Kappas, my boss at the nursery, came by the house to check on me but I was out on my other job. My mother appraised me of this and I knew the jig was up. The next day, I went to Cal and fessed up. When I told him I was getting $1.50 per hour for brick layer work, he immediately increased my pay to match it and I was back on the job with Durrant the next day. Working at the Durrant Nursery was advantageous because it was much closer to our house, and I would save quite a bit in gasoline and other auto-related costs. Mischief at the Durrant Nursery included an episode in which we nailed George's lunch pail to the workbench. He kept it close to the door so he could snatch it on his way out so you can imagine his surprise when he pulled the handle off instead of leaving with his lunch pail!

My job at Durrant Nursery motivated me to purchase over $1000 worth of seedlings which I planted under snow fences on my dad's ten-acre farm. Every year or two, I transplanted them increasing the space for each plant to grow. When I was in college, dad sold the farm but it was with the stipulation that he could return to harvest any of these plants he wanted for his new property.

Of the $55 per week I earned, about $50 of it went to my parents. The remaining $5 was mine as disposable income for gas, movies or other expenses. In those days, gasoline was about $.15-.20 per gallon and, despite parental objections, some of it went for movies which were about $.50.

On one occasion when I was working with one of the MSU college interns (I think his name was Bob Kline) we decided to use our lunch hour for a wrestling match. I surprised us both when I threw him completely over my shoulder abruptly ending the contest.

At my brother Ike's funeral service in December, 2004, I was surprised to see one of my old friends, Harold Postma. I was reminded of fun days racing our cars. At that time, I had a 1955 Chevy and he had a 1955 Ford. My Chevy was faster than his Ford. He told me he left Durrant Nursery to work for Avery Tree Company. I think he also dated my sister, Lena for a while.

I was driving our Nash Ambassador when Dave Walma's generosity prompted him to give me a baby skunk which he promptly sequestered in the trunk. Arriving home with my new pet, I opened the trunk to retrieve the little critter only to discover he had crawled into the springs of the back seat and I couldn't get him out. I removed the entire seat and shook him out! My efforts resulted in the little fellow spraying his defensive musk which required extensive effort and a lot of time before the odor faded. Dave Walma had an uncle who lived with his family. As kids we thought he was weird because he collected stuff we didn't appreciate. His nail kegs of Indian head nickels in today's values was likely a great deal of money. He also had other collections we didn't appreciate but, in retrospect, I suspect he had more money than most people. My recollections of time with Dave Walma include a fall evening around Halloween when he and a couple of his buddies picked me up and we went grape gathering at an abandoned farmhouse Dave knew featured a grape arbor. We harvested several buckets of red table grapes.

One favorite prank around Halloween was to tip over any outhouse that we could find. At that time there were still a few genuine outhouses around; although I must say they were getting harder and harder to find.

One time Joe was driving one of the Nash cars back home from church and I guess dad felt he was too close to the center curb and proceeded to slap him on the side of his head. Joe hit the center curb, stopped the car and said to dad: "You drive it home!"

Our family car, a 1953 Nash Ambassador featuring a naked lady hood ornament had problems with the starter. Making a favorable impression on dates with Louise Langerak (who was my girlfriend) was difficult with my head under the hood, hammer in hand banging on the starter to release the solenoid.

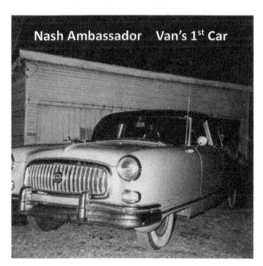

Nash Ambassador   Van's 1st Car

My cousin Rob reminded me of the time when I was driving my Nash Ambassador on the West Beltline when one of the front wheels folded underneath the car. I did not remember this, but Rob did.

One time Ike and my cousin, Rob Boot, were cleaning a 22 rifle and the cleaning rag got stuck in the barrel. They tried to get it unstuck but the more they worked on it the tighter and tighter it got. Then Ike said, "I will fix that," and put a bullet in the chamber and pulled the trigger. What happened next was that it split the barrel in two and thus ruined the rifle.

An old barn stood on the lot next to ours. It was owned by Mr. Lucas who stored an antique phonograph in it. We delighted in sneaking into the barn to play records on the old wind-up relic. In retrospect, I suspect it would be a valuable artifact today commanding a significant price if it was presented on the PBS Antique Road Show.

We were living on Cascade Road when, without fanfare or explanation my brother, Joe, left home. We assumed he had simply decided to strike out on his own. However, one morning, about two weeks after Joe left home, when the family was sitting down for breakfast, dad left and went to work but he returned home within minutes to tell everyone he saw Joe hitchhiking just down the road and that he appeared to be heading home. Dad warned everyone not to mention or bring up the topic of Joe running away from home. Using money intended to purchase four new tires, we soon learned Joe had gone to New York where he enlisted in the army.

When Joe finished his tour of duty, he returned from Germany and brought with him a VW Karmann Ghia. At that time, Ike had a new '56 Chevy Bel Air. Joe drafted Ike and me to drive to New York to retrieve his German Karmann Ghia. On this trip an epic blizzard struck as we traveled the Pennsylvania Turnpike. Attempting a turnaround between two toll booths, we were stuck requiring assistance from the booth operators who expressed their unflattering opinions about us and the impact our disturbance created on their paperwork routines. Ike and I thought the popular song at the time, Connie Francis' hit, "Who's Sorry Now", was a perfect description of our circumstance.

Volkswagen Karman Ghia

About this time, Joe and Ike were dating and bringing their dates home on Sunday afternoons. My mother did not believe in doing a whole lot of fancy cooking on Sundays; so, most of the time she would serve something simple and easy to make—sloppy joes fit the bill. When Joe and Ike brought their dates home for dinner, the older kids sat in the dining room. Since I usually consumed four or five (sometimes six) sandwiches, my plate was loaded with eight to twelve slices of bread which never failed to ignite a conversation about my voracious appetite and ability to consume sloppy joes. I preferred sloppy joes to rice pudding with raisins or prune pap. In later years, sloppy joes, rice pudding and prune pap were replaced by baked ham for Saturday and Sunday special dinners. Mom also made incredibly delicious homemade soup; in fact, the memory makes me wish I had a bowl right now. Mom's attempts to preserve her homemade cookies by locking them in the china closet were less than effective. I enjoyed these delectable treats at my leisure by cleverly picking the lock.

Joe was so proud of his 55 Buick Century he washed and polished it about every week. His enthusiasm for keeping it sparkling resulted in a few bare spots on hard creases where he actually rubbed through the paint.

Dad never missed an opportunity to remind me of his place as owner of our house and chief enforcer of his rules. Following an altercation between Joe and me during which I decked him for slugging me in the back, my dad chose to defend Joe by hitting me on the side of my head with a blow so hard my ears ring from it to this day. The original cause for the tension between Joe and me was nothing more than my decision to ride home in the back seat of Joe's car from an afternoon of tobogganing with Joe, Harry Mast, Ike and me. Joe hit me for what he perceived as my disrespect for his authority when I failed to clear enough snow from my pants to satisfy his expectation. When he hit me, I knocked him on his butt. I rode home with Ike and Harry but Joe had already given our dad his side of the story. The moment I stepped through the door into our kitchen, dad hit me. He then proceeded to tell me he didn't care "---whether I got so wide (from body building) I would have to turn sideways to come through the door, as long as I lived at home, he was the boss ---". I never questioned that.

I think the miles we rode on our bikes delivering papers on Casey's paper route in Cascade contributed to my leg muscle strength. Riding our bikes from home to Cascade provided opportunities to collect empty pop bottles we could exchange for cokes which, at that time, were only $.05. We also picked up beer cans along 28th Street. This was also our source of revenue for saving enough to buy my first set of weights.

When we older boys were just sitting around the house and jostling back and forth sometimes the term "old man" was used to refer to dad. He kind of got upset about it. He did not like to be referred to as the "old man." I guess now that I am older I understand how my dad must have felt.

I witnessed the tornado that tore through Allendale. Lena had finished a babysitting job on the west side of Grand Rapids and we were on our way to take her to catechism when, off in the distance, a funnel cloud had touched down and we could see the extensive damage it was doing.

Our pastor, Rev. Lamain, was a cigar smoker. The consistory where he and the elders met, reeked with the disgusting odor left behind by cigar smoke.

In September, 2005, when we were dining out together my cousin, Rob Boot, reminded me of the prune pap or rice pudding we ate as kids when he visited us on Sunday afternoons. Occasionally I enjoyed a reprieve from Sunday afternoon church services when I was allowed to go to his house but I don't remember the menu served at his house on these occasions.

Then as now, a good suntan in the summer was almost mandatory. When we were allowed to stay home from church on Sunday afternoons to babysit our younger siblings, the minute our folks left, we donned our swimsuits and, in defiance of our responsibility for staying inside with the younger ones, we chose to be sun worshippers in the back yard. Mixing iodine with baby oil was our preferred suntan oil but it did little to hide the red burn from our folks when they returned home. Suntan mania went to new levels when we obtained a heat lamp. On Sunday afternoons, at Rob's house, we innocently became crispy critters tanning under this artificial sun. Rob's house had a semi-flat roof over their kitchen that also served as an ideal tanning bed. My determination to sport a suntan continued beyond our back yard. On an auto trip to Niagara Falls with Ike, Rob Boot and Harry Mast, the sandy beach of Lake Erie beckoned and I made the mistake of falling asleep there. When I awoke, I was so sunburned I could not find any way to sit, stand or lie down comfortably. I paid dearly for these adolescent errors of judgement when, in my adult years, I have had to endure many corrective treatments for skin cancer.

I was introduced to commercial turkey farming when I was in high school. During Thanksgiving and Christmas vacations, Gary DeArmond and I worked at the Beltline Turkey Farm where we processed live turkeys into commercially viable birds ready for being cooked. Placing each individual turkey into a specially designed funnel allowing their head to poke out for the stroke of a well-positioned guillotine, each bird lost its head. Allowing a few minutes for the blood to drain, the decapitated carcass was then subjected to a tub of very hot water where they soaked till they were extracted and placed on a large drum featuring many rubber fingers designed to pluck the hot wet feathers. From there they were hung upside down on an assembly line for further processing which resulted in all the innards, lower legs and feet being removed.

During my senior year in High School, I bought a pair of blue suede shoes. This was at the very time that Elvis Presley was singing his song about, "Don't you step on my blue suede shoes."

A particularly large blue racer snake provided the prop we needed for a bit of mischief. One summer night, Rob Boot and I killed one we found crossing the highway. We drove to downtown Grand Rapids and threw the dead snake on the sidewalk in front of one of the popular theaters – I don't remember if it was the Savoy or the 4-Star. Regardless, the ensuing reaction of the patrons provided hilarious entertainment for us. You might get the impression I spent a lot of time with my cousin, Rob Boot, and you would be right. On Saturday nights we often drove his '46 Oldsmobile convertible to the drive-in movie in Caledonia. Rob had his own sense of fashion and always wore his blue jeans with the cuffs rolled up.

Once Lena had her driver's license Dad sold her his '53 DeSoto. It wasn't long after she bought it that she totaled it. Lena fell in love with Dave Marsman, an ex-marine without gainful employment. Dad wasn't impressed with Dave and attempted to dissuade Lena from tying the knot. Alas, Lena's determination was stronger than Dad's protests and the wedding went on. It is my pleasure to report this was a successful union that prevailed for many years.

Pete and Jeni mastered the art of whistling with their fingers in their mouths. I was unable to accomplish this but it was comforting to watch my other siblings unsuccessfully attempting this simple practice. One thing we all had no trouble mastering was chewing on any number of naturally occurring fauna – sprigs of alfalfa as well as simple weeds often decorated our lips.

The Michigan area provided delightful entertainment for visiting relatives. Coming over from the old country, our relatives enjoyed tours of the Oldsmobile plant in Lansing where they watched amazed as production lines delivered car after car on an assembly line. They were no less impressed when they visited the Kellogg cereal factory in Battle Creek and, of course, the incomparable Niagara Falls.

One of our neighbor's sons, Edgerd Lucas, had a 1956 Packard with a load leveling device on it. Thus, it kept the car level regardless of the load in it. Sometimes, when he would park it by their barn away from their house, we would sneak over and sit on the trunk to ride it up to where the car was level again.

Predigital analog odometers registered the miles any vehicle logged during its lifetime. When our '52 Chevy station wagon rolled over 90,000 miles, we decided this many miles would reduce its value; thus, using our mom's sewing machine, we ran the odometer past its maximum 99,999 mile maximum to 35,000 miles. This took all night. We justified this action by convincing ourselves these were "highway" miles rather than the more common "stop 'n go" miles which we were convinced reduced the impact on wear and tear. Actually, however, there weren't any interstate highways at that time so our logic required a bit of imagination.

Our neighbors, Leo and Flossie Blocker, convinced my folks to buy a Kirby vacuum cleaner—no doubt a good machine but certainly a bit more expensive than we could afford. Leo in his spare time was a Kirby vacuum cleaner salesmen. However, the Blockers were ambitious and we enjoyed the benefit of Leo's employee discount at the Herrod Meat Plant where he purchased meat for us using his employee discount and Flossie, who had her hair salon in her home, was Lena's and Casey's hair dresser. The Blockers eventually left Michigan to manage a sportsman's lodge in Canada.

One of my high school buddies, Steve DeVries, lived on Laraway Drive next to Gary DeArmond and we rode the same school bus. After graduating from high school, Steve became a Michigan State Police officer. He was killed by a motorist he had pulled over along I-94 near Kalamazoo and I don't know if his killer was ever apprehended.

As the Elvis Presley song goes: "Memories, pressed between the pages of my mind," is what this is all about.

Between High School and College

Shortly after high school graduation, I bought a '55 Chevy Bel Air hardtop that had suffered an electrical fire from Welder's junk yard in Grand Rapids. Ike and I put in a new "pigtail" which is a wire harness that runs under the dashboard to under the hood that includes all the electrical wires necessary to get the car up and running. We also had to replace all the sparkplug wires, etc. under the hood of the car. Since both Joe and Ike worked at a body shop, I got my car sanded and painted for no charge. Jack Buist, one of the owners and full-time mechanics at the Marathon gas station in Cascade, had to come over to our house and drop the distributor back in its hole correctly to get the car to fire. What Ike and I did not know was that there was a slot in the bottom of the distributor that had to drop in exactly right for the timing to be correct.

This was about the time that Ike was dating Jennie and she used to come over to our house in Cascade occasionally. They might have been engaged at this time. My mother was expecting a baby. It must have been Jeni since she was born April 9, 1957.

Even in today's world of high speeds, a passenger vehicle rocketing along a public street or highway at 110mph as my '55 Chevy Bel Air was doing deserves an explanation. On a Sunday morning returning home from church, Ike and I decided to race. Ike's '56 Chevy and my '55 Chevy were well matched. We were blowing through Eastmont at speeds near 110mph when a sheriff passed us going the opposite direction. I made the irresponsible decision to attempt escape by jumping the median intending to hide in a neighbor's driveway. The cop wasn't fooled and he arrested me. From the Kent County Jail, I called home but Dad refused to get involved. Ike rescued me and my escapade ended with me paying a $150 fine – over $1000 in today's dollars.

Van's '55 Chevy Bel Air with Continental Kit

Following this escapade, I installed fender skirts and a continental kit (spare tire) on the back of my '55 Chevy. This was kind of an "in" thing for a young stud to do.

Before the auto makers made it a standard feature, we were packing yellow and brown bread wrappers into our parking lights. At one point, Ike was pulled over to be advised his "amber lights" were illegal. Now we take them for granted.

46

1958

Following my high school graduation, I took a job at Wolverine Brass Company in Grand Rapids. This firm made all kinds of brass plumbing fixtures such as elbows, tees, faucets, etc. In taking my physical exam to start to work, I was watching the nurse inject a needle into my arm to take a blood sample and I actually fainted.

I started off working in the mold room and then transferred down to the foundry. There I was introduced to what is called "the brass chills." When the furnaces are charged on Monday morning, the humidity creates a mist (fog) inside the plant. In this humidity, physical exertion heats the body while the cool humidity artificially cools the surface. This is particularly problematic for workers pushing pots of hot melted brass and men charging the furnaces. Toward the end of the day, workers experience chills despite their sweating bodies. The only remedy is to get home, drink hot milk and go to bed. Mornings commonly include yellow rings of moist bedding marking where the worker slept. I experienced this phenomenon a couple of times.

Many Wolverine Brass foundry workers left their homes in nice dress clothes and then changed into work clothes at the factory. I cannot think of many jobs that are dirtier than a job in a foundry. I suspect that some of our neighbors thought I had an exceptionally good job which it was not. It paid good money but that was about it. Convinced I would be dead by age forty if I stayed at Wolverine Brass, I knew I needed a better education and that translated to college. I will expand on this decision a bit later in this work. At this same time my body building interests peaked. What little money I kept from my employment after paying my dad for room and board, I invested in high protein tablets, cottage cheese, muscle magazines and a membership at American Health Studio. I was motivated by reading about Steve Reeves who had been honored as Mr. America and Mr. Universe for his body building success. He also starred in the movie, Hercules.

The Armstrong Health Studio in Grand Rapids sponsored a body building contest that my cousin Gerard Boot and I entered. Gerard won a third place trophy but my fourth place did not warrant any trophy. A year or so later, I placed third. Those were the only contests I ever entered.

Van and Gerard Boot

My political acumen was bolstered when I predicted Castro would overthrow Batista but that his success would be a pyrrhic victory since his dictatorship would not be much different than the Batista dictatorship he was replacing.

When Casey returned from his tour in the army he was earning about $100 per week but paying dad $50 per week room and board. Soon after his homecoming, he and Jim Verburg were in an auto accident and Casey was catapulted through the windshield sustaining life threatening injuries.

Mom visited him in Butterworth Hospital and came home to tell us his jaw was broken on both sides and his survival was in question. Despite his injuries, he recovered and returned home to convalesce. Even though he had no income, Dad demanded $50 per week room and board from him. When I left for college, Casey went to work for Wolverine Brass where he met his future wife, Jane who worked there as personnel manager.

A 'Necker's Knob' was a steering wheel accessory intended to enhance control of steering during the days before power steering. Most young men installed them allowing them to drive one-handed so they could put one arm around a girl sitting beside him and still safely negotiate curves, sharp turns and corners with the other hand. My cousin, Rob Boot, had a '50 Ford Coupe which was lowered, had a continental kit and a Necker's Knob. Rob and I double dated a few times. Because Rob's date was Catholic, she couldn't eat meat on Friday and this forced us to wait till after midnight on Fridays before we could stop at Big Boy or McDonalds for a burger.

Just after my 18th birthday, I enlisted in the Michigan National Guard. My buddies, Adrian Gilder, Gary DeArmond, Danny Koetsier and Dave Carpenter and I were all assigned to the same company and we were sent to Camp Grayling for two weeks of summer camp. I think they all completed their commissions but I received a deferment when I was accepted by LeTourneau College. Like most military boot camps, Camp Grayling could have been called Camp Humility because of the humiliating tasks PFCs were expected to perform. One of the more unpleasant tasks for a PFC at Camp Grayling was emptying the 30-gallon garbage can of urine in the morning after it had filled during the night. I was not excused from this unpleasant assignment.

All 7 Van Bemden boys, except for Butch my youngest brother, were in the armed services in one form or another.

The alcohol content of fermented beverages, particularly beer, was a more pronounced issue during my adolescent and early adult years than it is today. "Near Beer" was beer with an alcohol content of 3.2% as opposed to more mainline beers with 6% or more. "Near Beer" was the only beer we could buy at Camp Grayling so you can imagine why we would nickname a fellow PFC "One Can" when we discovered he would be inebriated after drinking one can.

My cousin, Rob Boot, reminded me of a time when Harry Mast bet me I could not climb up and down the stairway without stopping on Lookout Mountain. This was not really a mountain but rather a high hill with a great view of the western part of Grand Rapids. It was also an exceedingly popular place to park and make out with your date. Anyway, I not only ran up and down, but I did it two steps at a time. I think Harry was surprised at my physical conditioning. Nellie Russ (Ike's wife's sister) and Lena skipped catechism one Tuesday night and got into an auto accident with dad's car. She thought she would get killed once dad found out, but I believe the whole episode came off easy. I think Ike resolved the situation.

Sadly, I remember and know of many times when my dad's anger resulted in violence. One time Dad told Cora she could not go roller skating at Neibors Roller Rink but she went anyway. When she got back to the house, the back door was locked requiring her to get Dad out of bed to unlock the back door to let her in. When she got into the kitchen and proceeded to go up the back stairway, dad, wielding a hanger, sliced her back cutting her to the point where she had to have several stitches to close the wounds. Ike drove Cora to the hospital to get her stiches where she had to lie about how it happened, so she told the doctor she fell off the tractor. On another occasion, Cora changed from her work dress into red pedal pushers but dad ripped them off as a protest against the fashion of the day. Dad hated the color red.

Dad's temper was on display again when Pete and Adrian went hunting in Lucas's woods before they had all their chores done. Upon their return home, Dad threw their guns into the marrow pit destroying them. Casey experienced dad's wrath when he came home with "Blue Angel" painted on his '56 Ford Fairland and Dad scraped it off. After I left home and went off to college, disgusted with my brother Pete's interest in car shows and the trophies he had won, dad smashed a good number of them. My other brother, Butch, was downstairs hiding as many of Pete's trophies as he could but, when he heard Dad approaching, he ran through the screen door rather than be subjected to Dad's temper. My brother Butch made an interesting remark to me when I visited him and my other brothers and sister in Florida in May 2005. The comment Butch made was that dad never laughed and that was pretty much true. It was very seldom that you would catch him happy and enjoying himself. Although I believe he did, I never heard my dad say he loved my mother.

I believe my little sister Jeni was the only kid in the family who mastered the Hula Hoop. I could never keep it up for more than a couple of wiggles. I believe she could have done it all day long.

Shortly after graduating from High School, Leonard Face, senior class president, and one of the best all-around athletes during my high school days, was killed in a car accident. I think he owned a Chevy Corvette. Before I left for college, Leonard's brother, Keith, also lost his life in an auto accident.

Softwater Lake in the Plainfield Township of NE Grand Rapids was another popular place for swimming. There were always lots of kids our age there. The pool featured several different diving boards at various heights challenging us to choose the highest for showing off.

My College Days
1959-1960

My dad worked at Imperial Metal Products where the owner, Mr. VerWyse, was a staunch Christian layman. Mr. VerWyse pointed out that my first name "Urbanes" is mentioned in the Bible and is found in Romans 16:9. Everyone who worked at Imperial Metal Products was probably on the mailing list of R.G. LeTourneau's publication, "NOW," which was published every month. I knew from reading the NOW publication that LeTourneau Technical Institute of Texas had a work and study program where students could work their way through school.

LeTourneau University is a private, interdenominational evangelical Christian university in Longview, Texas. Founded as LeTourneau Technical Institute in February 1946 by R. G. LeTourneau with his wife, Evelyn, the school initially educated veterans returning from World War II. Total annual enrollment is nearly 3,000.
This is what Google has to say:

RG Letourneau Memorial Center, now the Nursing Building

R. G. LeTourneau founded LeTourneau Technical Institute in February 1946 on the site of the recently abandoned Harmon General Hospital, a World War II hospital that specialized in treating servicemen with neurological and dermatological issues. LeTourneau bought the site from the United States government with the help of *Longview News-Journal* publisher Carl Estes and other Longview community leaders for one dollar with the conditions that, for the next decade, the U.S. government could reclaim the 156 acres (631,000 m^2) and 220 buildings in the event of an emergency and no new construction or demolition could occur.

The State of Texas chartered the school on February 20, 1946, and classes were first held on April 1. At that point, enrollment at LeTourneau was exclusively male and predominantly veterans. For the first two years, LeTourneau provided an academy section to allow the completion of the junior and senior years of high school as well as a college section that offered two-year trade skill programs and a four-year technology program. Students attended classes on alternating days; while one half of the students were in class, the other half worked at R. G. LeTourneau's nearby LeTourneau Incorporated manufacturing plant (now part of Cameron International), thus satisfying the laboratory requirements of all of the industrial courses.

From 1946 to 1961, LeTourneau Technical Institute and LeTourneau, Inc. were one unified company under R. G. LeTourneau. In 1961, LeTourneau Technical Institute underwent a transformation into the co-educational LeTourneau College and began to offer bachelor's degrees in engineering, technology, and a limited number of arts and sciences. At this point, the college began to transition from the traditional wooden barracks buildings. The Tyler Hall Dormitory for men was erected in 1962, the Margaret Estes Library in 1963 and the Hollingsworth Science Hall in 1965.

Bell Tower and Mall – Center of Campus

The college continued to grow under the leadership of Allen C. Tyler in 1961 and 1962 and Richard H. LeTourneau (eldest son of R. G. and Evelyn) from 1962 to 1968. Harry T. Hardwick's presidency from 1968 to 1975 saw to the construction of the R. G. LeTourneau Memorial Student Center and the Longview Citizens Resource Center along with spearheading LeTourneau's accreditation by the Southern Association of Colleges and Schools. Richard LeTourneau again assumed the presidency from 1975 to 1985, during which time he oversaw the accreditation of the school's mechanical and electrical engineering programs by the Engineer's Council for Professional Development (now the Accreditation Board for Engineering and Technology) and supervised nine major construction projects.

Margaret Estes Library

LeTourneau College became LeTourneau University in 1989 under the leadership of President Alvin O. Austin, who served until 2007. Austin oversaw the development of an MBA program and the expansion of programs in business and education into educational centers in Houston, Dallas, Tyler, Austin, and Bedford. Austin also oversaw the removal of all wooden barracks from the Longview campus except the historic landmark known as Speer Chapel, which

Heath Hardwick Hall for Liberal Arts, Psychology and Continuing Education

Longview Hall – Center of Business

is the only remaining WWIIera structure and is a popular place for weddings and ceremonies. Under Austin's leadership, the university's main campus underwent considerable improvements including the construction of the university mall and Belcher Bell Tower, the Solheim Recreation and Activity Center, the Glaske Engineering Center, seven new residence halls, and the S.E. Belcher Jr. Chapel and Performance Center, a 2,011-seat auditorium that opened in spring 2007.

In the spring of 2006 Austin announced that he would retire from his position as university president in June 2007 and assume the newly created role of university chancellor. On March 8, 2007 Dale A. Lunsford was announced as the new president of LeTourneau University. He assumed the office on July 1, 2007. Prior to accepting the job as university president, Lunsford served as the vice president of student affairs and external relations at the University of Texas at Tyler. The school was in the spotlight in May 2015, when Outports reported it "updated its student-athlete handbook to ban gay athletes from "dating" and "athletes from showing support for gay marriage." Most of the university's undergraduate degrees are focused on engineering, aeronautics, computer science, business, education. A smaller liberal arts program provides educational balance to the largely technical concentrations. The school also offers extensive business and management graduate classes in Houston, Dallas, and Longview.

R.G. LeTourneau was one of the more famous Christian laymen of his day. Instead of tithing 10% of his money, he gave 90% of his income to the Lord's work. Anyway, his NOW publication always contained stories of his new and generally huge machines that he was building to clear the Amazon rain forest to build missionary stations, move mountains of dirt, etc. His claim to fame was designing and building gigantic earthmovers, front end loaders, log stackers and offshore drilling rigs which he built in his factories which were in Longview, TX and Vicksburg, Mississippi. Below are some examples of the type of equipment that R.G. Letourneau designed and built in the Longview plant.

A tandem earthmover

An early LeTourneau earth mover

Van at R G LeTourneau plant in front of huge front-end loader

Knowing that I would not qualify for a scholarship to any college and knowing that my dad did not have the money to put me through school, I needed to find a place where I could work and earn my way through school. Well, LeTourneau Technical Institute fit the bill since it was very much a work and study type of atmosphere that existed there at that time. Thus, I sent off for an admission application and soon I was college bound. Of course, not having prepared myself academically in high school, I could only enroll by being on probation until I could prove myself.

When September, 1959 rolled around, I was off to Texas. I took the Greyhound bus from Grand Rapids, MI to Longview, TX. About the only thing I remember about the trip was that it was long and hot. I had a couple hours lay over in Gladewater, Texas which I found out afterwards was only a few miles from Longview and my destination. I probably could have walked the distance before I got another bus to take me to Longview if I had known that beforehand and had the directions to LeTourneau Technical Institute.

Dale Dechert and Van in the dorm at LeTourneau

My first roommate was Dale Dechert, a young fellow from Wyoming. Dale had years of experience in every field you could imagine. With all his years of experience, he had to be 50 years old, and he wasn't any older than most of the rest of us. He had a motorcycle which he rode to the plant and around town. I believe we were only roommates for one semester. After the first semester, Bill Banker became my roommate and I roomed with him until I got married the last semester of my senior year.

After enrolling in school, one of the first things almost every guy that attended LeTourneau did was to apply for a job either at the LeTourneau plant or some other place in town that employed the college guys. I applied for a job at the R.G. LeTourneau plant and got a job running a turret lathe for $1.00/hr. Our department head was Mr. Clay Bennett. Mr. Bennett took a liking to me because I was an extremely hard worker, I was mechanically inclined, and I could set up my machine without too much help. Later, I also worked on milling machines, gear hobbing machines, arc welding, and brake press. I also worked a school year at Trailmobile in Longview. They had a huge contract to build semi-trailers and they hired lots of LeTourneau students.

The work-study was set up with an A and B schedule. Each student was either on the A schedule or the B schedule. One week the A schedule students would go to school Monday, Wednesday, and Friday, then the B schedule student would go to school on Tuesday, Thursday, and Saturday morning. The following week your schedule was opposite the days you were not in class you could either study or work. Thus, if you teamed up with someone from the opposite schedule you were on, the two of you could hold down a full-time job wherever you were working.

This arrangement I feel works out better than another similar program that I am somewhat familiar with and that was the General Motors Institute. The GMI program differed from LeTourneau in one significant area. With the GMI program one is sponsored by one of the GM plants and a student goes to school for 3 months and then works in the plant that is sponsoring him the next three months. This program is akin to public school where kids have a long summer vacation. By the time September rolls around, most have forgotten everything they learned before the summer break.

Daily chapel service attendance was mandatory at LeTourneau. We had lots of guest speakers which made it interesting and, if we did not have a guest speaker, our chaplain, Rev. Barney Walker, would speak. There was always a Bible verse hanging up in front of the chapel we recited and were expected to memorize. The task of taking attendance at the chapel service was the responsibility of Mavis Smith, the Registrar's Secretary. I believe that Lloyd Dechert, upon graduation, married Mavis and moved to Wyoming.

That fall there was a revival at the college where Mr. Don Lonie was the main speaker. These revival meetings were again mandatory. Coming from a Dutch Reformed background, I did not know what to expect since I had never attended anything like this. At the end of a good series of talks during the week of revival meetings given by Mr. Lonie, I decided to give my heart to the Lord and accepted him as my personal savior.

LeTourneau choir at Fall Revival

Van hard at work doing his drawing assignments

Normally, when we got home from either working and/or from the end of the school day, we would work on our various class assignments.

Bill Banker, my roommate for the next 3 years, was born and raised in Charlotte, North Carolina, and he grew up in a culture where there was a very distinct and separate black and white environment. I remember one time he jokingly said that if they get one shade darker, he was heading home. He was referring to some of the Indian students (from the country India) that attended LeTourneau College. What was puzzling about that statement was the fact that his mother had an African American nanny that helped raise Bill.

One time I drank some water out of a water fountain at Childs grocery store in Longview that was marked "Colored" and then proceeded to yell at my roommate, Bill Banker, that this water tasted just like the water out of the "White Only" cooler. The locals that heard me just gave me a dirty look. When I first got to Longview there was still a lot of segregation in the south.

Most of the students at Letourneau Tech attended one of the local churches in the area. Dale Dechert, several other guys from dorm 4A, and I went to the First Presbyterian Church in downtown Longview. It was while I was attending this church that our Sunday School class decided we should have a bowling party and each of us should invite some local girl. There were no girls attending LeTourneau Tech at that time, so we had to find a local girl. Well, Sammy Whitson, who was in the same

Our Bowling Outing

Sunday School class I attended, told me about this girl he used to date and that she probably would like to go. Well, I called Brenda and made a date with her for this party. The rest is history as they say. We began dating on a regular basis.

Brenda learned to drive in an old straight stick Studebaker. One of those where you could not tell whether it was going forward or backwards.

A car like the car Brenda learned to drive in

Occasionally, Brenda, with her friend, Ann Berry, would drive on campus in her mother's 1959 white 4-door Chevy Bel Air. I am sure her mother did not know they were going over to LeTourneau to visit with the boys.

Brenda and I had a telephone signal arrangement set up so when we wanted to talk to each other we could. I would call her home number and let it ring once or twice (I forget the exact arrangement) and that was the signal for her to call me and spare the 10 cents required to use the phone in the dorm.

One summer after I started dating Brenda my brother, Pete, and I drove to Texas in my '57 Chevy to see her. My car broke down Saturday afternoon in the middle of Arkansas. We had to hitch hike into town and pick up a new fuel pump. We replaced it and proceeded to drive to Longview where we arrived later that day. Pete could not get over how Brenda sounded when she asked, "Are you hungry?" in her Texas accent.

Some of my professors the first year at LeTourneau were Dr. K. F. McKinley who was the head of the Christian Services Dept, Prof Ed Roberts who headed up the Machine Science Dept. and Fred Smith who was my Engineering Drawing professor. Prof. Nelson my trigonometry teacher also was one of my favorites. Prof. Crawford who worked in the Math Dept. and taught algebra also was a very likeable professor and did an incredibly good job of making the math he taught apply to everyday tasks and problems.

I did not have a car when I arrived at LeTourneau because, in the admission papers that I filled out, it stated that freshmen could not have an automobile. Thus, as I stated earlier, I sold my '55 Chevy Bel Air hardtop with a continental kit on it to my sister, Lena.

When I arrived at LeTourneau, I realized the "no car for first year students" rule was not strictly enforced. Since I did not have any wheels, I quickly became buddies with others who did—generally an upper classman. Later that year, I bought a '57 Chevy for $150 from a fellow that lived in Henderson who had used it to race at the local racetrack. It was lowered all the way around and had the transmission welded

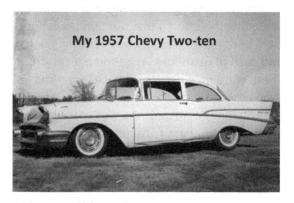

My 1957 Chevy Two-ten

permanently in 2nd gear. I drove it home that summer and raised it back up to the normal height by heating the leaf springs and letting the weight of the rear axle drop down to its normal height. Sometime later, I hit a hard bump in the road and the main leaf springs that had been heated up broke so that the car was riding on the axle with no springs whatsoever in the rear end. One could feel every bump in the road. I soon installed a new set of main leaf springs.

With hair cutting skills I learned practicing on my dad and brothers, I became the ad hoc barber for our dorm. At $.50 per head I made a little extra spending money. My fussiest customer, Gene McKay, demanded a perfectly flat "flat top" which was a popular hair style for young men in those days.

David Tobelmann became a good friend during my first year there. He was interested in bodybuilding and he and I hit it off right from the start. I did not have any weights at the

Van and David Tobelmann Working Out

Van doing a little boxing

school at that time and, if I remember correctly, he did, allowing us to work out in my room several times a week. LeTourneau didn't have much of a formal sports program. The only official sport was basketball. There were however, a lot of intramural sports/clubs. There was some goofing around boxing, weightlifting, etc.

Sidney Conklin, a quiet but very intelligent classmate whose home was in Charlotte, MI, and I drove back to Michigan together at the end of the school year. From that point onward, he always rode back and forth with me and helped pay for the gas. One time when Sidney was driving in the middle of the night on the way back to MI, and I was sleeping in the back seat, he was rocking the car back and forth and I woke up wondering what was going on. He said he was squeezing the last drop of gas from the tank to get us to a gas station. I would not have thought of that, but it worked and we coasted up to a gas pump on the remaining fumes.

1960-1961

Summer employment during my college years included working with my brother, Casey, as welders at D&D Welding (owned by a couple of Dick Vandertoorn's brothers) in Allendale, MI. Dick Vandertoorn, a friend of the family worked for his brothers and I believe got Casey and me that summer job. We devoted eight to ten hours per day to welding signs, pallets, and parts bins for several GM plants around the area. Arc welding requires very dark hoods to prevent the luminosity of the weld from damaging human eyes. Often this protective device failed when we were working together and one or the other of us raised our hood when the other wasn't protected. This resulted in "welder's eye," a painful experience at best and, at worst, possible blindness.

In the early days of telephone service, the phone company promoted a service they called "operator assisted person-to-person calling." This was an expensive way to ensure you could call a person rather than just a number hoping your preferred party would be available for a conversation. We used it as a primitive free "proof of delivery" message. When I traveled to college I would call home by calling person-to-person and asking for myself; thus, everybody knew I had arrived safely at my destination. Years later, we used a similar method at MDSI by asking for Mr. Goodyear who was never in.

I remember well many of my college professors. Prof. Phillips, my slide rule course professor, had a homemade 3-4 ft long slide rule hanging on the wall in his classroom. He generally had a short test every day to start the class with a practical application of slide rule calculations. He told the story of one of his students handing in his test paper with a bunch of decimal points circled on the bottom of the page with a notation stating, "Use where needed." Apparently, the student had trouble keeping up with the placement of the decimal point. It obviously was humorous, but Prof. Philips did not buy off on it. Keeping track of where the decimal point goes is probably the hardest thing about using a slide rule.

"Kansas City," recorded by Fats Domino, was a popular song during my college years; thus, when Dr. Moser, Chairman of the Chemistry Dept. and my teacher, during a discourse on corrosion, mentioned Kansas City to make the point that corrosion occurs everywhere, my roommate, Bill Banker, and I, devised a plan for using the song to play a prank on Dr. Moser. Capitalizing on a fellow classmate's access, Jim Yanke's part-time job in the maintenance department, a key was delivered to Dr. Moser's classroom facilitating our mischievous objective. Bill Banker and I sneaked into Dr. Moser's classroom and set up a clock radio connected to a phonograph in the plenum space above the ceiling close to the attic fan. With a 45rpm record of "Kansas City" on the turntable, we ran an extension cord from the adjacent classroom, Prof. Galyon's literature classroom, to the phonograph and set the clock to start playing the record during class time. We figured that Prof. Galyon would never notice the extension cord and if he did, he would probably assume the Maintenance Department did it. He was the kind of guy who you might say is out in left field or off in a daze in his own little world. Dr. Moser was just the opposite, he noticed everything. The following day, in chemistry class, Dr. Moser again talked about Kansas City. Not 10 seconds after he said, "Kansas City," the record player came on and Fats Domino launched into "Kansas City." The timing could not have been better! Dr. Moser attempted to continue his lecture ignoring the music but he finally surrendered by announcing:

"If anyone in here knows anything or has anything to do with this, speak now or forever hold your peace." We thought we had our bases covered but we failed to take it off of "repeat play," and it kept repeating the song till Bill finally fessed up and went into Prof. Gaylon's room to pull the plug. A year later Dr. Moser told my roommate Bill his little prank cost him a letter grade. I was unscathed.

The lure of mischief on the water tower beckoned and we responded. Late one night, Bill and I fastened a stop sign on top of it. Solving the first problem by commandeering a sectional ladder long enough to reach the first rung of the ladder to the catwalk, we had to conquer our fear of climbing 75 ft. above the ground to negotiate the catwalk that had no safety railing and finding the small fixed ladder to the top of the reservoir in the dark! We were terrified! Additionally, we had to continually monitor the ground below to prepare for discovery by campus security. The tower was situated in the easement bordering Fast Buck Avenue, the main traffic artery on campus. Our reward came the next morning when the main topic of conversation on campus was the stop sign on the tower.

I think it was this same year when a couple who were travelling across the country with a schooner wagon pulled by a couple of large horses stopped off at Letourneau Tech for a couple of days' rest. Bill Banker and I took one of the horses at midnight and put it in Dr. Moser's classroom. Once again, we got the keys to Dr. Moser's classroom from Jim Yanke.

Aware of our intense interest in all things cars, Carl Schroeder, a friend whose home was in Sebring, Florida, invited Bill Banker and me to his house to attend the Sebring 24 hour race.

Van looking at one of the racing cars at Sebring, FL

Despite the consequences of failing to pass an unannounced room inspection, Bill and I had my '57 Chevy motor in our room to work on it. Apparently, our efforts to hide it were successful since we never had any negative repercussions for violating this rule. Here is another photo of the four musketeers. I think we were getting ready to go to church, or just coming back, since we are dressed up. This is not how we attended classes!

Van, Jim Mullaney and Bill Banker moving my '57 Chevy motor into our room

Dave Tobelmann, Van, Lloyd Dechert and Jim Mullaney

Bill Banker, Van and Mullaney's Cadillac

1961-1962

Irrepressible young love prompted Brenda to ride the train one summer from Longview to Grand Rapids. This bit of bravado was uncharacteristic for young ladies at that time but she made the round trip safely and our summer was much more enjoyable together.

A couple of summers while I was in college, I worked at Allied Van Lines in Grand Rapids, MI. My cousin, Rob Boot, was working there and suggested that I apply for a summer job. It was a rather good job because the pay was particularly good, but it was hard and heavy work. The full-time guys all belonged to the Teamsters Union. We younger guys did most of the lugging and heavy lifting. He worked there a few years and eventually drove trucks for them and went all over the country.

I received an unexpected windfall when an uncashed paycheck I had failed to deposit fell out of a book when I was packing to return to LeTourneau after a summer of employment in Michigan. I don't remember how much the check was worth but, regardless, it was a welcome surprise.

"The heavens declare the wonder of His handiwork" – a Biblical passage made real to Brenda and me one warm fall night when we were out for a walk. Astonished, we were treated to an extraordinarily bright meteorite briefly lighting up the night sky. Momentarily frightened, we quickly recognized the special event as a gift of nature.

During a Christmas break when I was in college, Dad lost control of his temper when Casey and I came home late one Saturday night after midnight. With curfew at midnight, it was particularly onerous because it meant we had violated the Sabbath by being out on Sunday. Dad was waiting for us in the kitchen. As I entered, he hit me but I ran up the back staircase. He then extracted a knife from the kitchen drawer but Casey intervened assuming responsibility. This wasn't good enough for Dad, but it was enough to convince Casey to leave home and begin living with Dave and Lena.

Dad looking very tired

My dad was a very hard-working man. When he got home from work, he just plunked down. As you can see from the photo, he looked tired and I'm sure he was. I do not think he had a full day of rest in his life until well into his retirement. If he did, I sure cannot remember when.

Dr. McKinley, my Old and New Testament Prof., was talking to a student one time and the student kept on saying "but" this and that when finally, Dr McKinley said to him that he was going to go to hell on his "butt."

One night, Jim Yanke, Bill Banker and I sneaked into the garage where the maintenance department kept a small John Deere tractor. Determined to position the tractor on the porch of the administration building, we quietly

60

pushed it out the door and down the road before cranking it up. Jim was driving and we were almost to our destination when a car turned the corner in front of us and its headlights illuminated us. We abandoned the tractor and escaped by running to the dorm. We were about to enter when we heard a loud crash and realized the noise came from the area we had just left. We joined the crowd running to the source of the noise to blend in with the spectators witnessing the tractor ripped into two pieces and the car that had collided with it seriously damaged. Apparently, nobody involved in the accident was hurt so we simply added our surprise to the general consensus and, to this day, the mystery remains unsolved.

My '57 Chevy after Ed Poorman ran into it

On another occasion, my '57 Chevy was parked at the curb on Fast Buck Ave., the main thoroughfare on campus. On a spring fever impulse, drag racing turned it into an outlet for Ed Poorman with his hotrod (a 1935 Chevy featuring a V8) and Tom Brown with his '55 Chevy Bel Air convertible to turn a drag race into a demolition derby at my expense. With a sizable audience watching from their dorm windows, my parked car became the demolition target when Ed lost control and smashed into the front end of my parked car. Ed had no insurance; thus, repairing the damage fell to Bill and me. To his credit, Ed paid to rent stall time in the student garage where Bill and I were supervisors. Visits to the local junk yard produced serviceable parts and my car was once again road worthy.

Van and his '57 Buick Super

Later that school year, I found a '57 Buick Super with a non-working transmission I could get in trade for my '57 Chevy. Despite our minimum experience with automatic transmissions, Bill and I repaired it by replacing gaskets and other worn-out parts, and it ran smoothly. Since Bill and I ran the student garage, we had plenty of time to overhaul the transmission.

In the spring of 1962, Bill Banker and I approached the Administration requesting permission to form a fraternity in one of the dorms (34A). Approval was granted and one of the professors, Dr. Foley, was our sponsor. I was the first president of TKD (Tau Kappa Delta).

TKD Members

Bill Banker and Van

1962-1963

The summer between my junior and senior years I was working at Allied Van Lines in Grand Rapids which was right down the street from the Chevrolet dealer. I traded in my '57 Buick and bought a brand new '62 fire engine red Chevy Corvair coupe. Dave Marsman, my sister Lena's husband, was working at Ace Plating Company just across the street from where we lived on Cascade Road, and he was the night foreman in the plating department. I had lots of the removable parts of my Corvair chrome plated, which was the thing to do back then.

My '62 Chevy Corvair

My brother, Casey, who was living with my sister, Lena, left to go to Florida, Sept 9, 1962. I think he was driving a split rear window Corvette. He later bought a '64 Chevy Corvair. At one time he had a '68 Chevelle.

One of the fellows in my dorm, Arthur "Rover" Ayling had his own piper cub airplane he had flown down from PA. Periodically, he would take some of us up in his plane which he docked at the Gregg County Airport. I remember one time he took me up and intentionally turned the nose of the plane up and kept it there until the plane stalled. Of course, he knew what he was doing, but I never experienced that sort of thing, and I was holding on for dear life. Rover was one of the few guys who did not have a part time job while he was going to school. He could always sleep in; thus, many times late at night he would go to the Triangle (a local hang out) to get pizza.

Intramural weightlifting was introduced at LeTourneau in the Fall of 1962. I won the 181 lb.

Van Wins 181 lb. Class

class. Don Yocum, who was around my weight, wanted to know what class I was going to enter because he wanted to enter the weightlifting contest and win a trophy, but he knew that wasn't possible if he and I were in the same weight class because I could out lift him.

My best Christmas present ever was eloping with Brenda during Christmas vacation. December 29, 1962, standing before a Justice of the Peace in Standale, MI, with my brother Ike and his wife, Jennie, as witnesses, we tied the knot. The mother of Dave Carpenter, one of my high school buddies, did our blood work at a medical clinic in Cascade.

Mom hosted a small reception where we received some gifts and my Aunt Connie was there.

Brenda spent our honeymoon (between Christmas and New Years) typing up my 50 plus page term paper on an old manual Underwood typewriter. This was in the days before Microsoft "Word" and "cut and paste," and automatic indentation, pagination, spell check, etc. existed. Thus, if I screwed up on one of the footnotes for instance, it meant a lot of extra work!

When we returned to Texas, and broke the news of our marriage to Brenda's folks, they invited us to live with them; thus, my college dorm days ended. I made my own wedding band from a hunk of stainless steel in the LeTourneau plant. I wore it for many years but eventually lost it. During the time that I worked at Sundstrand and Lear Siegler, one could not wear a wedding band (ring) or a necktie unless it was a snap-on. This was to prevent accidents as we moved around various machines in the shop.

My graduation in 1963 with both sets of parents in Parkers' front yard

My Mom and Dad drove down to Longview, Texas for my college graduation. I was their first and only kid that graduated from college and my dad was enormously proud of me. They also met Brenda's mother and dad for the very first time. We have a picture of both sets of parents with Brenda and me that was taken in the front yard. Following the ceremony held in the gymnasium, we were at Brenda's house when my Dad asked to see my diploma. I handed him the folder and, when he discovered it was empty, that is, it contained no official printed diploma, I had to explain that, until I paid the amount due in my college account, my diploma would not be available. Well, the next morning, a Saturday, we went to the business office and dad paid the outstanding amount due - $600, and I had my signed officially conferred degree certificate! It is the only time my dad loaned me any money.

Armed with a bachelor's degree, I interviewed several companies including Sundstrand and IITRI, both in Chicago. IITRI was developing APT and it would have been interesting work. However, commuting to South Chicago every day did not appeal to me. Also, Sundstrand provided what I perceived to be the best opportunity for me to build my resume and the work environment was considerably better than any others I considered.

The Start of My Professional Career

Belvidere – Sundstrand 1963-1966

Upon my graduation, Brenda and I packed all our earthly possessions into the '62 Corvair and drove to Belvidere, IL. Visiting there with a gas station attendant who described an apartment he had recently renovated and was available, we grabbed the opportunity and moved into our first residence as a married couple. It was a small 2-room upstairs snuggery and the scene of the infamous chocolate pudding explosion. A double boiler Brenda was using built up enough pressure to create a relatively minor but very sticky explosion instantly decorating the otherwise freshly painted white walls with a coat of chocolate which we quickly restored to acceptable living condition but not before recording in these photographs.

Chocolate pudding

Our landlord's mother lived beneath us and she was the victim of water leaking from our 30-gallon aquarium into her ceiling. Because we weren't home at the time, our landlord exercised his right to enter our apartment and resolved the problem. We lived in that small 2 room apartment for about a year or so until we had an opportunity to move next door to a downstairs apartment which was much larger.

Having successfully interviewed with Sundstrand Machine Tool during my senior year at LeTourneau, my employment began immediately upon arrival in Belvidere. I reported to Darrell Cunnigham in the Industrial Engineering Department and my job included creating a time and motion study for various tasks in the plant. However, aware of the comprehensive numeric control research paper I had submitted for my degree, I accepted their offer to move from Industrial Engineering to Numeric Control Programming. Bill Fisher was in charge of the NC programming department.

Some of the people who were working in the programming dept. were:
- Harold Anderson who went to the same church where Brenda and I attended and became the godfather of our two boys, Jeff and Gary
- Paul Day who enjoyed marking up my program (as well as everyone else's) using heavy dark red ink pens
- Frank Norton who worked for years at Barber Coleman in Rockford and drove a '64 Ford Mustang Fastback
- Larry Gibbs, a young guy like myself

- Alice Hack, an exceptionally good mathematician who did a lot of work writing programs in Fortran for machining propellers, etc., which could not be programmed in SPLIT. Her husband, Bill, was also a LeTourneau graduate who, years later, used MDSI Compact II in a junior college where he taught

Another fellow whom I came to respect and learn a lot from was Hal Beaverstad, who oversaw the IBM computer dept. and wrote the SPLIT programming language. My very first exposure to computers was his IBM 1620. Ron Olsen, one of the night shift computer room operators, also became a good friend. Since we lived only a few miles from the plant where I worked, I always came home for lunch.

Belvidere was, for the most part, a bedroom community for Rockford, a much larger population center about ten miles away where we did most of our shopping and entertainment. Had it not been for Chrysler building a new assembly plant in Belvidere, I think the town would have dried up and blown away. We were on our way home from seeing the movie, "The Longest Day," in Rockford, when Jeff announced his imminent arrival. To our chagrin, we had locked our keys in the apartment requiring me to use a ladder to climb through a window to gather necessary items for Brenda's visit to the hospital. All this, added to the tense bumpy ride ending with delivering Brenda to the hospital, made for a very long day.

Aug 18th, 1963

Carol giving Jeff a good looking over in Belvidere

Brenda gave birth to Jeff the following morning. It was indeed the longest day of our young lives. Despite the local newspaper's daily "New Birth's" column predictably misspelling my name as "Vrpanes Van Bemden, I sent it to my folks. Misspelling my name was so common I could write a book about it. One particular occurrence stands out. Any time I needed to spell it out on a phone call, I would say: something akin to: "---Van, like a minivan, space, capital B---" and so forth. Well, this practice backfired when a telemarketer heard this and responded with a letter hilariously addressed to: "Urbanes Van 'minivan' Bemden."

It was during the first couple of weeks in Jeff's young life that my brother, Ike, and his family came by for a short visit on their way to Corsica, South Dakota, where they were checking out the possibility of buying a farm, which they eventually did. In this photo, Carol is really giving Jeff a good looking over.

Joe, Joan, Barb, Van and Jeff in Belvidere

It was customary back in the 60's, when you were blessed with a newborn, you passed out cigars to the men and chocolates to the ladies. One would go to a cigar store and buy a box of cigars that had a wrapper (band) around them that would say "It's a boy" or "It's a girl." So here is Van, the world's most anti-smoking protestor, passing out cigars. I guess you go with the flow.

My brother Joe and his wife Joan with their daughter Barbara came for a visit when we lived in Belvidere and are shown in the photo to the left.

Joe smoked a pipe when he was first married. I used to think the picture of perfect contentment was the image of a fellow sitting under an apple tree smoking a pipe. Years later, on a visit to Sydney, Australia I walked into a tobacco shop just to smell good old Prince Albert (PA) pipe tobacco. That is probably hard to believe but it is the gospel truth. However, I must say that there is nothing that smells worse than a pipe that hasn't been cleaned!

Lillian, Jimmy Parker and Jeff with new Mustang

Brenda's mother and her brother, Jimmy, drove up from Texas to see us that summer. Jimmy drove them up in his brand-new Mustang. This is the same Mustang he would sneak off in on Sunday afternoons and drive down to the drag strip in Marshall, TX.

I remember listening to a local radio station on one of the talk shows where listeners could call in and make comments on various topics being discussed. One time I called in to mention how to bring up a young child and quoted the verse out of the Bible, namely, `Train up a child in the way he should go: and when he is old, he will not depart from it. (Prov. 22:6.) I was nervous and hung up as soon as I got done reciting that verse.

After working at Sundstrand Machine Tool for about 6 months and adding to my responsibilities as a newlywed husband, father of a newborn boy, beginning a career in numeric control programming, and making a little extra cash by doing the bookkeeping for the Illinois Toll Road Oasis at Belvidere, I enrolled in an MBA program at Northern Illinois University in Dekalb, Illinois. An assignment in one of my classes was to write a critique of a chapter in a book the class was using. Imagine my chagrin when, in class, the professor read my work as an example of how NOT to write a critique! My embarrassment was obvious making the professor's insistence it was not identifiable completely ridiculous. Brenda had helped me with the assignment so my opinion of the professor's judgement dropped considerably.

This was also about the time they were having sit-down strikes in the South. June 11, 1963, Governor Wallace, who years later ran for the Presidency, stood in the front door of the University of Alabama to prevent a black student from entering the university. Eventually they called out the National Guard and she entered the school under their protection.

It was also around this time a very popular network television series, The Fugitive, aired. It was a weekly show in which a medical doctor, Richard Kimball, was accused of killing his wife but he maintained his innocence by claiming he had seen the killer who was a one-armed man. Poor police work and miraculous circumstances allowed the innocent doctor to avoid capture till the series ended when the police arrested the one-armed killer. A Hollywood movie starring Harrison Ford followed the TV series. I was hooked on the show when I was on the night shift so I made every effort to be home for my "lunch" break when the show aired every week. This is what Google says about The Fugitive: The Fugitive premiered in the United States on September 17, 1963. Over the course of the show's four seasons, 120 episodes were produced, with the last original episode airing in the United States on August 29, 1967. The series aired Tuesdays at 10:00 pm on ABC.

Friday, Nov 22, 1963, President, John F Kennedy, was assassinated in Dallas. All Sundstrand employees were permitted to leave work. We left Belvidere that afternoon and drove to Grand Rapids, MI.

Harold Anderson who worked with me in the programming department at Sundstrand and attended the Evangelical church suggested we should attend his church. We attended church services regularly but chose to sit in the back row pews in the sanctuary to deal with the responsibilities of a young boy. In the fashion of the day, my pants legs were short enough to qualify for being labeled "high water pants" which emphasized my white socks. I also taught Sunday School class to a group of teenagers. I guess having gone to a Christian College and taken several Bible courses made me the most qualified.

On one of our trips back to Grand Rapids, the news was reporting rioting in Watts, Detroit, as well as other major cities. We were very surprised when we arrived in Grand Rapids to find that gangs were setting houses on fire in the inner city of Grand Rapids.

There's nothing like firsthand experience to learn the real way corporate America works. I had a peer at Sundstrand who taught SPLIT programming to customers and wrote several manuals. He constantly complained about the fact that he had to work overtime to complete his task when we were all paid by the hour. Of course, this earned him more money than the forty hours management expected him to use to complete his work. Well, when the company changed our pay schedules from hourly to salary, Ron was suddenly able to complete all his work in forty hours. He obviously had been milking it!

Brenda's work experience as a high school student at Sears in the credit department in Longview made her an ideal employee for Sears in Rockford where she worked when we lived in Belvidere. Her hours dovetailed with mine when my boss, Bill Fisher, changed my hours to the second shift, allowing us to be home with the kids most of the time. As you can see from the photo, I enjoyed playing with Jeff.

Jeff getting a horseback ride

Second shift allowed me to enjoy the challenges of solving problems the machine operators encountered.

It was while we lived in Belvidere that we got Jeff his first tricycle. I had to put some wooden blocks on the peddles so he could reach them. He loved riding it.

Summer 1964.

Jeff enjoying his tricycle

Because Brenda's folks were both working, it was difficult for them to find time to drive to Belvidere; thus, the first summer after Jeff was born, we went to Texas to visit them. While we were there, we went to the Lake of the Pines, which is not too far from Longview, to give Jeff his first introduction to playing in a freshwater lake.

Summer 1965.

After living in an apartment for a couple of years we had a local home builder build us a small 3-bedroom house on the outskirts of town. We lived there for about a year. This small 1050 sq. ft. house had 3 small bedrooms, one bathroom and a one-car garage. One time when Brenda was giving Jeff a bath, I dropped one of my Angel fish into the bathtub and Jeff went bananas.

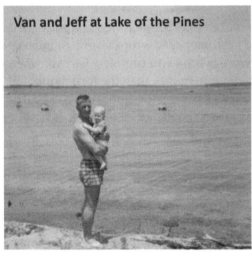
Van and Jeff at Lake of the Pines

Jeff with his little red wagon in Belvidere

While we lived there, Brenda's parents visited us. On one of their visits, they bought Jeff, who was about 1 year old, a small Red Ryder wagon. I pulled him around the block in his little red wagon.

While I worked at Sundstrand, I bought a 1953 Chevy Bel Air from one of the guys who I worked with. I drove it to work so Brenda would have the Corvair to run around town to run errands, take the kids to the doctor, etc.

A visit by Dutch relatives provided an opportunity to visit Ike and his family on the farm he had recently purchased in South Dakota. On the way, we enjoyed the Badlands and Black Hills. On

this trip, I pulled into a gas station and noticed some fellows sitting on a wooden bench made from a good-sized tree cut down the middle cleverly positioning the branches to form the legs of the bench. I thought this was a great idea and when I returned to Belvidere, I kept my eyes open for a tree I could use to make a similar bench. It wasn't too long afterwards that, during a good windstorm, several huge spruce trees surrounding a cemetery blew over. Inquiring how I could get possession of the downed trees; I was told I could have them free of charge if I would clean up the mess--in other word take the branches and the trees are yours. I made

Hennie Boot, Mom Van Bemden and Uncle Izaak Boot in the Black Hills of South Dakota

two wooden benches. 50 years later, one of those benches is still in the family. My son, Jeff, has it. I gave one to my dad and I don't know what he did with it.

Visiting my brother, Ike, on the farm near Corsica, South Dakota, I was in the garage with Ike and he was doing something with an old beat-up hammer. I bought him a new one and gave the old one to my son, Jeff, who still has it to this day. He calls it a gift from his Uncle Ike. Also, I went to the drug store while I was there to buy Ike's son, Mike, some cold medicine. I do not know for sure, but I believe Ike was on hard times and probably overextended himself making farm payments.

The only time I remember drinking enough alcohol to be inebriated was on a trip to Cleveland where saw two of my old LeTourneau dorm buddies, Bill (Mary Ann) Banker and DeWayne (I can't remember his surname). Crawling on my hands and knees to the toilet to heave my cookies taught me a lesson I've never forgotten.

In the mid 60's, folk music was extremely popular. There was even an hour long show on Saturday afternoon devoted to folk music, and I tried to watch it as often as possible. This was like "American Bandstand" that was hosted for years by Dick Clark.

Oct 7, 1965.

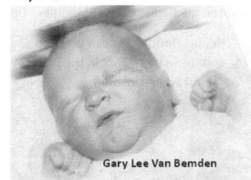
Gary Lee Van Bemden

On Oct 7, 1965, at Highland Hospital in Belvidere, Il Brenda gave birth to our 2nd son, Gary Lee Van Bemden. Back in the 1960's, when a woman gave birth, they stayed in the hospital for several days. I think Brenda was probably in the hospital for 4 days or so before she came home. We lived in our new house at 610 Greenwood Ave in Belvidere. Brenda's mother came to help us shortly after Brenda came home.

Our new house at 610 Greenwood Ave. in Belvidere, IL

Lillian Parker, Gary and Jeff

Photo of our new house with the tail end of Brenda's mother's car, a 59 Chevy Bel Air Brenda drove around town in Longview and to Letourneau College when we were dating. We drove to Texas to celebrate Christmas 1965. The photo below is of Gary's first Christmas, which was celebrated at Brenda's parents' house in Longview. Jeff has a few presents.

Jeff and Gary in Longview – Christmas, 1965

We spent most of our Christmases in Texas. That was one way for Brenda's folks to see the grandkids. Usually at Christmas time, Aunt LaPearl would come over from Bossier City. Jimmy and Romelle would also come into town. I remember Aunt LaPearl telling us the story of her standing on the hood of her car at the dealership because the problem she had with her car was not being addressed. I think she got the dealer's attention very fast!

My family never did much for Christmas when the kids were home. I don't think the Netherlands Reformed Congregation endorsed the traditional gift exchange part of celebrating Christmas. Because the church frowned on it, my parents never had a Christmas tree in their entire lives.

Our sons, Jeff and Gary, were both baptized in the Evangelical Mission Covenant church in Belvidere, IL. Harold Anderson, who worked with me in the programming department at Sundstrand and attended the Evangelical Mission church, was the godfather to both Jeff and Gary.

Jan 1, 1966

After our visit to Longview, TX, on our way back to Belvidere, travelling along Hwy 67 in southwest Arkansas (this was before they built I-30), we encountered a flooded section of the highway. Some local fellows were stationed at each end of the flooded section telling people to go slow and stay on the upper edge of the curved highway. Well, I proceeded to follow their instructions but I dropped off the cement and hit the brakes. The little Corvair could not go any further. With water up to the middle of the door, I proceeded to climb out of the window hoping to keep the car from floating away. Brenda exited the car with both kids in her arms. A good Samaritan in his "Sunday-go-to-meeting clothes", waded into the water to help Brenda and the kids get to dry land. In the meantime, a farmer and his tractor towed the car with me in it to the same place where Brenda had found safety with the boys. The fellow who picked up Brenda was a young minister on his way to church. Don't you think he had an interesting story to tell that morning? With my family safely situated, my first order of business was to drain the water out of the car. Successfully locating the drain holes, I pulled the plugs and soon had a wet but serviceable car. However, we had to rescue several cloth diapers (paper disposables were not yet popular) and get them dried out. I did not even want to find out how much water was in the trunk (which was in the front of the car). With the car's heater blowing full blast to dry the diapers, and fearing water had invaded the gas tank, I drove the car till the gauge registered empty. When we finally stopped the car to gas up, I checked the trunk and, to my surprise, there was not a drop of water in it. But what an experience that turned out to be.

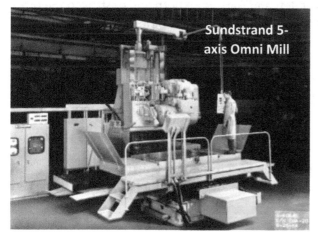

Sundstrand 5-axis Omni Mill

During my time at Sundstrand Machine Tool, I learned a lot about machining parts and NC programming. At one time we had more 5 axis machining centers in various stages of completion than existed anywhere else in the whole wide world. I truly was working in leading edge technology.

We had various DOD related customers the likes of Boeing, McDonnell, Rockwell Int'l, Dassault of France, etc. Since I was one of a hand full of people in the entire world who worked with 5 axis machining centers and I knew how to program them, I had several job offers from our customers. Boeing was persistent and flew me to Seattle to interview for a job in their new 747 plant in Renton. They treated me to dinner at the Space Needle but I wasn't ready to abandon our lifestyle in Illinois and the increased costs of periodic trips to Texas and Michigan prompted me to reject their offer.

Seattle Space Needle

At Sundstrand Machine Tool, I wrote special programming macros for the rest of the guys to use, etc. I also worked in our R&D lab where I could run the various machines (2-axis lathe, 3-4-5 axis machining centers, etc.) to try out various routines, master programs, and learn new capabilities that Hal Beaverstad added to the SPLIT processor from time to time.

After working at Sundstrand for a couple of years I approached my boss, Bill Fisher, for a raise. He said something like, "Do you know what other people are paying for a programming job?" to which I replied, "NO, but I guess I will find out." Thus, I put my papers (resume) on the street and soon landed a job at Lear Siegler in Grand Rapids, MI.

On April 21, 1967, after we moved to the Grand Rapids area to take the programming job at Lear Siegler, the small 3 BR house that we had built in Belvidere was destroyed by a tornado. It was a bad tornado that hit the hospital where Jeff and Gary were born and destroyed the office section of the hospital. The boys' birth certificates were destroyed by the storm requiring us to secure copies from the State of Illinois. The tornado went right down the street where we had lived killing a number of high school kids as school was just letting out when it hit. Our house was blown away and the only thing that remained was the foundation. We were fortunate to have moved away because Jeff would very likely have been playing in the back yard the time of day this tornado went thru Belvidere.

Google info...
A deadly tornado hit Belvidere on April 21, 1967. The **EF-4** tornado claimed the lives of 24 people, including 17 children, and injured as many as 500, destroying more than 100 homes and damaging hundreds more.

Grand Rapids–Lear Siegler 1967

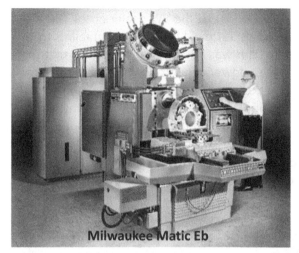
Milwaukee Matic Eb

I went to work at Lear Siegler on 44th St. in Grand Rapids, MI. I was now programming Kearney and Trecker Mod II and Eb NC machines using the IBM programming language called Autospot, which was a 2½ axis programming language. But Autospot was a decent language for the type of machines that we had. I was fast in programming the various components/parts that my boss, Ron Sherwood, assigned to me. Since we were machining mostly parts for the government, I think he wanted me to "milk it" more than I was. It was also a union

K & T Model 2

shop. I remember one time that I should have had another strap on the part that I was dry running. When it was lunch hour, I took the fixture to a drill press to drill and tap another hole so I could add another strap. Then the operator came over and asked what I was doing. I explained, he responded by informing me it was the job for someone working in the shop to do what I was doing. Apparently, my response (which I don't recall now) prompted him to file a union grievance against me.

Bob Guy, a co-worker hired about the same time I was and who was about my age, was a GMI graduate whose desk was right behind mine. We had a lot in common but when I learned he was working on his MBA at Western Michigan University, his encouragement prompted me to restart my MBA degree pursuit I had begun at Northern Illinois in DeKalb when I was working at Sundstrand Machine Tool in Belvidere. He and I took several classes together at Western Michigan's extension in Grand Rapids. A few years later, I talked him into accepting a job at MDSI.

When we lived in the Grand Rapids, Michigan area and I was working at Lear Siegler Instrumentation division, we rented a house on 52nd Street from my cousin, Gerard Boot. On one of our trips coming home from Texas with Brenda and the kids in our little '62 Chevy Corvair we went through Indianapolis. I rolled down the window to ask for directions at a STOP sign and the guy I asked for directions aimed a gun at me. This apparently was in a bad section of town where they were building the expressway and we had to pull off and detour around some side streets. It kind of shook us up.

Our VW bus, '62 Corvair and Jeff

While we lived in the Grand Rapids area my dad retired from Imperial Metal Products and was now working at the VW dealer on 28th Street. During this time, I bought a VW minibus from him. This was one of those VW buses that the flower power generation (in other words hippies) were using to travel around the nation to the various Woodstock type concerts. I installed a partition behind the front seat to shut off the rest of the bus, so we had at least a chance to get the front seat area warm. This vehicle had a heater that was warmed by the exhaust. VWs were air cooled and had no radiators. Thus, it was quite a challenge to get the vehicle comfortably warm. Also, they only had 32 HP, so when you were going down the highway wide open (the pedal to the metal), it topped out at about 60-65 miles per hour. When you went to pass a semi-truck and got to the point where you had to start cutting your own air, the speed would drop back down again and so it sometimes made it almost impossible to pass someone. Several years later we traded it in on a VW camper.

Jeff at John Ball Zoo

During our residence in Grand Rapids, we were frequent visitors to the John Ball Park Zoo that Jeff and Gary enjoyed.

Lear Siegler was building a new plant in Zeeland, Michigan that was to be a new division for LSI called Fabrication Technology. This was a job shop for machining various components and parts for the manufacturing plants around the mid-west. It was still partially under construction (3 sides were complete but one end was still open to move large machines into place, etc.), when Ron Sherwood, my boss at Lear Siegler in G.R., asked me if I would be interested in transferring to the Fabrication Technology division in Zeeland to help get the plant up and running. I told him I would since the environment there would be more of what I was used to, etc. I would not have to worry about getting my hands dirty and running the machines, nor would I have to be concerned about a union member writing me up with a grievance.

Lear-Siegler, Zeeland, MI

When we lived in Zeeland, we visited my folks quite often. By now, my parents had moved to a house on Boone CT, in Wyoming, MI (a suburb of Grand Rapids). Their house was on a *cul-de-sac* and there was nobody behind them.

Summer of 1967.

On one of our visits to my folks, Gary wandered into the woods and got lost. I panicked and had everyone hunting for him. It was getting late in the day and the sun was still shining but it was not going to be long before night fall when I found him quite a way from Dad's just merrily trucking along on his own along a trail that led to an abandoned rhubarb field where we harvested rhubarb from time to time, enough for "crisp" dessert. This episode really scared the daylights out of me.

One of the fellows who worked at LSI owned a dog that just gave birth to a litter of puppies. He talked me into taking one home for Jeff and Gary. We had it for probably 4-5 days and I gave it back. The puppy was not house broken, and I didn't have the patience to train him. I would put it in the stairwell at night and covered the entire place with newspaper; but somehow it found a place where there was no newspaper and there, he would do his job. I got tired of this very quickly.

I transferred to LSI in Zeeland and worked in the programming department there. Al Hutton was the plant manager. Norm Bork, commuting daily from Grand Rapids, led the programming department. We did a lot of bidding on various contracts because the fabrication technology division was primarily a NC job shop that LSI built because they thought they really knew how to operate NC machinery better than most other people. We had nothing but K&T machines—a couple of K&T model 2's with pallet shuttling capabilities and 4-5 K&T model Eb.

We used the same IBM NC programming language I used at the LSI plant in Grand Rapids. Again, it was sufficient for the type of NC machines we had and the type of machining we were bidding on. The major short coming was that we had no computer access at the Zeeland plant. Thus, any correction or modification to a given program was either done manually and /or resubmitted back to the computer in Grand Rapids. Luckily, two of the supervisors that worked at the Zeeland division lived in Grand Rapids. Thus, they would drop off the program on their way home and pick it up the next morning to return it to the Zeeland plant. As you can imagine, getting a good program to the shop often became a long-drawn-out procedure.

Occasionally, when we visited my brother Ike, who by now had moved back to Grand Rapids from South Dekota, we saw a portable TV sitting on the fireplace mantel in the family room. He could quickly slip it into the closet if one of the elders or deacons came over. The First Nederlands Reformed Congregation in America does not believe in TV because of all the bad stuff broadcasting networks deliver. However, when my dad came over to our house, and we happened to be watching a nature show or a National Geographic show, you could not get him away from it.

Jeff and Gary all dressed up

After living in the apartment complex, we bought a small house along Main Street in Zeeland. We must have been coming back from church in the photo where Jeff and Gary are all dressed up.

That winter we had a Christmas party for all the LSI fab tech employees and their families. In the photo on the left we have Jeff and Gary on Santa Claus's knee telling him what they want for Christmas. That is me on the left.

Jeff and Gary on Santa's knee

Spring of 1968

Around this time, (April/May of 1968) there were lots of local chapters of the Numerical Control Society in and around the mid-west. Virtually all Lear-Siegler NC programmers were members. The Western Michigan chapter of the NCS had scheduled a demonstration of an NC programming language by Chuck Hutchins and I signed up to attend. When I saw what Chuck Hutchins had to offer, I recognized it as a "Split like" language he named **Compact**. Here was Chuck Hutchins demonstrating his newly created NC programming language named **Compact** (a SPLIT knockoff) at the Western Michigan Chapter of the Numerical Control Society. I, in the meantime, had left Sundstrand Machine Tool Company and was now working at Lear Siegler Instrumentation Div. in Grand Rapids, MI (1966). After working there a year or so, I had transferred to the new Fabrication Technology Div. in Zeeland, MI. We had several Kearney & Trecker Milwaukee Matic NC machines, several Model 2 with shuttle capabilities, a half dozen Eb, etc. and were using IBM's Autospot, a 2 ½ axis NC programming language to program them. As noted earlier, the computer we had access to was in Grand Rapids some 30 miles away. Thus, the turnaround time to correct programming changes and mistakes was not very good. We were looking for a solution to this problem.

Following his presentation at the NCS meeting, Chuck and I met to arrange a time for him to visit our plant for a demo of Compact. A few days later he and his trusty ASR33 teletype (10cps) came out to show us what he had and how it could solve our turn around problem. Thus, I sat down and wrote a program for one of the parts we were running on one of the K&T Eb. After processing it via Comshare Timesharing Xerox Data System 940 (XDS 940) computer, we ran it on one of the Milwaukee Matic Eb machines. The K&T Milwaukee Matic Eb was one of the first links that Chuck and Bruce wrote and everything appeared to be fine. Following this exercise and a discussion of associated costs, we went to lunch during which I mentioned to Chuck that I was considering returning to Sundstrand as a member of their sales department. Chuck said: "You do not want to do that! Why don't you come to work for me?" That evening, I talked to Brenda about it and the following Saturday I was in Chuck's house in Ann Arbor discussing what would become a major career decision.

While we pretty much take it for granted in today's 21st Century world of home computing, the thing that struck me the most was being greeted by Chuck still in his underwear working at home on an ASR33 communicating with a computer jock in Hackensack, N.J., where Comshare had one of the XDS 940 computers. We then went to the Huron Towers to see the XDS 940 timeshare computer and where my office was to be. I accepted his job offer and moved our family to Ann Arbor.

Ann Arbor–Comshare—MDSI

When we moved to Ann Arbor, we rented an apartment at Traver Knoll which was below the hill where Chuck Hutchins lived and right next to the railroad tracks. I taught Jeff how to ride his bike (which we bought from Chuck's son, Stewart) in a Traver Knoll parking lot.

The school where Jeff started was not too far from our apartment. We often walked there so Jeff and Gary could use the swings. On windy days we would sometimes fly a kite on the schoolhouse yard. The photo below shows Jeff teaching Gary how to fly a kite.

Jeff teaching Gary how to fly a kite: March '69

We lived in the Traver Knoll apartment for a year or two and then rented a house on Glastonbury Street in Ann Arbor.

One of our favorite things to do during certain times of the year, especially in the wintertime, was to go to the Ann Arbor Arboretum.

Jeff & Gary, already mechanically inclined, working on Jeff's bike

Another favorite thing to do was to go to Zingerman's Deli. Menu Item #2 – Corned beef packed so high that first bite is as challenging as it is delicious—just the memory makes my mouth water. Brenda and I often shared one of these and it was enough to satisfy both of us. We often treated out of town visitors to this delectable local culinary delight.

Joe and Harvey Vredeveld, Roger and Norma Verhey, Chloris Patrick and Mary Lee

In Ann Arbor, we attended the Christian Reformed Church and this photo shows some of our church friends.

Ken Ludema (not shown in this photo) was Dean of the Engineering School at the University of Michigan. I was impressed with his story of being a high school dropout and lying about his age to join the service after which he enrolled at MIT where he earned two PhDs. He and I met serendipitously occasionally in US airports and international airports as we were both involved in careers requiring extensive overseas work. Roger and Norma Verhey went on a sabbatical to Sir Lanka which was a remarkably interesting experience for them. Our memories of living in Ann Arbor are, for the most part, very pleasant.

Despite the increased commute, I continued working on my MBA at WMU. Occasionally, Bruce Nourse helped me with some of my homework. He was exceptionally good in math, and I enjoyed spending time with him in his apartment.

When I went to work for Comshare in 1969, the concept of computer time sharing was in its infancy. Remotely connecting small computers with limited core power with larger mainframes using phone lines and a new product they were calling "modems," was an IBM-led business strategy. Large companies who could afford to buy large mainframes were encouraged to lease time on their equipment to smaller companies who needed the calculating speeds of mainframes but whose business could not justify purchasing an in-house system.

My office was in a large complex across the street from the VA hospital on the Huron River in Ann Arbor. Comshare had one of their XDS940 (see note below) timesharing computers in the same building with my office.

NOTE: Here is Wikipedia's HISTORY OF THE XDS940 – We have come a long way!

The **SDS 940** was Scientific Data Systems' (SDS) first machine designed to directly support time-sharing. The 940 was based on the SDS 930's 24-bit CPU, with additional circuitry to provide protected memory and virtual memory.

It was announced in February 1966 and shipped in April, becoming a major part of Tymshare's expansion during the 1960s. The influential Stanford Research Institute "oN-Line System" (NLS) was demonstrated on the system. This machine was later used to run Community Memory, the first bulletin board system.

After SDS was acquired by Xerox in 1969 and became Xerox Data Systems, the SDS 940 was renamed as the **XDS 940**.

The design was originally created by the University of California, Berkeley as part of their Project Genie that ran between 1964 and 1969. Genie added memory management and controller logic to an existing SDS 930 computer to give it page-mapped virtual memory, which would be heavily copied by other designs. The 940 was simply a commercialized version of the Genie design and remained backwardly compatible with their earlier models, with the exception of the 12-bit SDS 92.

Like most systems of the era, the machine was built with a bank of core memory as the primary storage, allowing between 16 and 64 kilowords. Words were 24 bits plus a parity bit. This was backed up by a variety of secondary storage devices, including a 1376 kword drum in Genie, or hard disks in the SDS models in the form of a drum-like 2097 kword "fixed-head" disk or a 16384 kword traditional "floating-head" model. The SDS machines also included a paper tape punch and reader, line printer, and a real-time clock. They bootstrapped from paper tape.

A file storage of 96 MB was also attached. The line printer was a Potter Model HSP-3502 chain printer with 96 printing characters and a speed of about 230 lines per minute.

END NOTE

The first week at work, Chuck and I traveled to Traverse City to attend a conference where we could perform COMPACT demos. Chuck enjoyed telling the story of me saying by Wednesday evening we had our 40 hours in. I do not know if that was literally true or not, but back in the early Comshare days, we worked a lot of hours

When I was not doing demos, I was trying to rough out a COMPACT manual. Our first attempt was a simple flyer describing the program Ann Hutchins developed and some vocabulary we used for the COMPACT language. While the three of us (Chuck, Bruce, and I) were working long hours at Comshare we were spending a lot of our own money doing demoes. Bob Guise suggested we do a search for financial support to start our own enterprise. This activity occurred simultaneously with the appearance of Ken Stephanz.

Chuck hired Ken despite his concern for stretching the payroll beyond its ability to support me – in his words: "I just hired this Dutchman with a wife and two little kids requiring him to relocate to Ann Arbor and I wasn't sure how I could pay you, Van."

The founding of MDSI. FEB 1, 1969

Manufacturing Data Systems, Inc. officially spun out of Comshare on Saturday, February 1, 1969.

Chuck asked Bruce and me to think of a name for our new company. We tossed a few names around and settled on Manufacturing Data Systems which would be abbreviated as MDS. However, that abbreviation was already used by someone else, so Ken suggested we incorporate creating the abbreviation, MDSI. We were off and running. I had no idea what lay in store for us. I just knew it was exciting and remarkably interesting. I had the good fortune of being in the right field (NC) at the right time and now I was again in a new field called computer timesharing. How blessed can a man be!

When we founded **MDSI,** the acronym **COMPACT** changed from "**Com**share **P**rogram for **A**utomatic **C**ontrol **T**ools" to "**COM**puter **P**rogram for **A**utomatic **C**ontrol **T**ools."

From the start MDSI followed a convention of numbering employees sequentially, creating a list that would quickly expand. Ken was considered employee #101, Chuck#102, Bruce #103 and Van (me) #104. Chuck liked to tease Ken that "rank has its privileges" since Chuck really was the first member of the company, and in fact, Bruce and I preceded Ken as well. An employee's number was a clear marker of how long he or she had been with the company, and from then on, employees would know their own numbers to compare with others.

Though everyone was hired for a specific role, in the early days it didn't matter what your job title was, everyone wore ten hats. We simply did what needed to be done. As an application engineer, I was doing demos to potential customers and working on a software manual, but I also trained new employees and customers to effectively employ COMPACT II. We moved to new offices on 2223 Packard Road and began hiring people: John Morris, Roy Winn, Paul Bearden, Ron Pinnow, and others. I was thrilled when MDSI hired Ron Pinnow (#110) in Sept of 1969 to take over COMPCT II customer training. Capitalizing on his employment at Sundstrand Aviation where he had mastered the SPLIT language, Ron required very little training to master COMPACT II. Additionally, we enjoyed the advantages of having previously worked together at Lear-Siegler who had a large contract with Sundstrand Aviation. Paul Bearden was one of our first salesmen. We lured John Morris away from Burgmaster for our VP of Marketing and Sales.

He brought Roy Winn with him and Roy became our first sales manager. All these guys came from Burgmaster, one of the first producers of a relatively inexpensive NC Turret Drill. They sold thousands of them. Paul Bearden was an interesting fellow. Consistently late, his breakfast habits were predictably annoying. First, he would rarely appear on time; then, he would harass the waitress demanding hurry up service and then he would always complain about his breakfast not being exactly right. I was teamed up with Paul Bearden and, despite his annoying habits, he did a good job of soliciting demos in Western Michigan on the days I had night classes at WMU in Kalamazoo. Paul supported his heavy cigarette addiction by mooching off others anytime they produced a pack. I can still hear him say: "Can I have one?"

During these early days with MDSI, I continued my pursuit of an MBA with night classes at Western Michigan University in Kalamazoo. One of MDSI's first customers was Jack Clausnitzer, a former colleague of Chuck's from Buhr, who had opened his own shop, Brighton NC, in Brighton, MI. Jack's interest in COMPACT was primarily the savings in turnaround time for producing the punch paper tape he needed for his NC lathe. Before he signed up with MDSI in April 1969, Jack used a computer located twenty miles from his shop that was only available at night. As a point of interest, years later when I was officially laid off from Schlumberger/Applicon, I went to work for Brighton NC.

Another early customer was the GM Tech Center in Warren, Michigan. When I performed a demo of a part on a trunnion, I knew COMPACT only had the ability to rotate a point in the XY plane. I needed the ability to rotate in the YZ plan and ZX plane. When I called Ann Arbor from the tech center and explained the situation to Bruce and Chuck, overnight, they added that advanced feature. The next day, I was equipped to convince the customer of our commitment to our customers. This is an example of how our business was conducted in the GOOD OLD DAYS!

Claude Wilson, founder of Wilson Concepts, a large NC shop in Dayton, Ohio was a real wheeler-dealer. John Morris and I presented our MDSI program to him and, during dinner that evening, he signed a contract on the back of the restaurant's placemat. Sometime later, on a Saturday morning, Chuck Hutchins called me: "Guess who's in town?" I said, "I have no idea." It was Claude Wilson. He had an immediate need for a couple "hot" jobs demanding my production that day (Saturday). I responded prompting Claude to request my services in Dayton to produce the parts on his equipment. I called Brenda for her assistance in packing my bags. Claude accompanied me to our house where, upon meeting Brenda, he thanked her profusely for allowing me to leave on such short notice. Upon my return following the successful completion of the job, I learned Claude had emphasized his appreciation by slipping Brenda two $100 bills along with his suggestion she use them to "—buy a new dress." He was a smooth and classy ladies' man. Claude and I went to dinner several times during my stay there. Our dining often included evenings in restaurants featuring live music. Imagine my delight when Claude, retrieving his saxophone from the car, would join the band. In addition to entrepreneurial talents, he was a woodwind virtuoso having traveled with the great Jimmy Dorsey orchestra.

On my frequent visits to Wilson Concepts, the shop foreman challenged me to arm wrestling contests. Despite his above average strength, I always prevailed, making me wonder why he persisted. It was friendly competition.

Like many new enterprises we struggled through our share of trials and tribulations. On one occasion, Bruce and Chuck wrote a new link for a Lodge and Shipley lathe and Bruce had one little mistake in it that caused me a lot of grief. The machine would not come back to home position and I kept adding and subtracting the numbers, etc. They all seemed to add up but what I did not catch was that a "G" function wasn't reinstated after a "G04" dwell cycle. Thus, the following blocks were not really interpreted as axis motion but just additional dwell blocks. That was the reason the machine was not returning to its home position. I was crawling all over the machine with dial indicators etc. trying to figure out what was wrong. I would go back to the office and add and subtract all of the X and Z motions and everything seemed to add up. It was not until we discovered the problem with not entering a G00 or a G01 after the G04 block that we realized what the problem was. A call to headquarters implemented the necessary fix and everything was A OK.

On July 20, 1969, my former colleague at Sundstrand, Harold Anderson, invited Paul Bearden and me to the General Electric plant in Cincinnati to do a demo of Compact II. He was faced with the same problem I had when I was at Lear-Siegler – no ready access to a computer for programming – and this was a golden opportunity for our fledgling business. Paul and I accepted Harold's invitation and went to Cincinnati. Harold's familiarity with the SPLIT program allowed him to follow my demonstration of COMPACT II without any problems. Adding General Electric to our growing list of customers was an exciting achievement. FYI General Electric had a competitive programming system based on a scaled down APT language, namely ADAPT.

Following our day of successful business transactions, Harold invited us to his house for dinner. It was made more memorable because we shared that night's exciting televised Apollo moon landing.

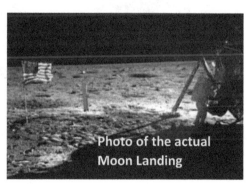

Photo of the actual Moon Landing

1969

Van, Jeni, Gary, Brenda, Jeff, Mom, Dad, Uncle Adrian and his wife

When friends and relatives from the "old country" visited my folks, we often took them to the Kellogg plant in Battle Creek for the tour. This photo records one of those visits when we lived in Ann Arbor.

1970

We moved out of the Traver Knoll apartment into a house on Glastonbury Rd. on the west side of Ann Arbor. We enjoyed the extra room and privacy until we relocated to Texas. During this time, we were hosts to my folks and their friends who visited from time to time from "the old country."

Training for new account executive salesmen and AEs required them to come to Ann Arbor for two to three months of intensive training. Successful completion was often celebrated at Bimbo's Pizza Parlor where live piano and band were featured on weekends. A favorite aspect of Bimbo's was their reputation for littering the floor with peanuts which inevitably led to

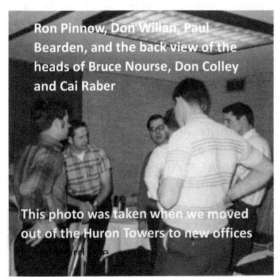

Ron Pinnow, Don Willan, Paul Bearden, and the back view of the heads of Bruce Nourse, Don Colley and Cai Raber

This photo was taken when we moved out of the Huron Towers to new offices

boisterous behavior of patrons tossing them at each other. I was not immune to this behavior. A memorable event occurred when I slammed my fist on the table spilling a stein on Don Young's suit. He wore the soiled suit to work the next day (Saturday) to say farewell to our staff before returning to his home in Pittsburgh. I learned later his preference for wearing the same suit every day was a common habit in England, from which he had recently immigrated.

It wasn't rare for employees of customers to join our firm. Following a demo Chuck and I made at a plant in Port Huron, Frank Roberts, a programmer, came to work for us. Frank lived in Port Huron which is right across the St. Clair River from Sarnia, Canada, where Chuck kept his 36' sailboat. Chuck occasionally treated MDSI employees and customers to a day of sailing on Lake Huron. It was not much later after we hired Frank, we hired his counterpart, Frank Rose. After a few years working out of the Ann Arbor office, Frank Roberts was promoted to District Sales Manager requiring him to move to California. After a few years as AE, Frank Rose also went on to become a salesman in the Michigan area.

One way the MDSI team tried to save money was by limiting long-distance telephone charges. We had an 800 outgoing number we used extensively. We had field people all over the country, and when they ran into a problem, they would call the home office person-to-person and ask for Mr. Goodyear. He was never in, so the call would be disconnected, and there was no charge. Betty or Judy, who would answer the phone, generally would let you know when they might expect him back in the office. That was a signal as to how soon we could expect a call back.

Brenda and I bought a 6-unit apartment complex in Grand Rapids from my cousin, Gerard Boot. We fixed it up a bit and enjoyed revenues from it for several years. My sister, Cora, managed it for us which included interviewing prospective new tenants. When one of the tenants asked for permission to paint his apartment, we authorized it. Imagine our consternation when we learned he had painted the walls and electrical outlet plates purple! Adding insult to injury, we learned he was a drug dealer selling to one of our nephews. Following his incarceration, our nephew attempted to convince us our tenant was a really nice guy. Give me a break!

Bedford, Texas

Jim Spencer, a seasoned perfume salesman, had been our MDSI salesman in Texas long enough to develop a customer base large enough to justify a full-time application support engineer. Our president, Ken Stephanz, knowing Brenda's family lived there, extended the opportunity to me resulting in our move to the mid-cities of the Dallas-Fort Worth area. In late 1969 or early 1970, we relocated to Bedford, Texas.

Bob Drewry, Dick Fisher and Jim Spencer

Jim was a tall, relatively good-looking ladies' man. He really tried to butter up Brenda by giving her lots of perfume. He also gave me a set of Texas longhorn cattle horns which I later gave to my Uncle Adrian when he visited us on one of his trips from Holland. Several years later, on one of my trips to Europe, when I took a few days off to visit Holland, I saw them mounted in the front hallway of his house. I do not think he ever saw a set of horns on any cows that big in Holland where cattle agriculture is almost exclusively dairies with dehorned Friesian Holstein milk cows.

Dick Clark, Bob Drewry and Dick Fisher, three guys Chuck hired away from Boeing in Omaha, were all in the same training class in Ann Arbor with Jim Spencer the salesman that I was going to be teamed up with later. In this photo, they are sitting on the couch in our rented house on Glastonbury.

Rented Parsonage and Chevy Impala

Upon our move to Texas, I needed a company car. Thus, when Bob Ricker, one of our salesmen in California, was terminated, I flew from Texas to California to retrieve his company vehicle, a Chevy Impala which became my company car. My flight was booked on a 747 out of Love Field in Dallas and there weren't fifty fellow passengers on the plane. It was my first flight on a 747 jumbo jet and I was astounded at the size and roominess – I couldn't help but wonder how an airplane this big could get off the ground.

When we moved to Texas, we gave our Corvair to Butch, my youngest brother. We had to have air conditioning to survive the Texas heat and there was no way an air-cooled rear engine Corvair could support it. We had driven it over 100,000 miles but Butch wrapped it around a telephone pole within six months. He insisted he drove it longer than that and claimed the brakes failed causing the wreck.

Life in Texas included frequent visits to Brenda's folks in Longview. They had a small house trailer at Toledo Bend Lake where Brenda's father satisfied his appetite for fishing. Toledo Bend Lake was created by a dam on the Sabine River. Fishing was exceptionally good due to the many trees in it resulting from the construction process. The photo is evidence of the fishing experience our boys enjoyed with their grandpa.

Jeff and Gary with their Toledo Bend catch – June 1970

We had two encounters with the water moccasin population of Toledo Bend Lake. Once, not ten feet from the boat, sunning himself on some branches, a huge snake caught our attention. While they aren't overly aggressive, they are venomous prompting us to slowly exit the area drawing as little attention as possible to ourselves. On another occasion, we had just cleaned some fish and I decided that I would go in for a quick fresher upper and Jeff decided to join me. We were enjoying ourselves and suddenly I noticed a snake headed toward us. I swam as fast as I could pushing Jeff toward shore, and we got the heck out of there.

The oil industry in Houston included some large companies and it wasn't long before Houston became our biggest customer base. We soon enjoyed orders from: Cameron Iron Works, National Supply, Baker Oil Tools, Gray Tool Co., Schlumberger and others. Schlumberger ultimately purchased MDSI.

Because our home in Bedford, Texas, was close to Fort Worth where Putnam Machine Co. was located, I spent quite a bit of time there assisting them in getting up and running with COMPACT II. Putnam's business included machining parts for General Dynamics. The owner's son-in-law, Dave Livingstone, was their lead programmer and he eventually left them to join us in Ann Arbor.

MDSI's sales engineers had closer working relationships with customers than our application engineers; thus, I made it a point to instill in the SEs the habit of using the client's names when we worked together as a team. I'm convinced this practice was an effective tool that set us apart from our potential competitors. Coupled with my insistence that MDSI's application engineers would be better prepared to be of value, I also developed the practice of being escorted through our customers' production facilities to better understand their manufacturing processes.

Often, after spending a week in Houston, returning home on I-45 driving 75mph, I roughed out my customers visits reports on my briefcase lying beside me on the seat of my car. Our secretary, Judy Foster, whose job it was to type and file the final file copy, loved deciphering my wriggles and scribbles that, I'm sure once in a while, included a few Dutch influences in the notes. The extraordinary time I spent on the road resulted in speeding violations threatening my license. When I was pulled over for speeding by a state trooper on my way home from Houston, the points it would have generated would have exceeded the legal limit and my ability to make customer calls would have been severely restricted. Fortunately, an attorney attending our church advised me to challenge the citation demanding a jury trial. He reasoned that, because the court for that jurisdiction would be in a town too small to successfully gather a jury for something as minor as a speeding ticket, the violation summons would likely be vacated. I followed his advice and never heard another word about it.

At National Supply in Houston, Luis Mandell, my principal contact, recognized my work ethic "90 miles per hour serving customers ", by describing it as "burning the candle at both ends." Years later, on a trip to Traverse City, MI, visiting a candle factory, I found a candle on display with a wick on both ends boasting the following verse coined by the American poet, Edna St. Vincent Millay in 1920:

First Fig by Edna Vincent Millay
"My candle burns at both ends,
It will not last the night;
But ah, my foes, and oh, my friends—
It gives a lovely light!"

Hired Dick Weeden.

After Jim Spencer was let go, Mike Long, the National Sales and Marketing VP, hired Dick Weeden. Dick Weeden told me the story of how he met Mike at the old Dallas Love Field Airport with his own bottle of wine for his interview for the sales position. The DFW airport was just beginning construction.

Dick Weeden and Family

When Dick and I were on the road we often roomed together to save the company money. We got along quite well and never had any problems. It was only years later when Brenda met Sharon during a trip to California that Sharon told Brenda that Dick was a recovering alcoholic. Sharon was still selling real estate and Dick was a house inspector.

Demonstrating our product, COMPACT II, required us to carry an ASR33 terminal with us. The standard protective case for transporting this equipment was a fiberglass case we called the Blue Goose. It wasn't an uncommon experience to arrive at our prospect's office with a non-working terminal. However, with the assistance of the phone company, we discovered the problem was generally created by rough handling by baggage handlers. As a matter of historical record, on one occasion I personally witnessed our Blue Goose being physically tossed on the conveyor belt as it disappeared into the belly of the plane we were taking to our meeting and I dreaded the moment when I would open the case to find a damaged demo terminal. However, we had learned that the culprit was most commonly a loose "H" plate relatively easy to repair. We should have had "HANDLE WITH CARE" painted on the cases.

Once when Dick Weeden and I were in Kansas City demonstrating COMPACT II to a large steel company, Tom Ingraham, a trainee, flew in from Ann Arbor to watch us in action. Sitting in the plant supervisor's office, a room in the middle of the plant surrounded with windows, I was asked to program a huge form roll for the steel mill. The blueprint had to be 15ft long. Tom Ingraham was holding up one end of it when he fell asleep allowing the blueprint to fall to the floor. Somewhat embarrassing to say the least. We later learned that Tom had narcolepsy, a fairly common disorder causing its carrier to involuntarily fall asleep. On another occasion, Tom and Bob Guy requested my opinion prompting me to join them in Tom's office. To explain my opinion, I turned my back to them to use the white board. As I turned back to face them, I realized Tom had once again fallen asleep at an inopportune time. I think what bothered me the most about Tom's condition was that he was a pilot and flying when one is afflicted with narcolepsy seems more than a little irresponsible. It just blows my mind.

On a cloudy windy day, returning home from Oklahoma City, I stopped to pick up a hitchhiker. When he got into the car, I noticed he had a bunch of newspapers under his shirt. When I asked him why, he said they were a good insulator to keep the cold wind out. When I dropped him off in downtown Fort Worth, I noticed he left something in the car. I drove around the block and found him walking along the sidewalk so I stopped to give him the package that he had left behind. I guess I never thought about newspapers being a good insulator; but years later, when I went with Jeff and his family to Leadville, Co and visited an old mining shack from around the turn of the last century, that too was insulated with newspapers glued to the wall.

Being one of the world's most anti-smoking human beings, imagine my reaction when my sister, Jeni, came to visit us when she was a teenager. Despite our family relationship, when she went into the bathroom and opened a window to smoke a cigarette, I smelled it and immediately confronted her telling her: "I won't have you or anyone else smoking in my house!"

Spring 1970

The house we were renting from the Baptist church backed up to a large ranch; thus, I bought a horse and boarded it at the ranch. The horse was a cross between a pony and a quarter horse and we named it Cricket. I built a pen close to our house so we could feed, saddle and ride him. Jeff and Gary really enjoyed riding Cricket.

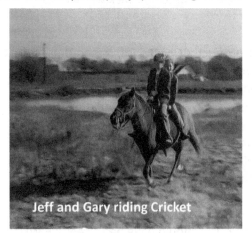
Jeff and Gary riding Cricket

After living in the rental house for about a year, we bought a house from one of our friends in the First Methodist Church we attended. It was a ranch with some Japanese influence. It had a fenced off back yard. At the front door, it had a small pond with a waterfall and some bamboo. Not too long after we bought this house, I added a couple dozen goldfish to it. Sometime later, two of my

Backyard Waterfall and Fishpond

brothers, Adrian and Pete, came up from Florida and we built a large cement (5 cubic yards) fishpond in the back yard.

Clayton Davis, the newly hired Application Engineer supervisor, made field trips to check up on how the application engineers were doing. He always carried a small bottle of liquor with him in his suitcase--like what you see in old movies where an actor takes a swig of it. Clayton Davis called me from Ann Arbor during the Christmas Holidays one year when they were having an office party. He let me know everybody was enjoying themselves with champagne and *hors d'oeuvres*; then he proudly informed me he had awarded me another fifty shares of MDSI stock. Insulted, I considered this to be a stingy reward so I told him to keep them. Clayton wasn't with MDSI very long; perhaps a year or so, before he accepted an offer from Clark Equipment, one of our customers, relocating him to Belgium. I lost track of him after that.

When I was on the road and spending many nights in motel rooms, I spent hours proofreading a Beta version of the CII programming manual. As I found errors, I reported them to our HQ team in Ann Arbor.

Executives in our Ann Arbor headquarters were eager to visit the milder climate in Texas, especially during the winter. On one occasion, Jim and I picked up our CEO, Ken Stephanz, at the Houston airport, on our way to do a demo at Baker Oil Tool Co. The demo went well and they signed a contract with us. When we got back into the car, we always did a mini critique. Ken took this opportunity to teach me a valuable lifetime lesson. He said, "Van, you were chewing gum through the whole demo. You probably should have swallowed it." I knew Ken was right, and I was embarrassed. At that point in time, I made a silent vow with myself that Ken would never again be able to hang that mistake on me again. Thus, to this day I seldom chew gum. My group of friends today all know this story, so often they tease me by trying to offer me a stick of gum, knowing full well that I have not chewed gum in fifty years.

An application engineer working for us in California resigned and went to work for one of his customers. Not long after his departure, we discovered he was logging into our system using an unauthorized staff account in England saving his new employer thousands of dollars in

Us and Dan Davis Family

computer time. Rather than settling for a slap on the wrist, the company took him to court where a fine of $25,000 was levied plus forfeiture of his MDSI stock. This case later became a textbook reference studied by law students for several years.

Jeni and Mary Ann Brown

We attended the Methodist Church in Bedford. Here we developed close friendships with the Dan Davis family and the Ron Brown family. The Browns were experiencing financial problems and, on one occasion, when the offering plate was passed, Ron put in a $20 bill. When the plate reached Mary Ann, she retrieved it.

Back to Ann Arbor 1975

Georgetown BLVD.

Responding to Ken Stephanz's (MDSI CEO) request, we moved back to Ann Arbor. My assignment was to create and manage the Quality Assurance Department. We had been living in Bedford, Texas, for a couple years and I had spent that time developing the MDSI market for the Southwest, primarily Texas.

Most of the initial task of the QA department was to review hundreds of machine tool links to see if they met the required specs for that particular machine tool, promptingus to add **IF** and **GOTO, DVR** (Define Variable #), etc., repeat major command (;), capabilities. With these commands, we developed **MASTER** programs for lathes and mills to help debug the new link. This significantly accelerated the process of checking links which were rapidly increasing in numbers.

We had purchased a home on Georgetown Blvd and the day of our move, Brenda was left by herself at our new home in Ann Arbor while I flew back to Texas to perform more customer demonstrations and to conduct additional training. After a few days she realized the wardrobe containing my clothes was missing. Our unfenced yard adjacent to the Thurston School grounds provided an ideal short cut for kids as well as treating us to the noises common to Little League Baseball games on the companion baseball field. The yelling those kids did to rattle opposing batters drove me nuts. The Thurston Pond Nature Center supported a variety of wildlife including ducks, turtles, dragonflies, salamanders and other critters. Jeff and Gary enjoyed riding their bikes around the pond and on trails through the adjoining woods. On family walks around the pond, we competed skipping rocks. On one occasion, the boys and I had a contest to see who could pee the farthest. Sometimes we would go fishing. We never caught any big ones, but we sure caught lots of them. To a young kid, size was not the most important thing. If you were catching something everything was A OK.

Gary and Jeff fishing at Bill's Lake

By this time, MDSI's strategies for managing customer interactions had become more structured. Software bugs reported by customers or AEs were documented on software problem reports (SPR's) and forwarded to the link engineering group. When the problem was fixed, my QA group checked to make sure it really was a legitimate fix and would work in the field.

Living in Michigan allowed us to encourage our boys to love the outdoors and camping. Memories of camping trips in our pop-up trailer we took to the upper and lower peninsula areas include one trip when Brenda's folks went with us and we camped below the Mackinaw Bridge. Brenda's dad was a warm weather guy – he preferred ninety degrees or more. The colder climate wasn't his cup of tea for pleasure camping. We camped several times at Tahquamenon Falls in the U.P. One time Jeff, Gary and I hiked from the lower falls to the upper falls and had Brenda pick us up there. Of course, we had to stop along the way and carve our initials into one of the trees along the trail. I am sure if you follow that trail today, you would see our initials there. Another common thing to do while you were in that part of the state was to drive to the town of Newberry and watch the black bears raid the dump.

Despite the perennially cold water temperature, camping at Painted Rock and along the beaches of Lake Superior were family favorites. The water in Lake Superior never warms up and most adults won't swim in it; however, kids generally enjoy frolicking in it.

Brenda with Jeff & Gary feeding swans in Grand Traverse Bay

Van and Brenda at Sleeping Bear Sand Dunes

Several times we camped at Sleeping Bear Sand Dunes. Then the boys and I would hike down to Lake Michigan and back around to the campground. This was quite a hike, but we enjoyed it immensely. One time when we were camping, and I believe it might have been at Sleeping Bear Sand Dunes State Park, I had just bought a BB gun for the boys, and I was

Camping up north with the Parkers

Jeff and Gary at Painted Rock along Lake Superior

Keith J. Charters Traverse City State Park is a 47-acre state park located on the east arm of the Grand Traverse Bay just 2 miles from downtown Traverse City. The park is home to a modern campground, a fully equipped lodge, mini cabins, and day-use area. The day-use area is located directly across U.S. 31 and features a quarter mile of sandy beach, a small beach house and picnic area. Our family enjoyed camping there.

Footprints in the Sand

91

showing them how to use it. Well, there was a blue jay that had just landed in the tree high above where we had set up our camping trailer. I proceeded to show them how to fire the gun. I aimed for the blue jay (which is a protected species in Michigan) never expecting to hit it, but I did, and it came tumbling down from the top of the tree deader than a doornail.

Dec 1971

We learned firsthand how dangerous the seemingly innocuous fun of sledding or "tubing" can be. On a snowy hill in December, 1971 our son, Jeff, flew headfirst into a tree sustaining a large bump on his forehead. My dad's house on Boone Court backed up to a hill ideal for sledding and tubing (large inner tubes facilitating exciting rides on downhill snowy slopes). My brother, Butch, with Jeff on his back, careened down the hill on a large inner tube, slammed into a tree catapulting Jeff headfirst into the tree. I cleared the fence on a dead run, picked up my injured son (unaware of whether or not he was conscious) and deposited him on his bed in dad's house. My memory

Butch and Jeff

is foggy, but apparently, he recovered soon enough to assure us he wasn't in mortal danger but not before his mother and I had the daylights scared out of us.

On a trip to the bank near the Kroger store at the bottom of Broadmoor Hill, while Jeff and Gary were conducting their business in the bank, Jeff's bike was stolen. Despite being acutely aware of the less than stellar reputation of this particular neighborhood, we devoted the following days to driving around in it unsuccessfully looking for the stolen bike.

Occasionally Brenda and I found time to enjoy dinner at the Win Schuler Restaurant. Located just a few blocks from our house on Georgetown Blvd., it featured an old English motif with relics and décor to immerse its customers in a relaxed medieval ambiance we found relaxing and comfortable.

Brenda and Van enjoying a meal at Win Schuler's

Other favorite Ann Arbor restaurants included: the Real Seafood Co, Metzger's for authentic German food and beer, the Gandy Dancer, and Weber's on Jackson Ave. Many of these restaurants offered a free meal on your birthday.

One of my preferred dining spots was Zingerman's. Established in 1982, it became an Ann Arbor institution and "must try" experience for visitors from around the world. Featuring over-stuffed sandwiches made with bread from their bakery, cheese from a local creamery, homemade sauces and some of the best meat selections in the area,

Zingerman's never disappointed its patrons. Their star of the menu was a Reuben, stuffed with corned beef, topped with Swiss Emmental cheese over Brinery sauerkraut on Jewish rye bread was my favorite sandwich. Big enough to satisfy two appetites, this was a treat we shared when Brenda was working at Deloitte and Touche and she would bring it home for dinner. I don't remember what it cost in those days but I Googled it in 2022 and it was $20.99!

Finally got my MBA.

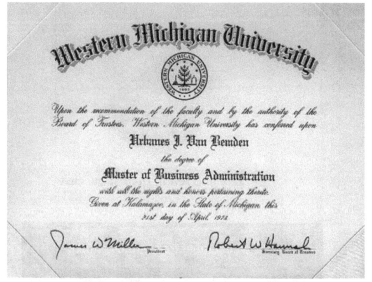

In the spring of 1973, ten years after earning my bachelor's degree at Letourneau, I finished my MBA program. It had been a circuitous route beginning at Northern Illinois University when I worked at Sundstrand Machine Tool Co. in Belvidere, IL, transferring credits to Western Michigan when I took the job at Lear-Siegler, then transferring again to North Texas State in Denton, Texas, when we moved to Bedford, and finally, once again back at Western Michigan, where I was granted the diploma for my MBA (see photo).

Winter of 1973.

Jeff, Gary and their friends found ways to enjoy the Michigan winters with their frigid temperatures and heavy snow storms. The winter of 1973 was memorable with its severe snow storm in Ann Arbor. Nothing was moving and schools were closed allowing the kids to make the most of it. These photos tell the story of those winter entertainment activities.

Gary, John Watson and Peter Watson

Gary and Jeff in their snow cave

1974.

Ron Pinnow, a fellow MDSI employee I recruited in 1970, suffered job-related burnout and resigned in 1974. Leaving MDSI allowed him to purchase a small resort on Houghton Lake where he hosted a group of us for a delightful weekend. Later in the fall a bunch of MDSI'ers spent the weekend at his resort having a wonderful time just relaxing and having fun.

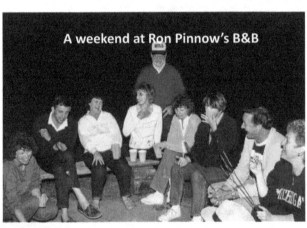
A weekend at Ron Pinnow's B&B

At the shore of Lake Michigan in the Silver Lake area

In this photo, from left to right: Brenda, Tom Ingraham, Judy Foster, Joan Pinnow, Ron Pinnow (standing), an unknown, Sandy Ingraham, Dick Brushe and Mary Ann Guy.

Converting Volkswagens into dune buggies by removing the roof, fenders, doors, etc., was a common practice in the mid-1970s. These dune buggies provided great entertainment on the many sand dunes in Michigan. Silver Lake, a popular dune buggy area, gave us a memorable weekend when my sister, Wilma, invited us to use her place and jeep one spectacular weekend. Close to Lake Michigan, we joined others who migrated to the shores to rendezvous there.

1974.

In 1974, MDSI acquired a minor competitor out of Cleveland called NCCS-Word. Inc. The original Numerical Control and Computer Services (NCCS) was the company that Richard "Dick" Stitt founded after he copied SPLIT to create his own NC program called Action. As a point of interest, the original name for Dick's package was ACTION. When he added the capability to define lines and circles, he changed the name to ACTION II. We followed suit when we added the capability to define lines and circles prompting us to change the name from COMPACT to COMPACT II.

Carl Harrison, who came over from Dick Stitt's group when MDSI bought NCCS, and I roomed together when we went to an X3J5 meeting in Tucson, AZ. One way Carl dealt with his weight problem was by dumping a dozen or so Sweet 'n Low packets on his cereal which I thought was a bit much. On this trip to Tucson, Carl and I drove down to Nogales and crossed the border into Mexico. In Mexico, Carl bought a bottle or two of various liquor but, when we got back to the border ready to go back into the good old USA, the border patrol told him he had more than the allowable number to legally cross the border. Carl was not just going to hand it over – he proceeded to pour it down the drain so the officers would not get it. I could always count on Carl to buy several boxes of candy from Jeff when St. Paul Lutheran school was having a candy sale.

Carl boarding the bus in Mexico

A year or two later, Carl was found dead in his apartment. I do not remember what he died from but I couldn't help but wonder if abusing Sweet 'n Low may have been a contributing factor. Years later I read that a test on rats eating Sweet 'n Low demonstrated they would have to eat 10 pounds of it to die. Thus, I do not think that Carl died from using too many Sweet 'n Low packages.

Summer of 1975.

During the summer of 1975, my cousin, Gerard Boot Jr., invited Jeff and me to accompany him, his dad, and our Uncle Izaak, on a Canadian fishing trip. Accepting the invitation, we drove from Grand Rapids to the straits and into Canada via Sault Ste. Marie. "Boot," as we called my cousin, drove his Chevy Blazer pulling a trailer with two small boats on it. The gravel roads we traveled in the boonies of Canada punctured the trailer tires several times along the way. Anyway, the fishing was good, mostly pike. I remember we ate fish morning, noon, and night.

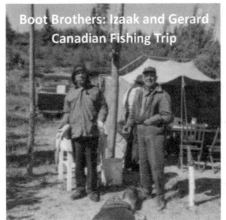
Boot Brothers: Izaak and Gerard Canadian Fishing Trip

I enjoyed visiting with Uncle Izaak since he was over from the Nederlands and I did not get to talk to him that often. I remember Jeff and I were in one of the boats when a storm came up and we headed back to our camping site. The waves were pretty big and, every once in a while, the prop would be out of the water. Jeff would look at me and wonder whether or not we were going to get back to our campsite safely.

A Chrysler 300 we bought from Joe made our annual trips to Texas to visit Brenda's folks more pleasant than earlier trips in smaller cars. In addition to the roominess for passengers and extra trunk space, my dad made a bench to insert between the front and back seats converting the entire back seat area into a play area. Of course, this pre-dated compulsory seat belt laws. On one occasion when we left our place on Georgetown Blvd to drive to Texas, we got stuck in the snow getting out of the driveway. We slipped and slid all the way thru Michigan and Indiana.

When Jeff was 13 or 14 years old, several of his buddies had scooters. Jeff eventually got one and his Uncle Pete sent him a cast iron Tecumseh air-cooled engine. It was powerful and Jeff could perform wheelies; however, it was also very heavy and made the scooter dangerously lopsided.

Jeff riding his scooter with the Tecumseh motor

Country roads lined with hardwoods, especially walnut trees, around our area of Michigan, provided an abundance of readily available walnuts. The outer husks of walnuts are notorious for staining clothing and, on one occasion, we demonstrated the effectiveness of this natural staining product. On this occasion, Harvey Blankenspoor and his wife, accompanied our family on a walnut gathering expedition. We gathered a bushel or so of the nuts still encased in their husks and took them home. When we dumped them on the driveway, Jeff's friend proceeded to dehusk them by stomping on them. Unfortunately, he was wearing a new pair of tennis shoes and the stain from the nuts all but ruined the appearance of the new shoes.

The Upper Peninsula is connected to the Lower Peninsula by the famous Mackinac Bridge. Once a year, on Labor Day, it is opened to pedestrian traffic and walking the five miles across it has become a relatively popular event. One year, beginning in St. Ignace at the north end, Jeff and I walked the five miles to Mackinaw City on the south end where Brenda was waiting in the car to welcome us after our successful completion of the five-mile walk across the Big Mac.

Considered by many as the "8th wonder of the world," the Mackinac Bridge is the longest suspension bridge in the western hemisphere with 7,400' of 4 lane roadways suspended in the air over the beautiful Straits of Mackinac. That is **950' longer** than the Golden Gate Bridge in San Francisco.

Gary is hit and killed by an Automobile June 24, 1976

On the morning of June 24, 1976, I flew from Detroit to Milwaukee to meet Paul Breniser who was to accompany me to a business meeting with Kearney and Trecker, one of our customers in Milwaukee. Upon arrival at the customer's office, I was alerted to a family emergency requiring an immediate phone call to our home office. Our company secretary, Betty Ruddy, could not provide details other than arrangements in place for me to board a flight waiting for me at the Milwaukee airport to return me to Detroit. Aboard this flight, I was left to wonder and imagine the nature as well as severity of the accident.

Roger Verhey met me at the arrival gate and took me directly to Children's Hospital at the University of Michigan. We left my car at the airport to be retrieved later. On our way to the hospital, Roger told me Gary had been riding his bike to Vacation Bible School where Brenda was the co-director when he was hit by a car but he did not know the current situation as it related to the seriousness of Gary's injuries.

When I arrived at the hospital, Ruth Mieras directed me to the hospital chapel where I could join Brenda. Brenda told me that we had lost our son in the accident. This tragic news rippled out into our family as well as the extended circle of friends and MDSI employees, many of whom attended Gary's funeral service.

June 28, 1976.

The day of Gary's funeral, my Plymouth Satellite, parked on Georgetown Blvd in front of our house, was stolen. I called the police and our State Farm Insurance agent to report my stolen car. It was never found. Later, when our policy was up for renewal, State Farm canceled our policy. To this day I will never take out a policy from that company. I guess I was turning in too many claims. A stolen car, a stolen bike, a large broken window, and we lived in one of the newer, better and safer areas of Ann Arbor.

```
              Funeral Service                              "WAITING"
           Gary Lee Van Bemden
               June 28, 1976                  We went one day at eventide,
                                                  To stroll where fancy led,
                                              Our son with restless dancing steps,
 Prelude                                          And we with slower tread.
                                              He loosed his hands from ours
 Invocation Prayer                                And looking up he said,
                                              "You walk so slowly, Mom and Dad,
 Scripture Reading  John 11:17-27                 I'll just run on ahead."
                                              And soon his eager rushing feet
 Hymn  "I am the Resurrection"                    Had carried him from view,
       (see back of this service order)       Around the bend far down the land
 Scripture Reading  I Corinthians 15:51-58        Where wild flowers grew.
                                              And when with measured steps we came,
 Hymn  205  The Tender Love a Father Has          And made the turning too,
                                              He called to us amid the flowers,
 Prayer                                           "I'm waiting here for you."
                                              And now those restless feet are still,
 Message  The Joy of the Lord- Jeremiah 31:13     The eager spirit, free,
                                              Has gone ahead to be with God
 *Hymn  469  By The Sea of Crystal                Through all eternity.
                                              And though our hearts are heavy
 *Benediction                                     For days that cannot be,
                                              We know among God's fragrant flowers,
 Postlude                                         For us he's waiting happily.



              Pastor  William C. De Vries
              Organinst  Charlotte Larsen
```

Bulletin for the Funeral Service for Gary

All of my brothers and sisters, with the exception of Pete who was in California, attended Gary's funeral. Since Pete was not there, I had Jimmy Parker, who is about the same size as Pete, stand in for him, thinking that I could Photoshop Pete's head in later. I never did. This photo was taken in our backyard when we lived on Georgetown Blvd.

VanBemden Family at Gary's Funeral

Shortly after Gary died, Rev. John Malestein, guest minister at the Ann Arbor CRC church, used an interesting quote in his sermon about the curiosity of young kids. I requested a copy and he sent it to me. It's posted below.

"Life's supreme tragedy is not poor health, lack of wealth or beauty or great gifts, a disappointment in marriage or having a boring job, grievously hard as they may be to bear. It lies in the fading of our youthful vision, our greatest sorrow is always the death of that sparkling spirit of wonder we possess as children, that deep joy in the world and in living, that pure faith and believing heart, the bubbling of divine joy within us"

How true this is!

A week or so after Gary's funeral, a friend of the Larsens who had a cottage in Vermont gave us a week's use of their cottage. Thus, Brenda, Jeff, Kirk Larsen, and I were off to Vermont. Their cottage was on Lake Champlain. Jeff and Kirk really enjoyed their time there fishing and canoeing on this huge lake. While we were there, we also did a few short road trips around the area.

Jeff and Kirk Larsen at Lake

The flower bed Kirk Larsen built

On his return to Ann Arbor, Kirk Larsen built a flower bed at the Ann Arbor Christian Reformed Church in honor of Gary. He did this to earn his Eagle Scout award. **EAGLE SCOUT** is the highest rank attainable. To become an Eagle Scout, you must earn a total of 21 merit badges and demonstrate Scout Spirit, Service, and Leadership.

A few weeks after Gary's funeral, a policeman came to our house. Discovering nobody home, he went to neighbors to inquire into my location. He explained to our neighbor, Gertrude Platner, that the young lady who had hit Gary was accusing me of removing lug nuts from her car's wheels. Gertrude explained I was in Japan and could not be guilty of the lug nut accusation. Quite frankly, to this day I do not know her name nor what she looks like, and I am OK with that. One time our company lawyer told me if I wanted to sue her, I would probably win the case. I told him I was not interested since it certainly would not bring Gary back.

Kcn Stephanz and I went to Japan to determine the advisability of expanding our markets there. I flew over ahead of Ken and Brenda and they were to join me there a few days later. Brenda had planned to fly over with Ken but she was unable to secure her visa by personally negotiating the process in Chicago in time; thus, she flew over by herself. It was her first visit to Japan and her unfamiliarity with customs and baggage claims in an airport where the only other people looked and behaved very differently was unnerving for her.

Brenda and Van on their way to Mt. Fuji

Brenda's first experience in a Japanese restaurant was also a bit less than comfortable for her. The restaurant featured fresh shrimp cooked on a hibachi – a hot plate the size of a small table. Live shrimp are tossed onto the hot grill where they jump around till the cook cuts them into bite-sized pieces.

Our Japanese host and guide was named Yoshi. He showed us Tokyo's places of interest before taking us to Mount Fuji.

With Dutch as my first language and English as my second, there are a few words I have a little difficulty pronouncing. Dave Price, a fellow MDSI employee, teased me when my pronunciation of "specific," sounded to him more like "pacific." He could only speak one language and I was blessed with 2 ½! He always came across as though he thought he was better than everybody else.

Brenda in one of many gardens we visited

MDSI's National Sales Manager, Dave Meissner, was a staunch Christian who consistently projected a positive and healthy outlook on life. When I was struggling, he would say, "Van, smile!"

March 1977. We had a family get together at Cora's house and had the entire family there and I took some photos and one of them is below.

Van Bemden clan – March 1977

Jeff attended St. Paul Lutheran school thru the 8th grade. Being a small school, class sizes were relatively small; thus, all the boys in each grade participated in the various sports.

**Jeff playing basketball at
St. Paul Lutheran School**

The summer of 1977, we traveled to Florida, and stayed with my brother Pete, who had a house right on the Gulf of Mexico north of Tarpon Springs. While we were there, we visited Cypress Gardens. We also went to a small island in the gulf and looked for sand dollars. Jeff's school friend, Kurt Firnhaber, also came with us on this trip to Florida.

Kurt with a parrot at Cypress Gardens

Jeff with a parrot at Cypress Gardens

While we were there, we also visited the harbor in Tarpon Springs and watched the boats coming in and out. I have also included a photo of my brother Pete's 2 young daughters with their German Shepherd.

Angie and Lori Van Bemden

Jeff and Kurt at the harbor in Tarpon Springs

The winter of 1977 we had a pretty good snow storm. I remember we could not look out of our front windows, because the snow drifts were so high. It took a while for us to shovel the driveway so we could drive our cars, etc. Kids were jumping off the Thurston school roof and really enjoying themselves.

Jeff admiring all the work we have done

Jeff jumping off the Thurston School

Look closely at the photo of our driveway. You will see our canoe hanging from the ceiling of the garage. This was a fiberglass canoe I enjoyed paddling on the Huron River which flowed through Ann Arbor. We didn't use it very often so, when the strap securing it to the garage ceiling broke allowing one end to hit the floor requiring repair, we got rid of it.

A bike built for 12! Only in Holland

A bike built for 12!
On my trip to Holland in 1977, I was lucky enough to catch this photo of a bike built for a dozen people. I caught it as we were driving down the road so it is a little blurred.

1978.

On one of my trips coming back from Japan, I routed myself to go thru customs in Anchorage, Alaska. Before I left the states, I talked to Al Hettinga, who had a brother in Anchorage, about stopping there to visit him. Al's brother showed me around and we went for a drive to Alyeska Ski resort. Alyeska Ski resort is located on the Alaska Pacific coast, just forty miles south of Anchorage. On the way there, we had to stop off at the famous Chicken Coop bar. The outside is shaped like a huge chicken. This is a real hole in the wall; however, when you're in the neighborhood, you must stop in. It is a real dive! He also had built a small plane that he flies around. As you can probably imagine, there are not miles and miles of roads in Alaska and lots of the getting around is done with planes.

Al Hettinga's brother at the Chicken Coop Bar

Al's brother with his plane

Early in 1978 Yoshi was in Ann Arbor and we went skiing at Mt. Brighton. Mt. Brighton is a former landfill and was about 8 miles from where we lived. This is where Jeff and I learned to snow ski. Years later it was bought by Vail Resorts, Inc. This is what Google has to say about Mt. Brighton. Mt. Brighton is a ski and snowboard area in Brighton, Michigan, that opened in 1961. As no hills large enough for commercial skiing or snowboarding exist naturally in Brighton, Mt. Brighton's slopes are man-made and reach a maximum height of 230 vertical feet.

Yoshi and Van skiing at Mt. Brighton

My cousin, Joe and his wife – Muiden Slot

On one of my trips to Europe, I stopped in Amsterdam to visit my cousin, Joe, (whose mother was one of my dad's sisters) in Muiden Slot. He gave me a particularly good tour of that part of Holland which I was not all that familiar with. We visited the Muiden Castle which had a moat around it, and a heavy draw bridge. It was remarkably interesting to tour the castle. He also showed me the local church where he rebuilt the internal workings of a huge clock by hand. I did not ask him how long it took him, but I believe it was quite some time.

Muiden Slot Castle and Harbor

The clock my cousin Joe, rebuilt

The summer of 1977 my cousin Gerard Boot, invited Jeff and me to a fishing trip on Lake Michigan. He had a boat and the lake was famous for Coho salmon. Jeff hooked one and handed the pole to me to reel it in. I had the fish close enough to the boat to scoop it in, but it dove under the boat snagging the line on the propeller allowing it to escape.

Jeff and Van fishing in Lake Michigan on Gerard Boot's boat

Some of the summers the alewives dying along Lake Michigan would create a stench so bad no one would use the beaches in Holland and Grand Haven.

Sept 1978, we had put together a big international meeting in Paris, France. I brought along several people from Ann Arbor to present various topics. Cai Raber, Tom Ingraham, Dave Meissner, and Bob Samson are shown in the photo below. You would think they are moving by looking at the cart with their belongings!

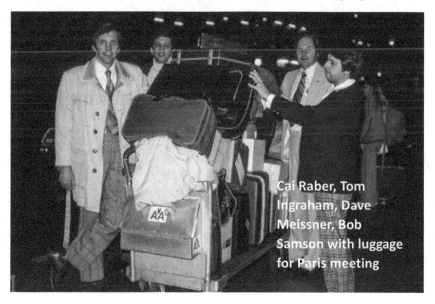

Cai Raber, Tom Ingraham, Dave Meissner, Bob Samson with luggage for Paris meeting

Oct 27, 1978. My 40th Birthday.

I celebrated my 40th birthday party in Ann Arbor on Georgetown Blvd. My mother and many of my siblings drove to Ann Arbor for the festivities.

Mom, Carol, Cora and Brenda

Brenda, Van, Jennie, Lena and Fred

Nov 1978.

The Van Bemden clan celebrated Thanksgiving at Ike's house. In the photo below it shows: Uncle Gerard, Aunt Connie, Mom, Harry with some of Mom's grandkids.

Carol, Brenda, Lena and Char

Uncle Gerard and Aunt Connie

Dec 1978, we drove down to spend Christmas in Longview, Texas. Carol Van Bemden came along with us. Jimmy, Romelle, and Michael were there as well as Aunt LePearl.

Christmas in Longview

Jeff filling up the car at Hudson Station

Gas was expensive. Generally, around this time, it was quite a bit cheaper than the price displayed above.

We must have gone to Caddo Lake during our stay in Longview, since the photo below shows Brenda at Caddo Lake. This is what Google has to say about Caddo Lake:

What is so special about Caddo Lake? The lake and bayou comprise an internationally protected wetland under the Ramsar Convention and includes one of the largest flooded cypress forests in the United States. Caddo is one of Texas's few non-oxbow natural lakes. For centuries, spring flooding eroded riverbanks, toppled trees and increased logjams. The raft disrupted river flow and water spilled into

Brenda at Caddo Lake

Louisiana's Cypress Valley, forming a lake around 1800. That lake was named for the Caddoan people. The Caddo Indians were farming people. Caddo women harvested crops of corn, beans, pumpkins, and sunflowers. Caddo men hunted for deer, buffalo, and small game and went fishing in the rivers. Traditional Caddo foods included cornbread, soups, and stews. Does Caddo Lake have alligators? YES! Alligators live in the park.

Van Bemdens at Aquarena Springs, TX

Once we were in Texas, we strived to make the most of the trip. Thus, we visited as many interesting places as we could.

I just **Googled** the Aquarena Springs and it says: "Once a tourist staple of San Marcos, *Aquarena Springs* no longer exists—," thus, I am glad we visited it when we did.

Jeff and Brenda enjoying the wonders of Texas

We also visited the Natural Bridge Caverns near San Antonio, TX. Natural Bridge Caverns is the most extensive cavern within the San Antonio area and one of the largest caverns within the state of Texas, making it one of the top attractions in Texas.

Japan. Spring of 1979.

In the spring of 1979, cherry blossom time to be exact, on my trip to Japan, my boss, Steve Imredy, came along to see how things were going. Steve always had to stay at the Okura Hotel, which, at that time, was an upper-class hotel right across the street from the U.S. embassy. When I was by myself, I usually stayed at the Kio Plaza which was within walking distance of our office in the Shinjuku area.

A group of young ladies in beautiful kimonos in the lobby of the Okura Hotel

Van, Steve Imredy and Masataka Uesono

Native Americans in German parade

Parade with beer wagon pulled by decorated horses

Following my far eastern business trip, I did a turn around to Europe. When I landed in Frankfurt, a festival of some kind featuring a parade with a beer wagon pulled by a brace of beautifully decorated horses was going on. To my surprise, a group of native Americans (aka: Indians) was also in the parade. You probably did not know there were native Americans in Germany. Well, the truth is, neither did the Germans.

I never drank a lot of wine until I started spending so much time with Europeans whose customary habit was to enjoy it with meals. Jurgen Selig maintained an extensive wine cellar in his basement.

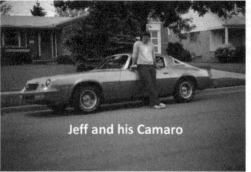

Jeff and his Camaro

I ordered a silver Mazda 626 from a young sales lady at the Mazda dealer in Novi. When she called to tell me, it was ready for delivery, Jeff and I went to the lot to take possession of it. We were confused when the sales lady, pointing to a brown model instead of the silver model we had ordered, said, "Well, how do you like it?" I responded, "It isn't silver". She was unprepared for my next statement, "You can keep it!" Jeff, who had just turned sixteen, and I, went directly to Rampy Chevrolet and bought the Camaro on the showroom floor.

Jeff got a ticket just after he started to drive his Camaro. I do not remember what for, but I think it was speeding. One Saturday morning I noticed some weeds hanging under his car caught in the rear springs and I asked him how that happened. He explained it must have happened when he ran through some deep puddles. Unconvinced, I pressed the issue and he confessed he had driven to his old school, St. Paul Lutheran, to show off his car and the weeds came from the playground.

MDSI, an early adopter of "healthy people make stronger companies" concepts, announced its intention to convert the underground parking garage into a gymnasium where employees could work out. Several vice presidents objected but lost their arguments when it was pointed out the company paid for their memberships to the Barton Hill Country Club. MDSI enjoyed reduced employee health insurance rates as a result of this decision.

Jeff, Brenda and Michael at the St. Louis Arch

Our Western trip Summer of 1979
8-1979
I had become good friends with Jürgen Selig, our Managing Director in Germany. Jürgen's son, Michael, who was about the same age as Jeff spent a large part of the summer of 1979 with us in America. During this time, we took a 3-week vacation out west. Our first stop was the

Chrysler Cordoba

St. Louis Arch.
Our trip was very enjoyable in part because we drove a Chrysler Cordoba I bought from my brother, Joe. This roomy vehicle featured a powerful 442 cubic inch motor. Other than our excursion driving it up Pikes Peak failing to adjust the carburetor for high altitude, it handled the Rocky Mountain highways with ease.

When we drove it up Pikes Peak with 4 of us in the car, it would hardly climb up the hill. I thought for a moment Jeff and Michael might need to push us. I found out years later from Rose Phillips that there used to be a gas station/garage at the start of Pikes Peak highway that would tune your car for high altitudes.

We also visited the famous Air Force Academy as well as the Garden of the Gods while we were in Colorado Springs.

Brenda and Jeff at the Balanced Rock

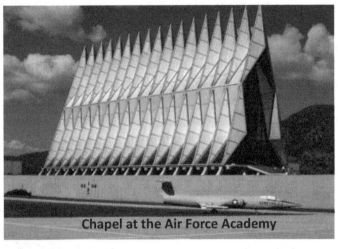

Chapel at the Air Force Academy

The Great Sand Dunes

Leaving Colorado Springs, we drove to the Great Sand Dunes near Alamosa. The Great Sand Dunes are the tallest sand dunes in North America. These dunes, formed by sand blown across the San Louis Valley to collect against the Sangre de Cristo Mountain range, reach heights of nearly 755 feet. The Sangre de Cristo (Blood of Christ) mountains, feature a few peaks exceeding 14,000 feet in elevation and cover about 39 square miles.

From there we visited Mesa Verde in the southwest corner of Colorado where we spent one night in a cabin. Walking the trail from our cabin to the visitor center and the cafeteria, we encountered a rattle snake which kind of scared the daylights out of us.

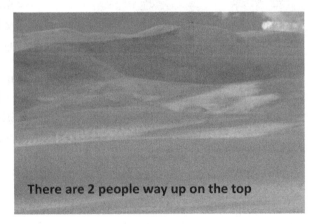

There are 2 people way up on the top

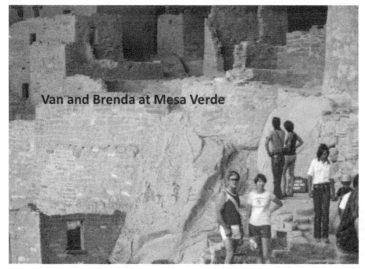
Van and Brenda at Mesa Verde

After spending some time at Mesa Verde, we traveled on to Four Corners. I believe this is the only place in the U.S. where 4 states meet: Utah, Colorado, Arizona, and New Mexico. Thus, as you can see in this photo, I was in 4 states at the same time! At four Corners, there were quite a few Native Americans selling jewelry. When I visited years later, the 4 Corners area had become a tourist trap. You must go into what amounts to a small Indian enclosure to do what I did years earlier.

Canyon De Chelly National Monument in Arizona during the summer months of Jeff's fifteenth year was extremely hot. Despite heeding a warning sign encouraging hikers to carry their own water, Brenda suffered terribly from the heat – she turned beet red and I think she was dangerously close to fainting from heat exhaustion. By removing our shirts, Jeff, Mike and I enjoyed the hike but we were almost as eager to get to

Van at Four Corners

the closest restaurant to cool off as Brenda.

From Canyon De Chelley, we visited the Grand Canyon. On the south rim, I was busily recording million-dollar photos to share with friends and family upon our return home. Arriving in Salt Lake City, I discovered I had failed to load my camera properly and my treasured Grand Canyon photos were lost. Fortunately, Michael

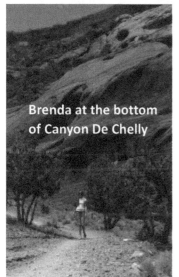
Brenda at the bottom of Canyon De Chelly

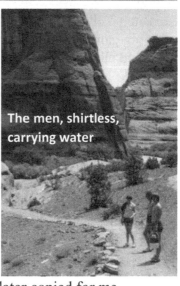
The men, shirtless, carrying water

had taken many of the same scenes on his camera which he later copied for me.

While we were in Utah, we also went to the largest open pit copper mine in the world.

In Utah, we saw the world's largest open pit copper mine

Van and Brenda swimming (floating)

Visiting the Platners in Salt Lake City

Jeff, Brenda and Michael at Yellowstone & Old Faithful

We went swimming in the great Salt Lake. I must not have much fat on me because I was really sinking!

We visited Yellowstone National Park and saw lots of big game animals like bears, buffalo, moose and elk. There was also a big fire burning in the park. I guess this was the first fire the forest rangers allowed to burn and let nature take its course. In other words, there was no attempt or effort to put it out. It eventually was put out by Mother Nature in the fall when it started to snow.

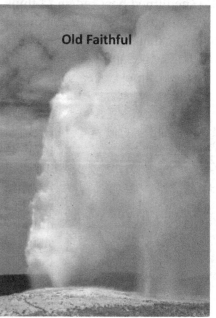

Old Faithful

Leaving Yellowstone, we traveled on to see Devils Tower located in the Black Hills of northeastern Wyoming. It is a 1262 feet high startling monolith rising out of the flat lands around it. In 1906, Theodore Roosevelt declared it the first National Monument.

Devils Tower

Although there are several theories of how Devils Tower was formed, scientists still do not all agree on its history. One theory says that it is a volcanic neck, also called a volcanic plug, formed when hot magma within a volcanic vent cooled and hardened. As the lava cooled, hexagonal columns formed. Over the years, the soil around it eroded until only the rock formation remained.

After visiting Devils Tower, we drove on to the Black Hills of South Dakota and went to Mt. Rushmore. I had been there several times before but Brenda, Jeff and Michael had not. They enjoyed it very much.

After visiting Mt. Rushmore, we drove to Custer State Park known for its free-ranging bison herd. With some 1,500 animals, it is one of the largest bison herds in the world. Pronghorn (aka: antelope), deer, elk (aka: wapiti), mountain goats, bighorn sheep, mountain lions, burros, prairie dogs, coyotes, eagles, and wild turkeys are other residents of the park's variety of wildlife.

Mount Rushmore

Van, Brenda and Jeff at Mt. Rushmore

Bison in Custer State Park

Mitchell, South Dakota's famous Corn Palace

After visiting Mt. Rushmore, we drove on to Mitchell, South Dakota, to see the famous Corn Palace. Built in 1892 the Corn Palace was created to dramatically display the products of the harvest of South Dakota's farmers, in the uniquely designed corn murals on the outside of the building. The murals are made from thousands of bushels of corn and other grains and grasses such as wild oats, rye, straw, and wheat. The World's Only Corn Palace is Mitchell's premier tourist attraction. Some 500,000 tourists visit from around the nation each year.

It was in this part of the country where we ran across this American Indian who sat at this gas station waiting for someone that wanted to take his picture for $1.

Native American – aka: American Indian

Van riding a donkey at Custer State Park

Our trip west took us to sixteen states and logged 7600 miles on our car. The dark line in the photo tracks our route. I believe Michael had an incredibly good exposure to the good old USA. I think we all did. It was a trip that all involved will never forget. This was followed the following summer when Brenda, Van and Jeff went on an extensive visit to Europe.

Our Western Road Trip the summer of 1979

Summer of 1980.

The CRC church in Ann Arbor had a picnic at a park I cannot remember. As you can see, it looks like Brenda is enjoying an ice cream cone. Some of the men enjoyed playing horseshoes.

Brenda enjoying an ice cream cone

Maija Kaldjian and Brenda at the CRC picnic

Some were playing volleyball and toss the egg. Toss the egg can be fun until the egg breaks, then it becomes messy. I cannot seem to find a photo with me in it. I guess it must be because I am always the one taking the pictures, and that's the price one must pay.

Roger Verhey and Larry Mieras playing horseshoes

Egg Tossing – oops, the egg cracked!

Our Extensive trip to Europe Summer of 1980

The summer of 1980, Brenda and Jeff tagged along with me when I went on a business trip to visit all MDSI subsidiaries in Europe. Starting in the U.K. where I visited our office for a day or so, we did a small/short tour of the countryside. Chris Jones was our tour guide for London and Stonehenge. At Stonehenge, I was reminded of the infamous 1969 large collection of Yuppies camped on the druids' graves at Stonehenge.

Hippies and Yuppies camped at Stonehenge

However, unlike Woodstock, these campers were demonstrating remarkable respect for the prehistoric ruins.

Having a cool one at an old English pub

Dinner at Chris Jones' house

Later that day, we enjoyed a lovely dinner at Chris Jones' house.

While we were in the London area, we visited many famous tourist attractions.

Jeff with famous Yeoman Warder

A few days later we went up north to the York area and Howard Barrett took us on a tour of the Lake District as well as the York area.

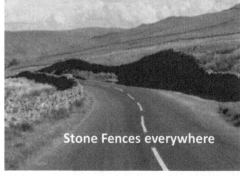

Stone Fences everywhere

We enjoyed the rural setting of these northern areas. A uniquely curious feature we observed was the plethora of stone fences dotting the landscape.

Our room in Shakespeare Hotel

Of course, while you are in the U.K. you must get some world-famous Fish and Chips.

Having some Fish & Chips

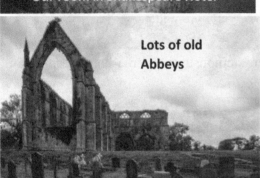
Lots of old Abbeys

While we were up north, Howard Barrett took us to The Narrows, in Shambles-York, England. The

Us in front of Shakespeare Hotel

reason it is referred to as The Narrows is people pay property taxes on the footprint of a house/building. Thus, the ground floor is small, but the second and third floors are extended past the floor below as you can see from the photo. We also visited lots of old abbeys, etc.

And you have to love the old houses with thatched roofs.

While we were in the York area, we went to

Brenda in "The Narrows"

York Minster

the York Minster where Christine Barrett sings in the choir. It is an incredibly beautiful building, and you can say with certainty that they do not build them like that anymore.

We also went by the Anne Hathaway Cottage which is a historical museum in Stratford-upon-Avon which was interesting. Bing has this to say about Anne Hathaway:

Anne Hathaway (1556 – 6 August 1623) was the **wife of William Shakespeare**, an English poet, playwright, and actor. They were married in 1582, when Hathaway was 26 years old, and Shakespeare was 18. She outlived her husband by seven years. Little is known about her life beyond a few references in legal documents.

Anne Hathaway cottage

A beautiful thatched roof cottage

One Sunday, Howard Barrett decided that we should visit the lake district. Thus, we were off again. After visiting our office in Solihull, and touring around the York area and the Lake District, we were off to the Nederlands.

The Lake District in England

And even old castles

MOSS

Nederlands 1980.

Arriving in the Nederlands, we spent a day in Amsterdam. The Rijksmuseum, one of the world's most famous museums, features masterpieces in its collection like *The Milkmaid* by Vermeer, *Self-portrait* by Van Gogh, *The Merry Family* by Jan Steen, and Rembrandt's *Night Watch*. Since Amsterdam has so many canals, we went on a canal cruise which was very interesting because you see a lot of houses/buildings that are centuries old.

On a canal cruise in Amsterdam

The Rijksmuseum

From Amsterdam we traveled on to Marken, which is an incredibly unique place to visit. We saw people dressed in the local costumes and the houses are unique.

Locals in local costume fashion

Unique wooden houses in Marken

Our next stop was to see all the old windmills in the Kinderdijk area. The windmills at Kinderdijk are among the most popular tourist destinations in the Netherlands. They are also a protected World Heritage site.

After visiting the Kinderdijk area we were on our way to Noord-Beveland and Kortgene. On the way to Kortgene, we crossed the Zeeland Bridge which now connects North Beveland (the island where I was born on and lived until we moved to America). When the Zeeland bridge was built, it was the longest in Europe. What follows is what **Wikipedia** says about the Zeeland Bridge.

Lots of windmills in the Kinderdijk area

The **Zeeland Bridge** (Dutch: *Zeelandbrug*) is the longest bridge in the Netherlands. The bridge spans the Eastern Scheldt estuary. It connects the islands of Schouwen-Duiveland and Noord-Beveland in the province of Zeeland.

The Zeeland Bridge

The Zeeland Bridge was built between 1963 and 1965. It was inaugurated on 15 December 1965 by Queen Juliana of the Netherlands, and was originally called **Eastern Scheldt Bridge** (Dutch: *Oosterscheldebrug*) before being renamed the Zeeland Bridge on 13 April 1967. At the time of its completion, it was the longest bridge in Europe. It has a total length of 5,022 metres, and consists of 48 spans of 95 metres, 2 spans of 72.5 metres and a movable bridge with a width of 40 metres.

The province of Zeeland borrowed the money for the construction of the bridge. The loan was repaid by levying tolls for the first 24 years. The following day we drove to Kortgene where I was born and spent a day or two there to visit various sites and attractions and many of my relatives. Whenever I visited Kortgene, I would generally stay with my cousin Izaak and Nellie Boot. He owned a landscape service, and he was my buddy when we lived in the Netherlands. While we were there, we also went to see the Delta Works, where one of my cousins worked. This is what **Google** has to say about the Delta Works.

The Delta Works under construction

The Delta Works were built to protect Zeeland's dry land after the 1953 North Sea Flood or *Watersnoodramp*. It is the world's biggest storm surge barrier, a unique structure well worth a visit! **The Oosterscheldekering** is 3 kilometers long and has 65 piles, making it the most impressive and famous part of the Delta Works.

Van, Brenda, Jeff, Nellie and Izaak Boot

Most of the time when I visit Kortgene, I enjoy visiting Middleburg, which is the biggest town around Kortgene. The city hall is an interesting building.

Van and cousins at City Hall in Middleburg

House built in 1579!

Most of the time when you go to Middleburg, you will see some folks dressed in the costumes of long ago. The photo below of the man who is probably on his way to sit in front of city hall and watch the world go by. The lady is doing some shopping and ran into an old friend so she has to catch up on all the latest news, etc.

Shopping in old local costume

Man in old local costume

Costumes of earlier cultural fashion in Middleburg – still

Our last house in Holland

I had to show Jeff where I lived before coming to America. Thus, the photo to the left is the house the Van Bemdens lived in before we immigrated to the good old USA.

Brussel, Belgium.

From there we went to Brussels, Belgium, and had a good mussel meal. Most of the mussels served in Brussels came from the Zeeland province where I was born.

Jeff and Brenda in the Grand Place, Brussels, Belgium

The Grand Place (town square) is surrounded by beautiful incredibly old buildings. I was there one year when the flower market was at its peak and that is when tourists should visit Brussels. From **Google**:

The **Grand Place** (French, pronounced [gʁɑ̃ plas]; "Grand Square"; also used in English) or **Grote Markt** (Dutch, pronounced [ˌɣroːtə ˈmɑr(ə)kt] "Big Market") is the central square of Brussels, Belgium. It is surrounded by opulent Baroque guildhalls of the former Guilds of Brussels and two larger edifices; the city's Flamboyant Town Hall, and the neo-Gothic *King's House* or *Bread House* building, containing the Brussels City Museum. The Grand Place's construction began in the 11th century and was largely complete by the 17th.

Nowadays, the Grand Place is

The Grand Place, Brussels, Belgium

the most important tourist destination and most memorable landmark in Brussels. It is also considered one of the world's most beautiful squares, and has been a UNESCO World Heritage Site since 1998. The square frequently hosts festive and cultural events, among them, in August of every even year, the installation of an immense *flower carpet* in its centre. It is also a centre of annual celebrations during the Christmas and New Year period, and a Christmas tree has been erected annually on the square since the mid-20th century.

Mannikin pis in Elvis's suit in Brussels, Belgium — his costume changes daily

The manneken pis statue is a must see for all Brussels visitors. This sculpture gets a different costume every day. They have a warehouse with close to a thousand different wardrobes.

Below is what **Google** having to say about manneken pis.

Manneken Pis (Dutch: [ˌmɑnəkə(m) ˈpɪs]; Dutch for 'Little pissing Man') is a landmark 55.5 cm (21.9 in) bronze fountain sculpture in central Brussels, Belgium, depicting a puer mingens; a naked little boy urinating into the fountain's basin. Though its existence is attested as early as the 15th century, it was designed in its current form by the Brabantine sculptor Jérôme Duquesnoy the Elder and put in place in 1618 or 1619.

Manneken Pis has been repeatedly stolen or damaged throughout its history. The current statue is a replica dating from 1965, with the original being kept in the Brussels City Museum. Nowadays, it is one of the best-known symbols of Brussels and Belgium, inspiring many imitations and similar statues. The figure is regularly dressed up and its wardrobe consists of around one thousand different costumes.

The Atomium is a landmark building in Brussels,

Belgium, originally constructed for the 1958 Brussels World's Fair. The ***Atomium*** represents one unit cell of pure iron. The ***Atomium*** represents an iron crystal enlarged 165 billion times.

Van in front of the Atomium in Brussels

Brussels is also known for its famous St. Michel Cathedral. The Cathedral of St Michel and St Gudula date back to the 9th century, making it one of the oldest buildings in Brussels. Inspired by Paris' Notre Dame, this hilltop church features a vaulted interior with 16th-century stained-glass windows with views of Brussels' skyline. Most people do not know that Brussels, a few centuries ago, was famous for its lace. If you walk around the Grand Place, you will see several lace shops, and you might come across the Fashion and Lace Museum.

St. Michael Cathedral

A Lace Boutique

Lace tablecloth – a Brussels specialty

France

While we were in Paris, I ordered escargot. I convinced Jeff to try them and he liked them. From that point on, whenever he saw it on the menu, he ordered them. Of course, he knew Uncle Ken (MDSI CEO) was footing the bill.

Notre Dame

Young boy with a hand full of snails

Eiffel Tower

One cannot really visit Paris, whether it is for business or pleasure, without visiting Notre Dame and the Eiffel Tower. And of course, we would do like everyone else.

After visiting Notre Dame, it was off to see the Eiffel tower. Other sites that are worth visiting are the Church of the Sacred Heart and Moulin Rouge.

Basilica of Sacre Coeur de Montmartre

The Basilica of Sacre Coeur de Montmartre, commonly known as Sacre-Coeur Basilica and often simply Sacre-Coeur, is a Roman Catholic church and minor basilica in Paris, France, dedicated to the Sacred Heart of Jesus. – Wikipedia

From **Google**. What is so special about Moulin Rouge?
Moulin Rouge is best known as **the birthplace of the modern form of the can-can dance**. Originally introduced as a seductive dance by the courtesans who operated from the site, the can-can dance revue evolved into a form of entertainment of its own and led to the introduction of cabarets across Europe.

Moulin Rouge

Statue of Liberty in Paris, France

One of the more interesting facts that most people do not know is that a ¼ scale model of the Statue of Liberty stands in Paris. Something one might not expect to see is a replica of the Statue of Liberty. And yet, just to the south, smack dab in the middle of the river, Seine, by golly, there it is. The quarter-scale replica sits on the southern end of Île aux Cygnes, an artificial island built in the Seine in 1827 to separate river traffic from the busy port of Grenelle.

Switzerland.

After spending a day or two in our Paris office, it was on to Geneva, Switzerland. MDSI did not have an office in Geneva, but an application engineer that lived in the area worked the eastern part of Switzerland, so I had a little bit of an excuse to visit Geneva. Below is a photo of Brenda and Jeff at a statue of a naked, emacicated, melancholy young woman named Clementine in the old town

Grandparents playing with grandkids

of Geneva. The statue was created by a Swiss sculptor named Heinz Schwarz.

Brenda and Jeff in Geneva

Geneva, home of Calvinism, was one of the great centers of the Protestant Reformation. It is also known for the famous Reformation Wall. The Reformation Wall is in Geneva's Bastions Park close to the Old Town. The monument features major figures of the Reformation in the 16th century –**John Calvin, William Farel, Théodore de Bèze and John Knox**.

John Calvin, William Farel, Theodore de Beze and John Knox

Leaving Geneva for Zurich, our next stop was Zermatt in eastern Switzerland. However, stopping to tour Chillon Castle on Lake Geneva was too good to pass up. Thus, we stopped.

Chillon Castle

Chillon Castle is an island castle located on Lake Geneva, south of Veytaux in the canton of Vaud. It is situated at the eastern end of the lake, on the narrow shore between Montreux and Villeneuve, which gives access to the Alpine valley of the Rhone.

Toilet facilities in the castle are called "privies" and the sewer is merely an open pipe discharging directly into the lake.

While we were in Zermatt, Jeff and I went on a short hike in the surrounding mountains. During this hike,

Jeff sitting on the "privy"

the fog rolled in, and we were kind of lost. We could hear a train whistle off in the distance and headed in that direction. We finally got to the railroad tracks and followed the tracks till we found a train station and boarded a train that took us back to town. Departing Zermatt, our next destination was Zurich where MDSI had an office. Visiting Switzerland was a pleasure because I always found everything in

Van in Zermatt with the Matterhorn in the background

order and our MDSI employee, Roger Bianchi, a good friend, also lived in Zurich. I spent many wonderful weekends around Zurich just wandering around town and/or taking a boat ride on Lake Zurich. According to Roger, despite their reputation of neutrality, lots of civilians own military grade rifles like M-16s. He also claims the Swiss Air Force uses highways as runways and fighter planes are hidden in caves along the highways.

Van taking a boat ride around Lake Zurich

While the Van Bemdens were doing their tour of Switzerland, we came across some farmers taking their cows out to pasture. Lots of the cows in Switzerland have large bells hanging around their necks. We also had to cross several passes, which still had lots of snow. As a matter of fact, Jeff and I had to dig our way out of one of them—just kidding!

Cows with large bells around their necks

During our trip in Switzerland we came across this interesting building. I do not know whether it is a house or a barn. I personally cannot think anyone would decorate a barn like this.

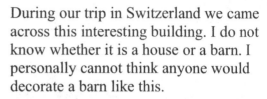

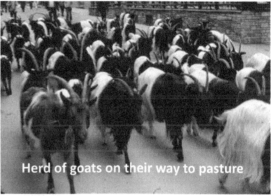
Herd of goats on their way to pasture

Van and Jeff on one of the snowy passes

Lichtenstein.

On our way to Germany, we stopped for a moment or two in the tiny country of Liechtenstein. This is one of the smallest countries in Europe. An interesting fact is that Liechtenstein's only billionaire is worth half of the country's GDP. The entire country has less than 50,000 people. Liechtenstein's per capita GDP is $165,028 – the second highest in the world—and it has no army!

Liechtenstein's famous postage stamps, renowned for their quality, are coveted by collectors the world over.

Lots of flowers hanging over railings

Lichtenstein Castle up the hill

An old castle along the road

Germany.

We were now on our way to Frankfort, Germany, where MDSI had an office. We would drop Jeff off to spend the rest of the summer touring Europe with his friend, Michael Selig who had spent the previous summer with us touring America.

Oberammergau, a city in beautiful Bavaria, is home to the Passion Play performed entirely in German. Had tickets been available, we would have attended. Disappointed when no tickets to the Passion Play were available, we were satisfied to explore this beautiful village situated among the stunning Ammergau Alps. We were also impressed by the beautiful murals painted on houses, churches, etc.

Oberammergau where the Passion Play is performed

Beautiful mural on the church

Castle Restaurant on the Rhine

While we were in Frankfurt, Juergen Selig took us for a trip along the Rhine River and eventually we wound up at an old castle that had been converted to a restaurant where we had a delicious meal.

The Old Castle

Us and Juergen Selig family enjoying a delicious meal at the old castle.

Brenda, Van and Jeff

On a rainy afternoon, we visited Rothenburg, Germany's best preserved walled city. The 2-mile-long walls around Rothenburg provide an incredibly good view of the city.

Juergen Selig family and Brenda

Rothenburg

Barge traffic on the Rhine River

Jeff, Michael and Juergen

We finally dropped Jeff off with Juergen and he spent the rest of the summer touring around Europe with Michael Selig, returning to Ann Arbor in time to go back to Huron high school.

Scotland.

Holyrood Palace in Edinburgh

Our Scottish SE's house in Dollar, Scotland

Brenda with our Scottish AE

After visiting our German office and spending a few days sightseeing, Brenda and I flew to Edinburg, Scotland, to touch base with our Scotland Application Engineer. While we were there, we stayed in our Scottish salesman's house (who happened to be in training in Ann Arbor) in Dollar, Scotland. There were several good MDSI-UK customers in and around Edinburg. Most of them had something to do with North Sea oil production.

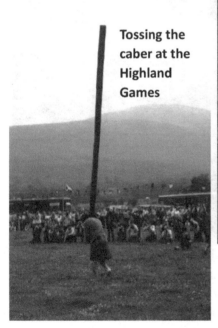
Tossing the caber at the Highland Games

Campbell Castle near Dollar, Scotland

One of the things I remember is that I was using the salesman's car to drive around and one time, after visiting Campbell Castle near Dollar, on the way back, I turned onto the main road, and it was not until I saw this car coming toward me, that I realized I was on the wrong side of the road. I woke up real fast! I have been trying to tell my English friends for years that **WE** meaning of course the USA, drive on the **RIGHT** side of the highway!

Rothenburg

The Scottish Highland games were a real treat. Traditional Highland games such as the **caber toss, tug o' war, and the hammer throw**, along with music, food, and Highland dancing, create a family friendly day for everyone in the community. Perhaps the signature event of the Highland Games is the caber toss, where competitors toss a 20-foot-long caber (a large log), which normally weighs around 150 lbs., as far as possible.

Dancing at the Highland games

We also got to see the sheaf toss for the first time in our life. The sheaf is a heavy bag (around 20 lbs.) that is tossed with a pitchfork over a progressively raised cross bar. Three attempts are allowed at each height. If the thrower misses all three tries at a height, he is out of the competition. You have to look closely and right where the hill meets the sky is where the sheaf is located.

Sheaf Toss

Scottish bagpipers at the Scottish Highland Games

I love bagpipe music and we certainly got to hear it. Travelling around the countryside, we came across a herd of Scottish Highland cattle. I have never seen any of them in person, so I had to stop the car and get out and take some photos. I managed to get really close to the fence, and then several bulls saw me and they came charging. It scared the living daylights out of me.

After spending several weeks travelling around the UK and Europe visiting the various MDSI subsidiaries we finally were on our way home. That pretty much concluded my lengthy European trip with Brenda and Jeff.

Scottish Highland Cattle – note the long hair

1977 -9.

This photo records MDSI personnel in Germany attending the EMI show in Frankfurt in September, 1977. Ken Stephanz, CEO, is at the head of the table prompting everybody to be on their best behavior; all kidding aside, these industrial shows, while a lot of work, are also informative and educational. They provided a forum for seeing firsthand what the competition was doing with machine tools and software.

CO meeting in Germany: Rich Pauli, Van, Paul Breniser, Sec., Phil Markham, Peter Kopeky, Ken Stephanz, Dave Price and Gerd Struckfuss

1979

Van at the Arch of Triumph, 10/1979

The Arch d' Triumph in Paris boasts the biggest and busiest roundabout in the world. It sits in a circular plaza from which **12 grand avenues** radiate, forming a star (étoile), which is why it is also called Arch of Triumph of the Star. Pierre Boudreau drove me thru this, and I must confess, I was glad he was driving and not me.

We were living on Georgetown Blvd when we observed a young kid trying to set Thurston School on fire. I immediately intervened but the boy escaped leaving evidence behind. On another occasion, Jeff and his friend, John Watson, escaped harassment by running into our house but I think they were guilty of teasing their antagonist from behind the safety of our big picture window because the kid through a rock through it leaving a hole in the glass.

Summoned to appear in court for jury selection in Flint, Michigan, I was eager for the experience; however, I was disappointed when the defense attorney dismissed me because, during jury selection, I admitted I had taken some business law courses. I think the man on trial was a gangster.

Terry Peterson owned a Glastron ski boat and a "collector item Corvette." Paul Breniser owned a house with access to Ore Lake. We were occasionally included in afternoons of water skiing on Ore Lake with Terry and Paul. Terry was fussy about his boat, particularly the way he insisted anyone else drove it. When he was skiing, he preferred to be towed in a straight line rather than the more common gentle circles – as a matter of fact, he objected to arcs less than ½ mile! He was similarly defensive about his Corvette and, on one occasion when Paul leaned against it, he almost physically attacked him.

Our Glastron boat we docked at Jan Bolthuis's lake house

A fellow Hollander who immigrated to the US in the 1930s, my friend, Jan Bolthuis, owned a cottage on Portage Lake. I eventually bought a boat and could dock it there. For the privilege of docking it at his place, I allowed him to use the boat at his leisure. One day I came back to use it and it would not start. Upon inspection and finding ignition wires loosely hanging behind the dash, Jan and I questioned his boys who admitted hot wiring it for an unapproved joy ride as part of their high school graduation high jinks.

One Saturday morning, Robert Neuerbourg, a German AE who happened to be in Ann Arbor for training, and I drove out to Portage Lake to do some water skiing. We were in the middle of the lake when a sudden violent storm arose. Bob's quick action averted disaster. He grabbed the steering wheel and skillfully kept the boat heading straight into the wind. We probably would have capsized had he not done that. Later, we learned a tornado had passed thru the area. I guess it did not touch down on the lake, but it came mighty close.

Jeff in our 'pull-me-over' red Fiat Spider

Coming home from work one spring afternoon, I observed fellow employee, Tom Ingraham, parked on our street in his red Fiat taking pictures of the flowering crabapple trees blooming in the median. I later bought this car from him. Jeff drove it more than I did. He drove it quite a bit while he was going to Calvin college in Grand Rapids. It was an interesting vehicle, in that the styling was OK; however, mechanically, it left a lot to be desired.

A popular prank common to high school kids during Jeff's teenage years was called the Chinese fire drill. Basically, stopping at a traffic light triggered the exit of all the vehicles occupants allowing them to race around the car and return to their seats before the light changed.

A list of teenage pranks popular during Jeff's adolescence would include:
- Hanging a fake human arm out of the trunk.
- Randomly calling a phone number from the phone book, the kids would ask: "Is Prince Albert in a can?" If the innocent party called answered, "yes," they would respond, "you should let him out!" and subsequently disconnect the call.
- Similar to the Prince Albert prank, the kids would place a call and ask if the refrigerator was running and then, assuming the called party said, "yes," the kids would respond with: "You better go catch it!"

White Castle hamburger sliders were popular with teenagers. These were about the size of a half dollar coin and satisfying an appetite required consuming a half dozen of them. I've never tried this but I'm sure I haven't missed anything.

My cousin, Gerard Boot was doing well enough financially to afford a good sized "cigar boat" when he worked with Ed Van Dyke. For ready access to Lake Michigan for recreational boating, he docked it in Holland, MI. Gerard's departure from Ed resulted in a downturn of fortune for Gerard and he fell on hard times.

A CRC church in Cleveland, Ohio, sponsored a weekend getaway to Ann Arbor for their youth group including housing several of the kids with us in our Georgetown Blvd. home. Eager to pick up our guests, my distraction led to my embarrassment when I failed to open the garage door before backing up the car! It was around 11:00PM when I very quietly started the car and proceeded to crack one of the sections of the door.

Jeff and I enjoyed riding our bikes together including occasionally challenging each other to race. On one occasion, racing to be first into the school grounds bordering Thurston Pond, we were neck and neck approaching the narrow gate with neither giving an inch. At the last second, recognizing imminent disaster, I slammed on my brakes and hit the dirt! The dirt consisted of scree (a surface layer of small stone gravel) which cut through my pants and produced a raspberry rash on my hip.

The Olds Cutlass with rear end damage

I bought this Oldsmobile Cutlass from Bev, one of the sectaries working in the international division of our company. It was parked in front of our house on Georgetown Blvd. when a distracted driver hit the rear quarter panel and damaged the driver side of the car. We drove it in that condition and eventually gave it to Karen DeJong, Jeff's girlfriend at that time.

Tahiti 1980.

Polynesian show at my hotel

Market Place

On one of my trips down under, I routed myself through Tahiti. This was to break the trip up and, never having been there, I decided I should stop in. My hotel featured a Polynesian show. The young ladies wore coconut shells for bras. Most people probably picture the big island with miles and miles of sandy beaches. Well, because many of the Pacific Islands are volcanic, what I witnessed was beaches of black pebbles. Also, because it is an island, if you visited the marketplace, you would find lots of different kinds of seafood. Below is what Google has to say about Tahiti.

The beach at Papeete

The island of Tahiti is the largest island in French Polynesia and is the most well-known. But, to new visitors, it is important to remember that the entirety of the 118 islands of French

Lighthouse at Matavai Bay

Polynesia are referred to as *The Islands of Tahiti*. The official languages spoken on *The Islands of Tahiti* are Tahitian and French, but English is spoken at most hotels and resorts.

I took a photo of Point Venus lighthouse in Matavai Bay. It was built in 1868. Also, I did not find nice sandy beaches around Papeete. All the sand and rocks around the water were black because it was all created from volcanoes.

Australia 1980.
During an EMO show in Germany, Hahn and Kolb, a German tool maker with offices in Australia, was contracted to represent MDSI products in Australia by Ken Stephanz. Their main office was in Melbourne, but they had offices in various places around the country. Shortly after Ken appointed Hahn and Kolb to represent MDSI, I was on my way for my first visit to Australia and work with them. The long flight, 13+ hours, seemed to take forever. From Detroit Metro, I flew to Los Angeles and on to Sydney, then on to Melbourne. Fortunately, Hawaii and New Zealand were overlay options I enjoyed a few times later on to make the flight from Detroit to Australia a little less stressful. Satisfying a long-time bucket list item, I was finally in Australia, land of kangaroos and koala bears.

Australians play a different kind of football they call Ausie football. Unlike American football, the players wear no pads. Even though I didn't know the rules, watching the game was fun.

Ausie Football Game in Action

The attacking emu

Driving through the countryside one weekend, I stopped the car to take photos of a wild emu. Imagine my surprise when it saw me with my camera and apparently was offended. I realized it was in attack mode and escaped to the interior of my vehicle.

Working with Kurt Schwotzer in the Sydney area was a distinct pleasure. As an invited guest, I enjoyed the hospitality of their home as well as being introduced to the popular game of cricket, which is nothing like American baseball. During one of my visits to Australia, Kurt and I enjoyed a brief trip to the Blue Mountains which are the highest in Australia. These mountains support varieties of birds including many colorful parrots we do not have in the United States.

Van playing cricket – missed!

Kurt and Wenie Schwotzer and their 2 daughters

Andy Lyons was Hahn & Kolb's designated Application Engineer to support Compact II customers in Australia. Andy had immigrated from the U.K. He lived in the greater Melbourne area. After his training in Ann Arbor, I flew to Melbourne and Andy and I traveled around Australia to do demos the Hahn & Kolb Machine tool salesmen and district managers had arranged for us. Andy and I went on several wine tours when we were out of town for the weekend working the market in such places as Perth and Adelaide.

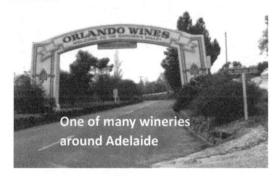
One of many wineries around Adelaide

Looking back to downtown Perth

Brenda enjoying breakfast in Bahamas

In the spring of 1980 Brenda and I took a trip to the Bahamas, courtesy of attending a time share/resort presentation in Florida. We said we would never do it again! We almost missed the ship that was going to take us there. While we were there, I got my first introduction to aqua agriculture. Because the island is

A very rocky garden in the Bahamas

quite rocky, aqua culture is their method for raising tomatoes. I guess as long as you can get water and a little fertilizer to the plants they will grow.

The Fall of 1980.

John Kidd and I were in Japan during the Aki Matsuri Autumn Festival. This is an

John Kidd and Van being served Saki

important cultural event for the locals as it is rooted in Shinto practice featuring traditional Aki Matsuri ceremonies featuring music, dance, prayer and food offerings like rice and rice wine to thank the kami (Shinto spirits) for a fruitful rice harvest. Thus, after our business dealings were over, we hit the road to find out what this festival was all about. Luckily, we found an area not too far from where we were staying where this festival was well on its way. Fortunately, we found a spot to sit down by a couple of elderly gentlemen who realized we were there to enjoy the ceremony. They even shared some Saki with us.

I even got to pose with some of the cast at this rice pounding ceremony. The local participants got a kick out of it and I certainly did also. It was a unique experience. As you can see a good time was had by all.

Van with the team

Part of the Aki Matsuri celebration

John and Van enjoying themselves

Germany 1980

I also found myself in Germany in the fall of 1980 and got to see what a real Octoberfest is in the country that invented it. It just seems that everyone wants to sit down and chew the fat over a big glass or two of beer.

Enjoying Oktoberfest in Heidelberg

Paris France 1980

Fortunately, I took this photo of the famous Notre Dame cathedral in Paris, France, before it suffered a tragic fire. The photo is converted from a slide I took in 1980; I am writing this in 2023 and the steeple you see in the photo is no longer there. Notre Dame is one of the most popular and visited sites in Paris.

This is what **Wikipedia** has to say about the fire:

Notre Dame in Paris, France

On 15 April 2019, just before 18:20 CEST, a fire broke out beneath the roof of the Notre-Dame cathedral in Paris, France. By the time the structure fire was extinguished, the building's spire had collapsed, most of its roof had been destroyed, and its upper walls were severely damaged. Extensive damage to the interior was prevented by its stone vaulted ceiling, which largely contained the burning roof as it collapsed. Many works of art and religious relics were moved to safety early in the emergency, but others suffered smoke damage, and some of the exterior art was damaged or destroyed. The cathedral's altar, two pipe organs, and three 13th-century rose windows suffered little or no damage.

MDSI Sold to Schlumberger for $210 Million.

January 21, 1981, Schlumberger shareholders approved the deal and Schlumberger purchased MDSI for $210 million – about $650 million in 2020 dollars. Ken called an all company meeting to announce the sale. The announcement was well received by MDSI employees who owned stock options redeemable for substantial sums of cash. At the time, MDSI supported about 700 employees worldwide with almost 500 in Ann Arbor. With 3850 paying customers and over 18,500 NC machine tools under contract, it was a newsworthy financial event.

Singapore 1981.

Singapore, one of the smallest city states in the world, was home to a Baker Oil Tool factory, my destination in the spring of 1981. Baker Oil Tool, headquartered in Houston, was one of our largest customers and their Singapore factory housed a number of the latest CNC machine tools.

Newer Singapore

After collecting the various specs the link building group needed back in Ann Arbor, I was off to see the sights. Singapore's reputation for being a "green" city and exceptionally clean, was exemplified by a city ordinance prohibiting spitting gum out of your mouth onto the street. If you are caught in this act, the police will cite you with a ticket levying a hefty fine.

Singapore is divided into two sections: 1) new part; 2) Old China Town. Old China Town existed primarily for its tourist attraction value. Walking the streets of Old China Town was a pleasant experience delivering some strange and more than interesting adventures. In one of the vendor stalls, I witnessed a butchered lizard hanging from a hook waiting for a patron to purchase it for the family dinner!

Butchered lizards for sale

Old China Town

More photos of my walk thru China town.

Batik is a traditional art form utilizing wax and colored dyes to create patterns on cloth. The word, "batik," can also refer to fabric made with "batiked" patterns. I was treated to a personal tour of a batik factory.

Sri Mariamman Temple

Batik Factory in Singapore

Walking the streets, one eventually comes to this Hindu temple. The Sri Mariamman Temple is the oldest shrine in Singapore and one of the most prominent places of worship for Tamil Hindus in the country. It was built to honor Goddess Mariamman, the deity of disease and protection. I was also privileged to visit the beautiful Chinese garden featuring a beautiful 7-story pagoda.

1981.
In the photo below, we are celebrating the completion of Bruce Bucher's medical degree program at the University of Michigan. Bruce (wearing a white sweater) was a good friend and fellow member of our

Main Gate to Chinese Garden

Bible study group. Bruce and his family left Ann Arbor to open a new internal medicine office in Tappahannock, Virginia. Harry McIntosh, our family dentist, is chatting with Van.

Congratulations

Dr. Bruce M. Bucher

On the
opening of
your new
medical
office.

May the Lord
bless your
work in
Tappahannock

From Friends in Ann Arbor, Michigan

Katherine Beaman	Floyd and Chloris Patrick
Tom and Sue Gillespie	Harry and Shirley McIntosh
William and Carolyn Gross	Kermit and Kathleen Stanton
Walter and Sandy Hahn	Hilda Too
Dotty Knol	Jacquin and Mei Mei Uy
Marion Malvern	Urbanus and Brenda Van Remden

Bruce Bucher, Harry McIntosh and Van

Jeff graduates from Huron High. June, 1981

In June, 1981, Jeff graduated from Huron High School in Ann Arbor. While I don't recollect him partying with his buddies the night before his graduation ceremony, I do remember his girlfriend, Karen, also graduated with him. His grandmother, Grandma Parker, flew into town for the auspicious occasion.

Looking closely at this photo – I think Jeff may have been attempting to grow a mustache.

John Watson, Jeff and Kurt Firnhaber

Van, Brenda, Lillian Parker and Jeff

Al and Cecilia Hettinga, seen in the photo below sitting in our living room celebrating Jeff's graduation with us, were good friends from the CRC. Al, a great favorite of the youngsters at church, was a retired US Post Office employee who kept his pockets full of peppermint candy. Al injured his back on the job earning him early retirement; but I observed him effortlessly position a rowboat on top of his pickup for a fishing expedition. They never had any kids of their own, but they loved little kids. Al had lots of wood working tools including a nice table saw. He and I made several shadow boxes in his shop. We had them for an awfully long time. The paintings on the wall in this photo were done by Jeff when he was taking painting lessons from a friend in our church. I do not know if they are still around.

This O'Brien waterski was Jeff's graduation gift. It resides in our basement and hasn't been used since we moved to Colorado Springs. Jeff and I now snow ski.

Jeff

Al and Cecilia Hettinga, and Brenda

144

Bangkok 1981.

My travels have taken me around the world several times. Sometimes I flew east to west and others I flew west to east. On one occasion, at Heathrow in England, I rendezvoused with a fellow Dutchman who was in Scotland during the oil boom following the discovery of large oil reservoirs beneath the North Sea. He worked for one of our customers, Cameron Iron Works, requiring him to visit Bangkok. He invited me to join him and, together, despite the extraordinary humidity, we enjoyed a weekend of sightseeing in Bangkok.

Van and friend enjoying their coconut drink

Van and friend enjoying a cool one

The pick-up in the photo provided public transportation service similar to a city bus. We counted a dozen passengers. Because it was a weekend, it did not make any difference where I spent it as long as I was in Sydney Monday morning; thus, I devoted as much time as possible to absorbing the local culture.

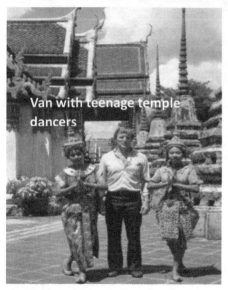

Van with teenage temple dancers

Located in the historical center of Bangkok within the grounds of the Grand Palace is the Wat Phra Kaew Temple, aka: Temple of the Emerald Buddha, or known locally as the Wat Phra Sri Rattana Satsadaram. This is one of the most revered Buddhist temples in Thailand. The photo above is with me and two teenage girls who perform dances at the temple. It seems there are temples all over the place, as well as monks.

A makeshift city bus in Bangkok

Young Monks in Buddhist training

145

Japan 1981.v

Cherry blossom time (Hanami in Japanese) in Japan is magical. In the spring of 1981, John Kidd and I were there enjoying the hospitality of the new Century Hotel as well as the ambiance of cherry blossom extravaganza. The hotel was within spitting distance of our office which gave us extra time to mix and mingle with the locals. Being in Japan at cherry blossom time, which I was fortunate enough to be able to do quite a few times, is really neat. Everyone is out enjoying themselves.

Van and John Kidd ordering breakfast at the Century Hotel

Van and Yoshi's family

Yoshi must have showed me around since he was with me taking his family out to see the cherry blossoms. Hanami is celebrated all over Japan when thousands of locals and tourists alike descend on popular viewing spots, gardens, and parks to view the blossoms. Picnics, food stalls, drinking, and songs are all part of the celebrations.

Mas Fukushima and I were visiting various parks in and around Tokyo. At one of the parks, a vendor

Flowering cherry tree at the Imperial Palace

Van at the Imperial Palace at Cherry Blossom Time

was selling foot long hotdogs where he had sliced the meat into thirds along the horizontal axis. This process delivered a 1/3-foot-long hot dog.

1/3 foot long hot dog

Another family enjoying the cherry blossoms

I kind of thought a 12-inch hot dog with 1/3 of the meat that you and I are used to was ridiculous prompting me to take a photo of it.

Young and old alike are out enjoying the cherry blossoms. As you can see, I am not the only one taking pictures when it's cherry blossom time.

Waiting for the couple to move

A young family enjoying sweet corn on the cob

Van skiing at Breckenridge

In December, 1981, Jeff and I flew to Denver to go skiing in Colorado. Back then we were still skiing on the long narrow skis. No helmet! I do not remember what ski resort we skied at but I believe it was Keystone since some of the photos I took show Lake Dillon in the background.

I do not remember for sure, but I don't believe there were any high-speed quad chairs at that time. As you can see from the photo below, Christmas break with 20-minute waiting lines to get on the chair was annoying.

Jeff skiing at Breckenridge

But, since Jeff was in college, that was the only time we had to go out west

Typical crowd at Christmas break

to ski. Thus, we tolerated it.

In December 1981, our small Bible study group had a Christmas potluck party at Dave Cole's house. Dave Cole was in charge of the automotive study group on the north campus at the University of Michigan. Dave's dad was the head of GM at one time. His dad was also famous for the Chevy small block V-8.

Google had this to say about Dave Cole.
Dr. David E Cole is one of the world's foremost authorities on the automotive industry. Born in 1937, Cole is the son of former General Motors President and fellow Hall of Fame Inductee, Edward Cole. His father was instrumental in developing some of GM's major breakthroughs, like the small-block V8, and there is little doubt that his father's position at GM had a strong impact on Cole's life. Cole attended the University of Michigan, where he earned three mechanical engineering degrees and a doctorate. While at Michigan, Cole worked extensively on internal combustion engines and vehicle

design. He later taught engineering at the university and became the director of the college's Office for the Study of Automotive Transportation.

Brenda Graduating from EMU, December, 1981

Brenda graduating from EMU

Van is immensely proud

Brenda graduated from Eastern Michigan University at the end of the fall semester in 1981 with a BS in accounting. She graduated Summa Cum Laude which means she had a GPA of 3.75 or better. She was a much better student then I was! A good friend, Floyd Patrick, was a professor at Eastern who helped Brenda by picking the best professors in the various courses she had to take in her chosen field. At Brenda's graduation, they asked all the parents of the graduating students to stand up; well, I stood up, even though I was not a parent, but I was very proud of her.

In the spring of 1981, I must have made a trip to New Zealand because I have this picture of me on a tour of Mt. Cook in a small plane landing on a glacier.

Van on glacier at Mt. Cook. New Zealand

Spring break in Florida, 1982.

In the spring of 1982, Jeff, Karen De Jong (Karen was Jeff's girlfriend), and I flew to Florida and attended a waterski school to learn how to barefoot. I had already done some barefooting by dropping the skis off after I got up. But now we would learn how

Van

to get up and barefoot without any skis. We had lots of fun and both Jeff and I learned how to barefoot with a side boom on the Master Craft ski boat. I do not know whether Jeff ever barefooted after the ski school or not. I had the good fortune of having one of our neighbors who had a boat specifically designed not to

Jeff, Karen, Van and 2 small kids

make a large wave include me in his boating adventures. He had a barefoot suit I could use. The photo above shows Jeff and Karen on a water board with the instructors 2 small kids trying to get up. That is me assisting them. Would you take a look at the guy's back muscles!

A large rocket at Cape Canaveral

While we were in Florida learning how to barefoot, we took a day off and visited Cape Canaveral. I could not get over how big some of the rockets were. Also on display was a mockup of the moon landing module. While we were in Florida, we also went to see the show at Cypress Gardens. In fact, the ski school we attended was on a chain of lakes. We followed the channel and took our boat to the Cypress Garden Lake.

Pulling 7 skiers

Moon Landing Module

Jeff getting with it

Van getting with it

Jeff and I were both pretty good water skiers; probably because we got to practice quite a bit. I would go waterskiing 2 -3 times a week in the summer time if I could get people to come out. We finally got our own portable course that we could put out as long as we had it out of the water by noon. Most of the time we would get up early in the morning, have it set up in 15-20 min and we were ready to go. Billy Bishop who moved into our neighborhood had a Mastercraft and they are considered the Cadillac of ski boats.

1982 February

Terry Myers, one of our programmers I recruited from Cameron Iron Works, and I flew to England together in 1982. He eventually worked in the International Division for me. Anyway, in a company car from our Solihull office, we drove to historical Bath, Plymouth and Wales. In the town of Bath, they still had pools the Romans built. While the pools are fouled with green algae, the water is contaminated by lead pipes feeding the pools making the water unfit for human consumption or bathing. Regardless, considering their age, being there so long after the Romans constructed them is a sobering and extraordinary experience. After seeing the sights in Bath and the surrounding area, we were off to Plymouth.

Near the Plymouth area

Coastal towns of Wales feature interesting harbors. We were there during low tide so activity was minimal.

One of the Roman pools in Bath

Terry was my chauffeur in Wales and I jokingly said he was blind in one eye and could not see out of the other. Really, his eyeglasses were as thick as the bottom of a Coca Cola bottle. Anyway, the streets in parts of Wales

Harbor along the Wales coastline

are very narrow and when Terry hit a curb, we had to deal with a flat tire. Rural Wales is a delightful excursion.

Reed thatched roof house

I loved the reed thatched roof houses and barns. The one in the photo to the right was precariously close to the road.

Narrow streets

The unique old stone bridge in the photo below must have required many hours of manual labor to mortar all those stones.

Neat Old Stone Bridge

April, 1982

The spring of 1982, I found myself in the Nederlands—probably on my way to visit our European offices. We had no office in the Nederlands, I do not even think we had an application engineer living there at this time. All customer support came out of the French office in Paris. On this particular trip I happened to be in Holland at the same time my dad and mother were there. Thus, I spent some time visiting some of dad's brothers and sisters I had never met.

A typical bunker dad built for the Germans

Dad and Mom with two of dad's sisters

During the war, my dad was forced to build German bunkers. The three of us visited this bunker my dad helped build.

During this trip, I visited Keukenhof situated in the municipality of Lisse.

If you are into spring flowers (especially bulbs), you have to visit Keukenhof. The Keukenhof Gardens, also called Gardens of Europe, occupying 32 hectares (79 acres), are the world's largest flower gardens. You have to see it to believe it, because it is a park where more than 7 million flower bulbs are planted every year. The gardens and four pavilions show a fantastic collection of: tulips, hyacinths, daffodils, orchids, roses, carnations, irises, lilies, and many other flowers.

Keukenhof Gardens

One of the many gardens at Keukenhof

Since I am talking about tulips, I must tell this story. I was in Ann Arbor in one of the bars around the shopping center when Gordon Beth and I were sitting next to a couple of guys who were playing backgammon. I noticed that one of the guys had an accent I did not recognize. I politely asked him where he was from, he wanted to know why I asked. Being an international guy myself, I told him I was from Holland. He proceeded to tell me that you guys (meaning the Dutch) stole the tulips from us. I knew right then and there that he was from Turkey. He was somewhat surprised that I knew that. Most people think the tulips were originally from Holland, but they really came from Central Asia. The Dutch just knew what to do with them.

Uncle Izaak's house in Kortgene

When I am in Holland, I always try to stop off in Kortgene, since that is where I was born but also that is where most of my relatives live. My Uncle Izaak Boot, the uncle who owned a painting business, has one of the nicer houses in all of Kortgene. Also, I took a photo of the beautiful thatched roof barn near the village of Kortgene.

Beautiful thatched roof barn in Kortgene

In Switzerland, I visited the famous Chapel Bridge. This is what Third Eye Traveler had to say about this bridge: One of the most famous bridges in all of Switzerland is the Chapel Bridge in Lucerne (Kapellbrücke). A gorgeous medieval wooden footbridge that allows you to cross over the Reuss River with an octagonal water tower

Famous Chapel Bridge

(Wasserturm) attached. Not only is this bridge one of the oldest covered bridges to exist in Europe, it is also the longest surviving truss bridge in the entire world! Today, it is an icon for Lucerne and also one of the main tourist attractions in Switzerland. So, you simply must pay a visit if you are in the city.

Now I am back in the good old USA. The fall of 1982 we took this picture of the 3 of us in our backyard on Georgetown Blvd. Why we took this, I do not know; maybe we were coming home from church and we were all dressed up. I just do not know. Regardless, I think it is a rather good shot!

Jeff, Brenda and Van

Japan Fall 1982.
The fall of 1982 I found myself in Osaka, Japan. I visited the Osaka Castle which is really a very interesting design. I believe it was either Saturday afternoon or Sunday afternoon and there were lots of people all over the place. Another thing I found interesting was the hippies/yuppies having a good time close to the castle.

Osaka Castle

Hippies and Yuppies doing their thing at Osaka Castle

One of the more interesting displays of mums I have ever seen was at the Osaka Castle which is shown below.

Beautiful display of mums.

Our move to Indianola
Summer of 1982

We moved to Indianola after Bob Guy ran into me in the hallway at work and asked me how things were going, etc. I was on the road and overseas a lot of the time and I had not spoken to him for some time. He went on to tell me that there were a couple of homes for sale in his neighborhood and that he had the keys to them. One night after work Brenda and I got in the car and went out to Strawberry Lake to see what he was talking about. The first house I did not care for but the second house which was semi-contemporary, and which happened to be right next door to where he lived, I thought had potential. Mike, the current owner, was getting a divorce from his wife and the bank was about to repossess it. Thus, he was willing to bargain, and the price was quite reasonable. We came to an agreement and soon thereafter it was ours.

Jeff spent a lot of that summer living there during the week working on it, but mostly driving the boat around the lake. His then girlfriend Karen De Jong also spent some time

Getting ready to do some painting

Our house at the time we bought it

there cleaning the kitchen, etc. But I do think that they were getting a lot of water-skiing it. Brenda and I would go out there after work to paint, etc. Every time we went out there, we would take a load of "Stuff" with us. Thus, when the final moving day arrived, we had all but the heavy stuff already at our new place. One of the first things we did to our new house on Indianola was to have TERAFIRMA build a nice deck on the back of the house. This same firm also put in our sprinkler system. Our lot was configured so there was a narrow bit of grass on the south side of the driveway. Well, when they put the sprinkler system in they had it spraying across the driveway to reach the narrow strip of grass. I told them this is not going to work, simply because in no time flat our asphalt driveway would turn red. The water from our well was very, very rusty. The water for the sprinkler system did not run thru the water softener. Subsequently they ran a water line under the driveway to get to that narrow strip of grass.

Since Karen DeJong (Jeff's girlfriend at this time) did not have any decent transportation the car I bought from Beth Cutler car, one of the secretaries that worked in the Int'l div., an old Oldsmobile and gave it to her. She drove it most of that summer and took it to Grand Rapids when she and Jeff went off to Calvin College. I do not remember how soon after that it died, and Jeff drove it to the junk yard in Grand Rapids. I do remember it had a bad oil leak and if it sat too long on the asphalt driveway at our new house on Indianola the asphalt started to get soft.

While we lived on Indianola, I entered the Ann Arbor Garden show several times and won several blue ribbons and first place honors for forcing Daffodils and other spring flowers.

The summer of 1982, Brenda and I took a trip to the Upper Peninsula of Michigan. I remember one of our favorite places to visit in the U.P. was the Pictured Rocks area on Lake Superior. We had visited many times before, but we never had taken a boat trip along the shoreline. So, we had to do it. The shoreline along the coast in this area is very picturesque with lots of cliffs.

Shoreline around Pictured Rocks in the UP of MI

Brenda at Lake Superior

Stopped off in Hawaii 1982.

The fall of 1982 coming back from Japan I routed myself thru Hawaii where I had arranged to fly from Honolulu to the big island of Hawaii to meet John and Loretta Miller. John and Loretta Miller were friends of ours who went to the CRC church in Ann Arbor and had a young son who was Gary's age and friend. They had moved to Hilo, Hawaii a few years earlier. Anyway, when I got to Hilo, Loretta was there to greet me with a Lai. My visit with the Millers was interesting in that I have been to Honolulu many times, but I have never been to the big island of Hawaii.

I have never seen so much evidence of volcano activity. There were lava fields everywhere. We walked a way

Our friend John Miller

inside of a Lava tube, which was interesting in that it was a good sized hollow tube. One could easily stand up straight.

At the Hawaii Volcanoes National Park

The Royal Kona Coffee Mill Museum

A record Tarpon

Later we visited the famous Royal Kona Coffee mill museum. While I was there, we witnessed someone bringing in a record catch Tarpon.

Parker Ranch

I was not aware of the fact that there are several huge cattle ranges on the big Island. There is the King ranch as well as the Parker Ranch. The Parker Ranch has over 130,000 acres. With over 17,000 head of cattle spread across the rolling country between Kohala and Mauna Kea, Parker Ranch is not only the largest active cattle ranch in Hawaii, but one of the biggest and most historic ranches in the United States.

1983.

One of the first things I did at our new house on Indianola regarding the lawn was to make some distinction between the lawn and the flower/shrubs beds. I used Landscape lumber (6x6), and that's the way it was for some time. There was a family across the street from us who had a young teenager by the name of Dennis who cut our grass. He used his dad's lawn mower and his gas. That went on for some time. Finally, when he was old enough to get a driver license, he started to hang around with the wrong crowd and was not interested in cutting grass anymore. Thus, it was now me mowing the grass. One of the first things I did was cut some of the low hanging branches that obviously interfered with the grass cutting but Dennis never complained about it. Here you can see the landscape lumber. The outline of the beds with the landscape lumber were all sharp corner. Gentle curves work much better, and make cutting the grass lots easier, but that was done a few years later.

Our Front yard shortly after we moved in

Note the bench on the Front porch. It was made from a large red belly cedar tree that I cut into 2 halves and made into a bench using the limbs as the legs. The other half was given to Brenda's brother Jimmy Parker. The cedar tree had blown over a short distance from our house when we lived in Bedford, TX.

One time after being told by Cal Kappas that I might just as well cut down all the elm trees in my yard because sooner or later the Dutch Elm disease which was rampant in Michigan was going to get them anyway. Well, Jeff and I cut down a couple of dozen elm trees. It looked like a tornado had going thru the place. We managed to cut them all up into manageable pieces and dragged them over into a vacant lot behind our house and burned them.

I developed the habit of using my turn signals when one Sunday afternoon when we were coming back from a Sunday afternoon drive and turning off of 4 mile road and onto Strawberry Lake road I didn't use my turn signal because no one was behind me and no one was coming toward me, but this gal was waiting at the stop sign getting ready to make a right hand turn when I turned right and she gave me the high sign, because I hadn't used my turn signal to indicate that I was making a right-hand turn she could have taken off and gotten down the road. Since that day I generally use my turn signal. I think the reason that I did not use my turn signals was because in earlier days the way they were made and mounted on the steering wheel they would periodically break. Thats not true anymore today.

Brenda had started to call me Mr. "T" and other nicknames. I do not remember when I started to call her Brenda Baby but several of my closest friends call her that from time to time. Whenever I talk to Howard Barrett a good friend that lives in the UK he always asks how is "Brenda baby?"

April 19, 1983, my youngest brother Gerard (Butch) married Julie Koning. Below is a photo of most of the Van Bemdens and their spouses taken at the wedding.

Most of the Van Bemdens at Butch and Julie's wedding. April 19, 1983

One time while driving to work on US 23 I had a fellow point a gun at me when we got to the Plymouth Road exit. I chased after him up and down some of the roads around corporate and I saw him throw the gun out of the window. I jammed on my brakes and looked for it and finally found it. I picked it up very tenderly as not to contaminate it with my fingerprints and drove back to my office. During the chase I managed to get most of his license plate number and make, color and year of car. I called the Washtenaw County sheriff department, and they tracked down the license plate number and matched it with the make of car. They called me and wanted to know if I wanted to press charges. I told them I did not, but the guy called me and apologized and mentioned that he had learned a lesson. The gun he had pointed at me turned out to be a flare gun, but I did not know that, and in retrospect chasing after him was a very stupid thing to do!

A year or two after we moved to Indianola, Billy Bishop who was one of the AE's that was working for me in the central Illinois region decided on his own that he was going to move to the Ann Arbor area and decided that he was going to build a house on the street behind our house. He owned a Mastercraft ski boat and he, Mike, Dave Taylor and I had become best skiing buddies. We would ski 4-5 times a week if we were in town and we could find people that wanted to ski. After a year or two of free style skiing Billy and I bought a portable ski course that we wound up getting permission from the DNR to be able to drop it into Strawberry Lake if we had it out by noon. We got to the point where Mike and I could have it set up in about 15-20 minutes. Sometimes we had some of the other more serious skiers on the Lake take advantage of the fact that it was set up and used it also. Before we bought our portable ski course we would go to Whitmore Lake, which was not too far from the house, and use the permanent course that the Whitmore Lake Ski club had installed there. Of course, when we were skiing free style, we mentally made all the buoys. When we started to ski using a real ski course and not an imaginary one, we realized how hard it really was to make all the buoys. We eventually got to the point where we were rather good at it.

Billy Bishop had a radar detector in his GMC SUV and always turned it on even to go to work when the traffic on US23 was bumper to bumper and moving at 30 miles an hour.

Major improvements that we made on our house on Indianola were:
Put in a sprinkler system.
Built a huge deck in the backyard.
Converted a 2 stall garage and built a 3 stall garage.
Remodeled the kitchen.
Created a gorgeous yard with many flower beds.
Built a huge deck and courtyard in the front of the house.
Stained the house a more pleasant color.

1983 - 5.

People in Hong Kong performing the Tai Chi

May of 1983, I found myself in Hong Kong and I was introduced and exposed to the Tai chi exercise. Every morning there were people out there doing the various form of Tai Chi. Tai Chi is a soft, internal martial arts style from China. It is practiced for self-defense as well as for health benefits, and as a form of meditation. They say Tai Chi helps reduce stress and anxiety. It also helps increase flexibility and balance.

1983 - 6.

My boss Steve Imredy was exceptionally good about me taking the international people that were in town to my house on Indianola for dinner. Brenda and I were empty nesters and enjoyed having people come over for a barbeque, etc. I never had any problem with Steve signing off on my expense account when for instance I bought a tray of shrimp for my guests in that they had to eat somewhere and it was probably cheaper at my house. In the photo below going from L to R: Betty Ruddy, Mary Ann Guy, Dianne Imredy, Steve Imredy, Bob Guy, and the back of John Ehrmann's head.

Enjoying a get-together in our backyard

The Van Bemdens at Point Pelee

The summer of 1983 we took a trip over to Ontario and walked along the beach at Point Peele. Point Peele is the point in Lake Erie where supposedly the Monarch butterfly crosses the lake either coming or going to the winter hibernation location. What makes Point Pelee unique is that the park is a peninsula which tapers out into a long, sharp point, surrounded by the waters of Lake Erie. Point Pelee is home to more than 390 bird species, 70 species of trees, and the 'Tip' of the park is the southernmost point of Canada's mainland.

7-1983

I happened to be in Japan the summer of 1983 and I remember that there was a rock concert going on not too far from our office complex. I never found out who was playing, etc. Do not know whether it was a group/band from oversea or a local band. Looking in the lower left corner it appears to be a Japanese group.

Rock Concert in Tokyo

9-1983

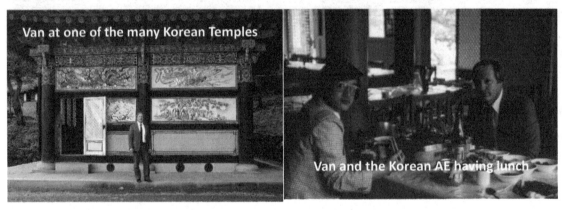
Skiing at Mt. Hotham in Australia

One time when I was in Australia, one of the men in the Hahn & Kolb Melbourne office decided he was going to go skiing that weekend and he asked me if I wanted to go along. I said yes I would love to go along. So later one that afternoon we headed to Mt. Hotham in Victoria, a couple of hours up the road. Mt Hotham is considered by many to be the Australian ski resort for serious skiers and boarders. Mt Hotham Ski Resort is rather flat on the top where the beginners' runs are, whereas the slopes get steeper as they drop into the valleys. I think I was on the top because as you can see from the photo, it seems that most were standing around and saying to themselves what do I do now. Further down the hill, there was a lot of low brush/bushes sticking out of the snow. This was probably one of the worst skiing adventures that I have encountered. But I can say that I skied in Australia. After spending some time in Australia, I packed up my bags and I was off to South Korea.

Van at one of the many Korean Temples

Van and the Korean AE having lunch

This was not all that uncommon. Most of the time when I went to the FarEast and down-under, I usually went on to some of the other countries in that part of the world that I was in charge of. Thus, most of my FarEast visits were a couple of weeks long.

Agawa Canyon Fall Color Tour Oct 1983.

October of 1983, Brenda, and I finally took the Agawa Canyon Fall Color train tour in Canada. We drove up to the Sault Ste. Marie straights, spent the night and the next morning we boarded the train to do the color tour. We talked about doing this several times, I guess things just got in the way, but here we are and finally doing it.

The woods were full of fall colors
Brenda taking a break

Van and Brenda

Many waterfalls

One winter Bob Guy my next-door neighbor borrowed one of my wool ski sweaters to go skiing at Whistler Blackcomb in British Columbia with his son in law and when he returned it, it came back about the size to fit a 2-year-old. Apparently, MaryAnn never told him how to wash a wool sweater.

The Guys had two small dogs which loved to bark whenever they let them outside. I think they barked to let the world know they were outside. One time they were out there, and I snuck up to them with a big stiff piece of plastic and I shook the daylights out of it and scared those poor dogs to death.

Another time we were over there sitting in their family room and Bob was bragging about the fact that those dogs were well house broken only to see one of them go to the bathroom then and there. Course I thought that that was funny and had to call it to his attention.

I remember experiencing the same thing at my sister, Wilma's house. She was bragging about how her little dog was house broken and while we were there visiting her, it had to pee on the floor.

Bob Guy was one of those people that did not know what end of the shovel to pick up, thus whenever I saw them trying to plant a plant I would go over there and wind up doing it for them. Of course, he knew that was going to happen and he and I both played along.

Whenever Sheri one of the Guy's girls would have car trouble, she would always come over to the house and ask me to help her. She wanted us to adopt her.

Speaking of dogs, I remember that on several occasions that I got pretty upset with my brother Ike's dog. It was a very nice-looking pure-white dog, but I thought it had a very mean disposition. I remember being at his place and it would growl at you if you looked at it eyeball to eyeball. One other distinct occasion when I really got upset was when the family was gathering at Dave and Lena's family cottage on Bill's Lake up near Newaygo, MI and Ike happened to bring his dog along. We were all sitting in a row on lawn chairs and his dog would just growl, etc. I told Ike then and there that I did not think that he should have brought it with him to an event where there were lots of people. I went on to tell him that if that dog ever bites me that that would be the end of it. I just do not believe that I should have to go out of my way to get back to my chair to stay away from a dog!

Brenda and Smokie

One time we were in Brighton, and we happened to go past a store front where there were people trying to give away some kittens. We saw one that we thought was nice in that she had beautiful long gray and white hair, and we brought her home and named her Smokie. One time she fell from the balcony down to the main floor. Later on, when she was a little bit older, she would jump up on the counter and drink out of the faucet in the kitchen sink.

It was also while we lived on Indianola that a person with his naked eye could see Echo I, a USA man-made object in the night sky. That was such a historical event that they would publish in the local newspaper when it passed overhead and where in the sky it could be seen.

I do not remember the exact year but while we lived on Indianola I had back surgery and I spent more than a month laying on the couch and reading every magazine and book twice over. I also learned Lotus 1,2,3 which was a spread sheet application, like the Microsoft Excel program we have today. I put all our finance info into the program. Again, that was quite a few years before the Quicken program we use today. I went back to work only to have Robin Kerr tell me I had to go get a doctor's order before I could come back to work.

1983.

The winter of 1983 when Jeff was attending Calvin College, he and I flew out to Salt Lake City, and stayed with our former neighbor who had moved to Salt Lake City. We spent a small week skiing the various ski resorts up and down little Cottonwood Canyon. The photo on the left shows little Johnny Platner who was a fairly good skier already, Jeff and me at one of the Utah's ski resorts.

Another time we stayed at a B&B resort in Cottonwood Canyon. We also enjoyed the B&B hot tub. We were

Enjoying the hot tub

told that we could not have GLASS beer bottles at the hot tub.

Coming back from having spent Christmas in Longview, TX. with Brenda's parents we got stranded in IL. because of the snow on the interstate highway.

Stranded at the Holiday Inn in IL

When we lived on Indianola we eventually started to go to the church in Brighton. We became good friend with Greg and Karen Spalding and Tom and Joyce Wirsing. Both couples worked at a Christian camp, I believe the name of it is Pine Hills Camps and its halfway between Hamburg and Brighton. **1984.**

Brenda watching the ice fishing

Occasionally, Brenda and I would hike around the lake at Kensington State Park which was near Brighton. I remember one time when we were coming back from the 12 Oaks Mall, we

Greg Spalding Family

stopped off along I94 and walked across the frozen lake at Kensington State Park where lots of people were ice fishing and had their vehicles parked on the ice. When Brenda and I were walking across the frozen lake we could hear the ice creaking and making loud noises. It was kind of scary for her.

The winter of 1984 Jimmy Parker and his family came north to visit us in Ann Arbor. We went sledding/tobogganing at the Veterans Park in Ann Arbor. I remember that it was quite cold, and the folks from Texas were certainly not use to that. The photo on the right is Jimmy Parker, Romelle Parker and Michael Parker. Jeff is steering the Toboggan.

The Parkers are tobogganing.

1985

Mom and Dad's 50th. March 7, 1985.

Mom and Dad celebrating their 50th Wedding Anniv.

March 7, 1985, the Van Bemden clan, and friends and relatives gathered at Plymouth Christian School in Grand Rapids to help Mom and Dad celebrate their 50th wedding anniversary. After we celebrated at Plymouth school where the public was invited, the Van Bemdens also celebrated my dad and mothers 50th wedding anniversary in that restaurant in Grandville where the family went a lot for various family events.

The photo on the left is Dad, Mom, Cora, Fred Roelofs, Eric, Butch, Julie, Wilma, Brenda, Urbanes and Lena.

Jeff's graduation from Calvin June 1985.

Jeff graduated from Calvin College in Grand Rapids in June of 1985. I did not attend his graduation because I was in the Far East with my boss Robin Kerr visiting Taiwan, Korea, and Japan. For his graduation from Calvin, I promised him a new car. So, he went to his Uncle Joe's office at Highland Plymouth-Chrysler in Grand Rapids and ordered a black Chrysler Laser. He told my brother that he did not want the Highland Plymouth-Chrysler sticker on his car. I believe it had a 5 speed on the floor transmission.

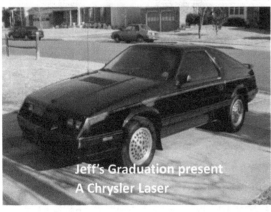

Jeff's Graduation present
A Chrysler Laser

Brenda was somewhat upset with the fact that I would not be at Jeff's graduation, but she got over it. I happened to be in Taiwan with Robin Kerr the vice president of the International Division. I was somewhat surprised that my mother and Dad were there. Al and Cecilia Hettinga were also there as well as Brenda's mother. I guess Brenda must have been busy calling various people.

Mom and Dad Van Bemden, Al & Cecilia Hettinga, Brenda, Lillian Parker, Jeff.

Karen DeJong (Jeff's Fiancée) also graduated and her parents were also there. Since it would be only days before Jeff and Karen get married, I think I need to also have her photo in this script.

Brenda and Jeff

Karen DeJong with her parents

Here is our 3-stall garage all finished

The spring of 1985 I added an extra stall to the garage. I got some help from Tom Wirsing and his son John. They helped me install the trusses and roof the new garage. They also helped me drywall and finish the interior of the garage, etc.

Jeff's Wedding July 13, 1985.

July 13, 1985, Jeff got married to Karen De Jong at the Christian Reformed Church in Ann Arbor, Michigan. Most of the Van Bemdens were there, even the ones from Florida. Brenda's mother and dad as well as Jimmy Parker and his family also attended. Between the wedding and the reception most of the relatives went back to our house on Indianola. The reception was held at the Brighton country club. There was no booze served at the reception so some of the guests hit the bar which was not very well viewed by some of the attendees. After the wedding ceremony was over, my brothers Ike and Joe got to meet

Van, Karen, Jeff, and Brenda

Van and Brenda

Brenda's parents, Brenda, Van and Jeff

Ike, Al Staal and Joe

an old friend Al Staal from the Nederlands Reformed Congregation back in Grand Rapids. They hadn't seen Al Staal in 50 years. Al parents came from the same island in the Nederlands as we did. As you can see everyone was quite surprised and happy.

That fall my dad and mother came over for a visit and I am sure it was Sat since they never stayed overnight at our house, and they had to be back in G.R. in time to go to church Sun morning. It looks like my dad is holding a small glass of wine. He never drank much!

Mom and Dad at our house on Indianola

1985 -12.

Christmas 1985 we were down in Texas like we always did and while we were there Jeff and Karen must have also come to Longview. They were now living in Keller and they did not have any family there so they joined us at the Parkers in Longview. While we were there, we went to visit Caddo Lake in East Texas. Caddo Lake is a very spooky lake; you almost need a guide to find your way around. It is saturated with Cypress trees that are covered with Spanish Moss. There are clearances here and there that allow you to navigate around the lake, but it is best to take a guide the first couple of times if you were to go fishing in the lake.

Jeff and Karen at Caddo Lake

Brenda at Caddo Lake in East Texas

Brenda's brother Jimmy and his family generally came down to Longview to spend at least part of the Christmas vacation with us and his parents. At times Aunt LePearl would also come to Longview to see her nieces and nephews.

Christmas morning at the Parkers in Longview

Jeff, Paul, Jimmy, Romelle, Lillian and Michael

1986

Important news event in Jan of 1986 was the fact that the space shuttle Challenger exploded after liftoff Jan 28, 1986. The immediate cause of the challenger disaster was the failure of two rubber O-rings to seal a joint between the two segments of the right-hand solid rocket booster.

Every once in a while, when we had relatives from the old country, and they were in America for any length of time, one of the things we would do is take them to see Niagara Falls. It's only a couple hours drive from Ann Arbor. It is a sight to behold. In the summer of 1986, I took my mother and dad to see Niagara Falls.

Niagara Falls

Mom and Dad resting
at the flower clock

One Summer I went back to Grand Rapids to visit with Cal Kappes, my former boss when I worked at Durrant Nursery when I was going through high School, who now has his own nursery. He agreed to come to our house and give us some landscaping ideas for the deck we planned to build. Shortly after I had the front deck built, I would eventually turn the area into a courtyard.

Liven Boot and his wife with Van and Brenda in Petosky, MI

The summer of 1986, my cousin, Liven Boot, and his wife came over to America and visited relatives. We went up north to Traverse City and Petosky and he enjoyed it very much. Liven is the son of my Uncle Izaak Boot back in Kortgene. His dad had been here several times. We refer to Uncle Izaak as the painter because he owns a large painting firm. He also painted landscapes and portraits.

Building our front deck
Our front courtyard

One winter when it was not all that cold out, I remember that a couple of snowmobiles went thru the ice on Strawberry Lake. They were obviously snowmobiling on thin ice.

Jeff and Karen's house in Keller, TX

The summer of 1986 we visited Jeff and Karen in their new house in Keller, TX. He had already done quite a bit of work to it. He put in an irrigation system, landscaped it and put a roof over the deck.

Jeff and Karen coming home to Ann Arbor after living in Colorado Springs a few years could not get over how green everything was in Michigan. I did not really appreciate her comments until years later when we moved to Colorado Springs and experienced the same thing on one of our return trips to MI.

171

The fall of 1986 I found myself back in Japan. One of the weekends I was there Yoshi took me on a tour to see the various sights. One was a large Buddha Statue, and another was a large Hindu statue.

Van at one of the largest Budda statues in Japan

A large Hindu statue

He also took me to see a monument that was dedicated to the atomic bomb casualties. Also, there is a photo of me below the pair of straw sandals that the big Buddha wore.

Monument to the Atomic Bomb Casualties

Van and a pair of huge sandals

Van and Brenda's 25th wedding anniversary.

Dec 1987. When my sister Lena had a 25th wedding anniversary party for us, she invited a lot of my high school friends over. Later, in the afternoon the biggest surprise of them

Celebrating our 25th at Lena's house

Brenda blowing on the money tree

all was when Jeff and Karen walked in. They were living in Texas at this time, and they had not revealed or let out the secret that they were flying up to Grand Rapids to join us for the party.

Jeff and Karen flew in from TX

Adrain Gilder and Van

Jeff and Karen with my sister Lena

One Saturday morning while we lived on Indianola, I was in the process of finishing painting (really staining) our house. It was kind of misty and damp, but I only had to finish underneath the overhang in the front of the garage. I proceeded to place a plastic sheet over the asphalt and pushed my sectional ladder up into the peak of the front of the garage. I then got my paint can and climbed up the ladder to where I could reach the peak and proceeded to begin staining. I no more than got started and the ladder which in retrospect had too much of an angle on it proceeded to slide out from underneath me. I tried to hang on for dear life, but the ladder kept sliding and dropped down to the asphalt driveway. I landed on top of the ladder with my face hitting the paint can. My legs we bruised and I was bleeding and hurting from head to toe. Both cars were parked in the garage and wound up with not a speck of paint on them. Brenda came out to see what I was doing, and I told her that I was going to clean up the paint before I did anything else. After I got the paint cleaned up, she drove me to St. Joseph Hospital, and they proceeded to X-ray me from head to toe. The only thing that was broken was my nose. That was not too bad because one time my nose doctor that I had gone to see if my breathing problem could be fixed told me that to straighten out my nose, they would have to break it again. I guess I must have had it broken during one of the times I got into a fight when I was younger.

Another time Brenda and I had gone to a Christmas tree farm around Howell to see about buying several spruce trees to plant in our yard. While I was following this tree farmer around, we were cutting through the trees, and he held back a branch which when he let it go hit me in the eye and I do not think I ever felt as much pain in all my life. My eye just kept on watering and watering, and I simply could not see anything out of it. As soon as that happened, we got out of there and Brenda drove me to emergency center at St. Joseph Hospital in Ann Arbor. We did not buy any trees from him!

One time when it had snowed quite a bit, Rob Raddack, one of the AE's that I had working for me was over at the house and we went out to eat at Burroughs Farms in Brighton. On the way back home, we did a 360 in the middle of Brighton Road that scared the living daylights out of us. It happened so quickly there was not anything I could do about it.

My sister, Wilma's trip, to Aspen. Jan 1987.

Van, Wilma and Jordon

Pete Van Bemden coming down the hill

Jan 1987 my sister, Wilma who worked at Steelcase in Grand Rapids had a friend who had a condo in Snowmass, CO. She apparently was able to rent it and called me to see if I wanted to join her and Rick and Jordon. Obviously, I did, and I told her so. She also invited my brother Pete. Thus, we all made our way to Denver where we rented a car and now it was on to Snowmass. The place she rented from her friend was a real ski in and

174

out. I do not remember exactly how long we were there, but I believe it was a week. We also skied at Aspen Mountain, and I do not remember whether or not we went to Aspen Highlands.

The Roger Bianchi Family at Mesa Verde

The summer of 1987, Roger Bianchi my good friend from Switzerland spent almost the entire summer roaming around the good old USA. They started off in Miami, Florida, rented a small RV and spent 5-6 weeks seeing the various sights. You've got to remember that over in Europe everybody gets 6 weeks of vacation. You do not have to be an employee for 25 years. You basically get this from day one. In the photo it is Eureth, Roger, Fabiana, and Manual Bianchi at Mesa Verde in August of 1987.

1988.
Dec 21, 1988, A Pan Am Boeing 747 airplane New York-bound exploded over Lockerbie, Scotland less than an hour after takeoff from London Heathrow airport, killing 259 people in the air and 11 people on the ground. Citizens from 21 different countries were killed. Among the 190 Americans on board were 35 Syracuse University students flying home for Christmas after a semester abroad. The bombing was blamed on Libyan terrorists.

Van's award-winning Daffodils and Hyacinth

While we lived in the Ann Arbor area, I started forcing spring bulbs and entered several flower shows in Ann Arbor for which I received several blue ribbons and 1st prize awards.

1991.

Our backyard spring of 1991

Lots of Trilliums

We had a beautiful garden which was the envy and talk of the neighborhood. Several garden clubs took tours of our yard. We also had people stop along the street and just admire our yard. Neighbors also asked to wander around and just look the place over. We had all of our beds numbered and thus when I told Brenda that I would be working in bed 3 for instance, she knew where I was. In the springtime we had more tulips, daffodils, and other spring flowers blooming in our yard than they probably did at the Holland tulip festival some years. In one of our more natural beds under lots of trees we had lots of ground cover consisting mainly of myrtle and pachysandra. In there we planted lots of daffodils and trilliums. I had dug up the trilliums in a farmer's woods halfway between Lansing and Grand Rapids. The woods where I dug them up was full of poison ivy and it seemed that every time I dug them I would wind up getting poison ivy.

While we lived on Indianola, I was president of the homeowner association. We had to approve all the new housing plans to make sure that they adhered to the covenants of the association. One day a fellow drove up into our neighborhood with his semi-truck and trailer which contained a crane to dig the basement for a new house. I went to see what was going on and he said that I am here to dig a basement for a new house. Well, I told him that we had not seen the blueprints, etc. and we needed to see them before anything happens. Well, he started to back the backhoe off of the trailer and I laid down in front of the tracks and he did not want to run over me, so he proceeded to put his machine back on the trailer and drive off. Sometime later, we received a set of blueprints to review, etc. This instance reminds me of an event that happened a few years later that the world witnessed because it was on TV and in the newspapers. This is what google had to say about the tank man:

Tank Man (also known as the **Unknown Protester** or **Unknown Rebel**) is the nickname of an unidentified Chinese man who stood in front of a column of Type 59 tanks leaving Tiananmen Square in Beijing on June 5, 1989, the day after the Chinese government's violent crackdown on the Tiananmen protests. As the lead tank maneuvered to pass by the man, he repeatedly shifted his position in order to obstruct the tank's attempted path around him. The incident was filmed and shared to a worldwide audience. Internationally, it is considered one of the most iconic images of all time.[1][2][3] Inside China, the image and the accompanying events are subject to censorship.[4]

I really get choked up when our national anthem is played and people just do not respond. I have had the good fortune of travelling over much of this world while I was employed at MDSI/Schlumberger and can verify that this has got to be one of the greatest places in the world to live and I cannot help it if I get teary eyed when "The Star Spangled Banner" is played and sung.

We had sales meetings in Las Vegas a couple of times, and I remember going to a show at the Mirage Resort and Casino where the 2 famous German magicians, Siegfried Fischbach and Roy Horn, are booked year around. I remember sitting in what probably was the orchestra pit at a certain show and they had these elephants walking within feet of us and they would pee, and it would splatter all over the floor. They also made the famous white tiger disappear, or move them from one end of the stage to the other end. It was pure magic. Years later one of the fellows was attacked by one of the white tigers and was dragged across the stage by his neck. It paralyzed him and I do not believe he is capable of walking to this day.

The summer of 1991 one of my second cousins, Jan Boot, came over to America and he came by to visit us while we lived on Indianola. Years later (Aug 1999) after he got married and he was in Denver he came by again.

Jan Boot and Brenda

John Adams and Van's visit to Sweden

Since John had a Swedish mother, John spoke and understood Swedish and so he really

Town Square Linkoping on Lake Vanern

Grass beach in Stockholm. Topless!

enjoyed working the Swedish market and the Scandinavia countries. I too enjoyed working the various countries trying to figure out whether there was a market there for us. I remember being over there in the winter and we were quite a distance north of Stockholm demoing CII and at 2 O'clock in the afternoon the streetlights were already on. When we were there in the summer everyone lays around on the rocks and grass like

Van at the Stave Church in Bergen, Norway

lizards soaking up the sun for the 2 weeks of summer they seemed to get. I remember water skiing in the Baltic Sea behind a boat of this couple that had befriended us. Water was cold. It seems that everyone had a place on one of the islands in the archipelago. Since the tax rates for the average person in Sweden were very high, their seemed to be a lot of bartering going on. "I'll do this for you if you do this for me." One time we were there around the Christmas holiday and got to witness how they celebrate the holiday. Even got to taste some real Swedish meat balls. Bought a small painting in Bergen, Norway when John Adams and I were demoing there and evaluating the marketplace. To this day I do not know what ever happened to this painting which I paid good money for. All I know it is no longer around. It was while we were demoing around Bergen that I also got to see an authentic Stave church. Below is what **Google** is saying about the Stave Church in Bergen.

The church was originally built around the year 1150 at Fortun in Sogn, a village near the inner or eastern end of Sognefjord. In 1879, the new Fortun Church (*Fortun kyrkje*) was constructed as a replacement for the medieval stave church. Fantoft Stave Church was threatened with demolition, as were hundreds of other stave churches in Norway. Fantoft Stave Church was bought by consul Fredrik Georg Gade and saved by moving it in pieces to Fana near Bergen in 1883.

10-1980

Old Sailing ship in Bergen Harbor

Bergen is an interesting town in that it is the center of Norway's North Sea oil activity. Thus, there is quite a bit of manufacturing relating to the offshore drilling rigs, etc. Come Saturday it seems everyone is out shopping. There is lots of activity around the harbor when the fishermen bring in their fresh catch. Surrounded by seven mountains and with a harbor of world heritage class, Bergen is perfect if you love mountain hikes, city walks, water activities and culture. Located in the heart of Western Norway, the city is also the gateway to some of the most famous fjords in the world. Bergen is also famous for its high levels of rainfall because it is located between seven mountains, which makes it particularly vulnerable to showers. The wind that comes from the Atlantic moves the clouds which strike the mountains surrounding the city.

Denmark. OCT 1981.

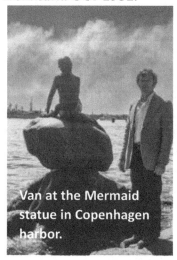
Van at the Mermaid statue in Copenhagen harbor.

Outside stairway

I received a call from John Adams who had arranged several demos in Denmark. Thus, I was on a plane to Europe via a stop in London. When I got on the plane in London that would takes us to Copenhagen, I sat down next to a man from Copenhagen and when the stewardess came around to ask if anyone wanted to buy some duty-free items, he bought a carton of cigarettes and since I was not buying anything he asked if I would buy a carton of cigarettes. I cannot believe I did since I am the world's most anti-smoking person alive. It turned out OK since he gave me a ride to the hotel that I was staying at. Since I generally took off from Detroit Metro on Friday afternoon, I had the weekend to do some sightseeing in Copenhagen. When you are in Copenhagen you obviously have to visit the harbor where the world-famous mermaid statue is located. While I was in Copenhagen, I also saw one of the most interesting church steeples I 've ever seen. It has the spiral stairway on the outside of the steeple.

My time in the International Division.

Before the official creation of the international division of MDSI, I had spent a great deal of time in Europe, helping to get the company operations up and running in England, France, Germany, Belgium, Luxembourg, Netherlands, Switzerland, and Scandinavia. I worked regularly with John Adams, the managing director of the Paris office.

On one of the trips to Switzerland, we had to take advantage of the fact that we were now in Switzerland and now was the opportunity to visit Zermatt. It was during our overnight stay in Zermatt, that John introduced me to a real Swiss dish, Raclette. Raclette is also popular in the other Alpine countries and is based on heating cheese and scraping off the melted part. It is typically served with small boiled potatoes.

By now my oldest son, Jeff, was a young teenager, and I taught him how to communicate with me when I was overseas using the ASR33 that was installed in our house. Jeff even attended a COMPACT II class when he was just 13 years old as an easy introduction to computer programming.

Yoshi and Seiji's 4 month stay in Ann Arbor 1975

Yoshi and Seiji in the Tokyo office

The two Application Engineers from Japan, Yoshi and Seiji, that came to Ann Arbor for 4 months of training to learn C II did not know how to drive a car, nor did they speak much English, although they had attended a Berlitz class in Tokyo. Thus, we wound up sending them back to a Berlitz class to speak rudimentary English so we could a least communicate with them. I learned later from Yoshi that Masataka told his two employees that if they left their jobs before three years they would have to pay back MDSI-Japan the $1500 cost of the Berlitz class they took in Japan.

When Yoshi and Seiji completed their MDSI sales training in Ann Arbor, I returned with them to Japan to assist in their first demos. At one demo with a potential customer Masataka and Yoshi carried on a long conversation with a large group of personnel. They seemed to be talking back and forth without getting anywhere so I asked Yoshi to ask them a particular question. At that, a young man (probably a computer geek), said, in almost perfect English, "That's a good question." Everybody laughed.

At another demo, the MDSI team (Yoshi and I) were invited to stay for lunch at the company cafeteria. I looked in dismay at my bowl of soup in a beat-up mess tin that looked like a relic from WII. It seemed to be floating with fish bones and squid. After Yoshi and I left the factory and were back on the train for the office. I told Yoshi, In the future, if a customer wants us to join him for lunch in the cafeteria, please tell him we have to go. Every time I was in Tokyo I would visit the famous camera and electronic districts. They always had the latest and greatest gadgets, etc. Being an avid photographer, I was buying much of my camera gear in Tokyo's "Electronic Alley" near the MDSI-Japan office. Eventually I wound up taking more than 10,000 photos during my overseas travels for the company, many of which were published in an in-house MDSI magazine.

I remember visiting a McDonalds not too far from my hotel and a street person saw me and shouted Yankee go home.

Parking in Tokyo is a disaster and awfully expensive, just like everything else. I remember being over there and the price of a cantaloupe was at that time the equivalent of around $10. We could get them all day long when they are in season here for $1.

Van and Brenda's visit to Israel June 1977.

In June 1977 Bob Drewry asked me to go to Israel and demo our programming system in the Tool show in Tel Aviv. He apparently assigned Dave Price to do this, but Ken Stephanz got wind of this and told Bob to assign me. Thus, it was Friday morning, and I was to be on the airplane the following day. I asked if Brenda wanted to go to Israel with me, which she did. I then had to get her an airline ticket; they apparently did not have any more seats available on the flight that I was booked on. Well, I told the airline that I was not going to go if I could not get a ticket for Brenda. They finally found a seat and we were off to Israel. We made arrangements to have Jeff stay with his friend Kurt Firnhaber. I had to make a wooden crate to carry the hard disc which had our system software on it and MDSI had made arrangements with DEC in Tel Aviv to use one of their computers when I got over there. I had to oversee the building and arrangement of our booth, etc. The show went off as planned, but it was not anything along our line of business. While we were there we saw lots of biblical historic sites when I was not demoing our system. We swam in the Dead Sea and the river Jordan and went to historical sites such as Jerusalem, Bethlehem, Capernaum, Jericho, etc.

Van swimming in the Jordan River

Van and Brenda at the Dome of the Rock

On the way home we stopped off in Paris and visited with Pierre Boudreau. He gave us a quick tour of Paris visiting such sights as Notre Dame, the Eiffel Tower, etc. since Brenda had never been there. We had dinner with Pierre and his wife. I remember ordering fish, and the fish came to the table with its head still on it and all I could see was a large pair of eyeballs staring at me. Pierre offered to trade plates with me and it worked out since he had ordered a nice steak dinner. I believe we must have spent Saturday in Paris also since the photos below are from this same trip.

Brenda and Pierre at the Eiffel Tower

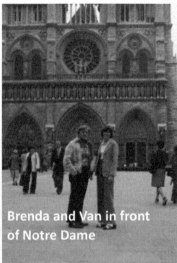
Brenda and Van in front of Notre Dame

One of the paintings in the Louvre

On that same trip Brenda got to go to the Louvre to see some paintings and that was remarkably interesting for her because she was taking an art course at Eastern Michigan University.

The Fall of 1977 Hiring Steve Imredy.
In the fall of **1977** Ken hired Steve Imredy as president of the international division. Sometime after Steve joined the company, I transferred over to the international division full time as director of technical services. My job was to see that each of our international subsidiaries had the right tools, training, and support to do their job. The big question was, "How can we, back at corporate, help you do a better job?" As a side note Steve Imredy was a Hungarian freedom fighter who had fought the Russians and eventually escaped to the west. One decision that I could not see eye to eye on was when Steve assigned Israel to Jürgen Selig, a German, to develop a potential market there. I had been to Israel the same year and demoed our product there during one of their tools shows and my conclusion was that there was not that big of a market there outside of the Department of Defense activities and they were pretty locked up since everything appeared to be a big secret.

Nov 1977. On one of my trips to England I had arranged for an appointment with the Prime Minister James Callaghan. Here you can see me waiting at Number 10 Downing Street for the Prime Minister to open the door. As you can see back in 1977, one could walk right up to the door at 10 Downing Street. Can't do that today. I really didn't have an appointment with the PM. This is a joke!

Van waiting for the Prime Minister

On that same trip I visited Trafalgar Square in Westminster, Central London where you can see there are a million pigeons. I do not recall whether or not I got out of there without some pigeon poop on my black winter overcoat.

Van with a million pigeons in Trafalgar Square

Yoshi and Van skiing at Mt. Brighton

Feb 1978, Yoshi was in Ann Arbor for additional training and he and I went skiing at Mt. Brighton. I believe I was just getting into skiing and I was not all that good. But being at Mt. Brighton which has a maximum of 230 vertical ft you do not have to be particularly good. Three good turns and you are back down at the base.

In the spring of 1978, we had an International Technical meeting in Geneva, Switzerland.

Dave Price, Chris Neylon and Bob Samson enjoying a lunch break

All of the international AE's flew and/or drove to Geneva for this meeting. I being the International Technical director took a few Ann Arbor based people Dave Price, Chris Neylon and Bob Samson with me to present various topics. Arriving a bit early we decided to buy a few bottles of wine, cheese, etc. and hit the road. Here is a photo of us enjoying a pull off to the side of the road lunch somewhere in Switzerland.

Sweden.

At noon in Sigtuna, Sweden

The Wasa Museum

On one of my trips to Sweden, John and I called on a customer way up north. I could not get over how low in the sky the sun was. Walking around at noon you got a little daylight, but by 2 o'clock in the afternoon it was time to turn on the streetlights. I believe it was on that same trip that we visited the Wasa Museum in Stockholm where they had on display a ship that had sunk years ago and was buried in the mud. To keep the ship from falling apart they had to spray it with mist 24/7. This is what **Google** said about the ship:

The ship sank after sailing roughly 1,300 m (1,400 yd) into her maiden voyage on 10 August 1628. She fell into obscurity after most of her valuable bronze cannons were salvaged in the 17th century, until she was located again in the late 1950s in a busy shipping area in Stockholm harbor. After sailing about 1300 meters, a light gust of wind caused the Vasa to heel over on its side. Water poured in through the gun portals and **the ship sank with a loss of 53 lives**.

On one of my trips to Sweden at customs they ripped open the liner in my suitcase looking for drugs, etc. I think the reason they did was because they could see in my passport that I had been in the Far East a number of times. Anyway, after tearing up my suitcase, they put everything halfway back together and I had now cleared customs in Stockholm.

1978 – 11. The fall of 1978 there was a Japanese International Machine Tool Fair (JIMTOF) in Osaka, Japan. I, Steve Imredy, along with Ray Gaynor and Larry Thomas from the states, flew to Japan to attend and work the JIMTOF Show. Masataka and Seiji from our Japan office worked the show. I remember one night that Masataka Uesono got pretty tanked up and as we were walking back to our hotel room he kept mumbling about this and that and I could see that Steve was upset about the whole situation. I got Masataka off to the side and got ahead of the rest of them and took him to his room and tucked him into bed. I probably saved him his job at least for a while. It was this same trip we got moved out of our rooms to another floor in our hotel because the Chinese Prime Minster Ling came to town with his entourage to visit the JIMTOF Show and for safety reasons, etc. they took over the entire floor. In the photo of us having dinner in

Dinner at the Osaka Tool show

Osaka. The people going from left to right are Ray Gaynor, Steve Imredy, Van, Larry Thompson, Masataka Uesono, and Seiji Kasaka.

One of the things you would notice as you walk around any downtown in Japan is the many Pachinko shops. Pachinko machines were first introduced to Japan in the early 1920s, and today there are over 9000 pachinko parlors across the country. Pachinko is similar to our pin ball machine except they are in a vertical position against a wall. And they are played with what I believe to be steel ball bearings. You go to the clerk and buy a small container with perhaps 50-100 ball bearings and drop them into the opening at the top of your Pachinko machine and watch as they come down from the top to the bottom. People sit there for hours and are almost hypnotized. You might ask why so many people play the pachinko machines and one reason surely is that it is Japan's one legal outlet for gambling, allowing players to try their luck and win money playing. In fact, during Japan's long economic downturn many turned to pachinko in a last-ditch effort to make ends meet. You have to be 18yrs old to play this game. At the finish they take the container with the ball bearings and depending on how many they have, that is their payout. Another game that was popular during my earlier days of visiting Japan was various machine like the arm-wrestling machines. There was also another one that was popular and that was to try to hit the gopher as they pocked their head out of the hole.

Lots of People playing

Larry Thompson watching a man play the Pachinko machine

Van arm-wrestling with a machine

My visit to Korea April 1979.

My first visit to Korea to select and appoint a distributor was in April 1979. What I found out was that the whole country seems to be run by a half dozen huge conglomerates such as Samsung, LG, etc. The first demo I was asked to program a TV tube; that was when they were still curved and not flat screen like they are today. Well, to make a long story short, our software did not have many

Typical subway entrance in Seoul

Open air market, anchovies, eels, spices, etc.

capabilities in that area. So, it was basically a wash. I do not think the distributor had a good knowledge of our capabilities. I love their subway entrances in Seoul. Very decorative! Doing some site seeing in Seoul I was going around some of the larger government buildings taking photos when suddenly, a guard/soldier was at my side and asking what I was doing. Taking photos of

government buildings was not allowed. I obviously got out of there and took lots of pictures from other sites, such as the street market where one can purchase just about anything. On one of my trips from Taiwan to Korea I had purchased a souvenir sword in Taipei that just fit in my large suitcase crossways. Well, when I got to Seoul I was at the baggage claim area waiting and

At the Korea Institute of Machinery & Metal

waiting for my bags. Finally, here came a couple of inspectors with my baggage and they wanted to know what I was doing with that sword. I told them it was a souvenir. To prove that I had no intentions of using it as a weapon I took it out of my suitcase and wiped it across my arm. I said it is duller than dull. They believed me and I was on my way. I

Manicuring the lawn by hand.

remember one of my first trips to Korea we made a call to the Korea Institute of Machinery & Metals in Daejeon, and I could not get over the fact that out on the front lawn were a dozen or so women, cutting and weeding the lawn by hand. By hand I mean cutting the grass with scissors. I asked our rep why they were doing this by hand and he mentioned the fact that it provided employment.

Dog Meat store

One time we were in Masan and our distributor pointed out this store where dog meat was sold. It so happened that South Koreans does consume dog meat! Bing.com: *Yes*, dog meat is consumed in Korea and other countries. In 2018 National Geographic reported 2 million dogs are consumed each year in South Korea. While slaughtering dogs and eating their meat may horrify Americans, it is *a longstanding custom in* South Korea and other Asian nations. I did not try it! Speaking of being in Masan and other cities in South Korea, it seemed as though we always stayed in Lotte Hotels whenever we left Seoul.

Open air market in Masan

Lotte Corporation is a South Korean multinational conglomerate corporation, and the fifth-largest chaebol (conglomerate) in South Korea. Lotte began its history on June 28, 1948, by Korean businessman Shin Kyuk-ho in Tokyo. Wikipedia

At the Korean Village

One of the things every visitor to Korea should do is take the opportunity to visit an authentic Korean Village. They are set in an environment taking you back 50-100 years. You will also see lots of very colorful Korean costumes.

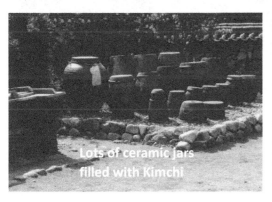
Lots of ceramic jars filled with Kimchi

A favorite Korean dish is Kimchi. Kimchi is a traditional Korean side dish made from fermented cabbage, radish, or cucumber. It is often categorized by the main vegetable ingredient used to make it. Kimchi is a staple food in Korean cuisine. Most Koreans have it with almost every meal at least once a day. If you are travelling around the countryside, you notice many big jars filled with this traditional dish. This spicy, fermented side dish has been a staple on Korean tables for thousands of years. Koreans believe that Kimchi can soothe an upset stomach, help you lose weight, cure a hangover, keep you from aging and much more. I personally can take it or leave it!

Sweden 1980.

Skinny dipping in the Baltic Sea

Early in the fall of 1980, I remember being over in Stockholm when Steve Imredy was also there and we got invited over to Olof's house for dinner one night. Olof's wife obviously went out of her way to fix a typical Swedish dish. It started out with pickled herring, and it was all I could do to down it. I certainly did not ask or want seconds. Olof Silverling, like many Swedes had a cottage out in the Archipelago in the Baltic Sea not too far from Stockholm. Olof, Steve and I went there and of course we had to go swimming, thus, with no swimsuits we just went skinny dipping. I am not sure the water in the Baltic Sea ever gets warm.

One time when I was in Stockholm John Adams and I went to visit the Milles Garden. This garden is incredibly unique. It was the home of sculptor Carl Milles and his wife Olga. Their home and grounds are now a fabulous sculpture garden and art museum.

Sculptures at Milles Garden in Stockholm

Van at the "Hand of God"

Probably the most famous sculpture is "Hand of God."

1981 Over the years while I was in the international division, we had International Technical meetings in various cities such as Paris, Geneva, Vienna, Frankfurt, West Berlin, etc. These were always fun and remarkably interesting because the various international personnel would get to see their friends from the other countries. However, it involved a lot of work on

International meeting in Paris

my part putting an agenda together, etc. At times I would bring people from Ann Arbor to present various topics. I would also use some local personnel whenever possible to present a topic.

An interesting sideline was when we were in Vienna and gathering at the bar, we ran across a Schlumberger wine. I do not know whether they were part of the same family that owned our company.

My visit to New Zeeland and Mace Engr.

One of my first trips over to New Zeeland was to visited Mace Engineering in Christchurch. I toured their plant which happened to be the largest machine shop in New Zeeland and tried to get an idea of what their needs were. Ted Mace, the owner's son, gave me a tour of the plant as well as discussed the type of machining they were doing. He took me over to his house and showed me the neighborhood that he lived in. The neighbors have a contest as to

Ted Mace in front of his house in Christchurch

who has the neatest yard and garden. His certainly was one of the nicer ones.

If you are in Christchurch, you must visit Cathedral Square in downtown Christchurch. It is beautiful. However, the steeple was destroyed in 2011.

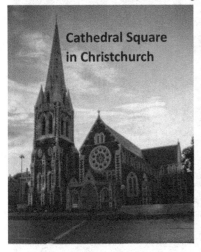
Cathedral Square in Christchurch

After the 2011 earthquake

As an interesting side note, a few years ago (2010-2015), I was sitting in a hot tub at The Gant in Aspen, CO, when I struck up a conversation with a couple from New Zeeland. I asked them where they lived in New Zeeland and they replied Christchurch. I told them that I had been there many times, and I had a good customer there by the name of Mace Engineering. They went on to tell me that they bought the house they were living in from Ted Mace. What a small world!

One time while I was visiting Mace Engineering, it was suggested that I go skiing at Mt. Hutt Ski Resort. This was back in the day when I was not all that good of a skier and the skis were exceptionally long and narrow. I remember we got to a certain place along the road that leads up to Mt. Hutt Ski Resort and we stopped to put chains on the car. All in all, it was a very neat experience. On that same trip I went on a Mt. Cook airplane tour where we circled Mt. Cook and finally landed on a glacier.

One of the many glaciers at Mt. Cook

Van's plane tour of Mt. Cook. Landing on a Glacier

International Managers meeting in West Berlin. June 1981

We had an International Manager's meeting in West Berlin and while we were there one evening we went over to East Berlin for dinner, and it was just an entirely different world. I remember getting on the train that took us over to the other side and there were East German soldiers with what looked like AK-15 rifles walking across the overhead bridges looking down

Van with most of the Int'l Mgr. in Berlin at the Brandenburg gate

on us, ready to shoot if necessary. Another thing I remember was that everyone that went to East Berlin had to exchange $40 dollars. They wanted hard currency, since theirs was not worth much.

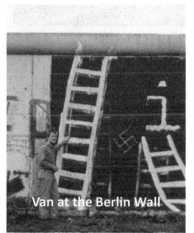

Van at the Berlin Wall

The Brandenburg Gate is Berlin's most famous landmark and a must-see for all visitors. A symbol of Berlin and German division during the Cold War, it is now a national symbol of peace and unity.

The Berlin Wall was still intact when I was there, and it was November 9, 1989, when it was finally torn down. Below is a photo of Van trying to climb over to the other side. Why he wants to go to the East Berlin side of the wall is crazy. What is wrong with this guy?

Kaiser Wilhelm Gedachtniskirche

Google. On June 12, 1987, in one of his most famous Cold War speeches, President Ronald Reagan challenges Soviet Leader **Mikhail Gorbachev** to "tear down" the Berlin Wall, a symbol of the repressive Communist era in a divided Germany. A few years later, during the night of **November 9, 1989**, crowds of Germans began dismantling the Berlin Wall—a barrier that for almost 30 years had kept the East Berliners from going to the west.

This is what Wikipedia has to say about the Kaiser Wilhelm Memorial Church. The original church on the site was built in the 1890s. It was badly damaged in a bombing raid in 1943. The present building, which consists of a church with an attached foyer and a separate belfry with an attached chapel, was built between 1959 and 1963. The damaged spire of the old church has been retained and its ground floor has been made into a memorial hall. The Memorial Church today is a famous landmark of western Berlin and is nicknamed by Berliners *"der hohle Zahn"*, meaning "the hollow tooth".

One time in the early 1980's when I was visiting our office in Frankfort, Germany, I was in my hotel room and heard a lot of noise down in the street and looking out of my window I saw many Turks' protesting. What they were protesting I do not really know, but I do remember that around that time there were a lot of Arabs and middle easterners escaping to various western European countries.

Turks protesting in the streets of Frankfort

8-1981.

Most of the time went I went overseas to Europe I would leave Detroit Metro Friday afternoon and arrive at my destination sometime Saturday morning. If possible, I would get a company car and go sightseeing over the weekend and I would be ready for business come Monday morning. I loved roaming around downtown Paris, it is so easy to get around. Most visitors strolling Luxembourg Gardens have seen kids pushing adorable little sailboats around the Grand Basin duck pond, but perhaps you did not know this is a tradition that's almost 90 years old.

Small sail boats for rent

Kids and Grownups enjoy a fun time at a large pond

One of the practices that Frenchmen have is drinking a Latte for breakfast. This is a large cup (almost a bowl), and they fill it up half full of warm milk and then they fill it up with coffee. It really does not taste like coffee anymore to me because it is so diluted. Then after lunch we normally would go downstairs in the office complex where we had our office and have an espresso. An espresso is extraordinarily strong coffee, so strong at least there that one could figuratively say "a spoon would stand up straight in it."

Spending part of my weekend in a Swiss Hospital. 1982.

It was during the winter of 1982 that I got the opportunity to go skiing in Switzerland. Our newly appointed Managing director had a house in the Films, Laax, Falera area and while I was visiting most of our offices in Europe and I happened to be in Switzerland he invited me to go skiing with his family. Well, everything was going along smoothly and all of a sudden, I hit a deep gulch in the snow that a heavy loaded ski mobile made and down I went. It cut a deep gash in my knee and was bleeding but I continued to ski down the hill and when we got down I knew something was very wrong since my left leg was kind of warm. We went down to his house and pulled up my pant leg and my leg was nothing but blood. We cleaned up my leg in the bathtub

Our Swiss Mgr. Family

and got into his car and drove down to the nearest village and to the doctor's office. When we got there, he took one look at my leg and suggested we go to the nearest hospital. So we get back into the car and drive to the nearest hospital. There they fix me up and I stayed overnight in the hospital. Here I am trying to communicate with the Swiss personnel (nurses, etc.) in my broken German. What was bad about the whole situation was that I had a plane to catch Monday morning to go to Frankfurt to conduct a technical meeting. So come Monday morning, our Swiss manager picked me up to go to the airport. Now I was on crutches, so it was kind of embarrassing.

To the folks in the various international offices, Van-from-the-home-office (whom they all knew that I had been with MDSI since Day One) surely had the answers to all their questions. Obviously, I knew that was not true, but whenever I traveled internationally, I faced awfully long days. I used to say, "They would meet me for breakfast and practically tuck me into bed at night."

Lots of MDSI employees in Ann Arbor would sometimes express envy at my trips overseas, and I did enjoy myself, but I also admit it was not all it was cracked up to be. "On the first trip to a new office, someone would meet me at the airport, take me to the hotel, maybe take me out to dinner and show me around. But after a couple of visits, they would say, "You know your way around. We will see you in the office Monday morning." I grew a lot professionally, personally, and culturally, but those trips meant a lot of time away from home."

Australia–Dave Bennett–1984.

When one is in Australia and playing golf, one does not encounter alligators like down in Florida, or geese like in Michigan, but one is likely to run into kangaroos like the photo on the right.

Lots of Kangaroos at the golf course

I do not know which trip to Australia it was, but before I returned, I bought a couple of red kangaroo skins. When I got back to LA, the customs people tried to confiscate them because they told me that they were a protected species. Well, I told them that some varieties of kangaroos might be, but the big red kangaroos are hunted down and shot regularly. They bought off on my reply and today the kangaroo skins are at my son Jeff's house, and one is at my grandson Paul's house and I still have 1 or 2 downstairs at my house.

Brenda, Van, Dave and Jan Bennett. Taken in COS

One of my best customers in Australia was Perfect Tune in Melbourne. Dave Bennett the owner bought a Series 1 system that he used to program his various machine tools in the shop. He also tuned up cars. Dave was into racing, and he did a lot of work modifying the cylinder head for GM cars. He became an incredibly good friend and even visited us in Ann Arbor and also after we moved to Colorado Springs. We still exchange Christmas cards. He invited us to visit him in his summer vacation home along the Golden coast. He had a large catamaran that he would love to give us a tour on along the Golden coast. He had a very successful business in Melbourne and none of his kids wanted anything to do with it, so he finally sold it to an outsider.

Open House at Hahn & Kolb in Melbourne 1985.

The winter of 1985 I was in Australia to be there for Hahn & Kolb's open house. We (MDSI) had our banners and systems up and running. They are a wholly owned subsidiary of Hahn & Kolb in Germany and had the latest machine tools, etc. on display. Most of their customers were invited and the Governor of the state/territory of Victoria along with some other high-ranking officials

Announcing the partnership with MDSI

were also there. It was quite a show. Premier of Victoria attending Hahn & Kolb open house in Melbourne Australia when they announced they were teaming up with MDSI.

Janise Terne?, ??, Van and Joell Small at Wim Schuler's

What the occasion was for me to take the secretaries out to Wim Schuler's I do not remember, but here am I with my secretary Joell Small and 2 other ladies who worked in the international division.

Winning the Intl salesman of the year contest. In the early to mid-1980's we had pretty much all the wholly owned subsidiaries in place and now we were working thru several distributors in the Far East (South Korea and Taiwan) and down under in Australia. I think it was in 1983 that **Steve Imredy** had an international sales contest going on and he had me working thru these distributors, as well as on my own, in places like **New Zeeland**, **Singapore** and he also wanted me to enter the sales contest. Now I had a potential customer by the name of **Mace Engineering** in Christ Church, New Zeeland (the largest machine shop in New Zeeland), that I had being working on for some time trying to get them to buy a big **Action Central** system. Lots of times when I would go to Australia to work with our distributor Hahn & Kolb, I would stop off in New Zeeland and try to get them off dead center. Well, the sales contest was coming to an end, and I needed this order! I telexed **Ted Mace**, the son of the owner who at this time was pretty much in charge of Mace Engineering, and suggested that if he were going to eventually place an order with us any time soon, I would love to have him place it NOW! He did it and his $200K + order allowed me to win the **International Salesmen of the Year** contest. If I recall correctly it was a $6K prize.

Saying Goodbye to the Far East.
Before I began my trip to the Far East to visit the various distributors, I approached Jon Erhman, MDSI CFO, and Dave Benoit in the finance department about adding the approximate $2k to my prize money if I elected to sit in the tourist area of the plane versus businessmen class. The company had a policy that any flight over 6 hours (which all of my international flights were) we could sit in the businessmen section of the airplane. Pan America had a special deal and I believe they called it "Tour the Pacific" and if you knew the exact date when you would depart and continue to your next destination the air fare would be much cheaper. Well, I had no problem knowing when I was going to depart one place and move on to the next planned stop. Thus, they allowed me to add the $2K to my prize money and that allowed me to fly our son Jeff to South Korea without spending any of my own money.

April 1984. Sometime later, I resigned from the International Division and turned it over to Gordon Creer who at that time was the International Div. Accountant. In the process of me turning it over, I had to introduce him to the various distributors, my contacts, etc. Thus, He and I and our wives were off to the far east, namely New Zeeland, Australia, Hong Kong, Taiwan, Korea and finally a stop off at our wholly owned subsidiary in Tokyo, Japan.

Van, Brenda, Janet and Gordon Creer

While in New Zeeland we called on **Mace Engineering**, where I picked up another **$25k** order for additional Machine Tool links. Mr. Mace (the original founder and owner) was still somewhat involved, and he asked me what we were going to do that coming weekend. I told him we did not really know for certain, and he suggested that we visit **Milford Sound**! Well, we told him that sounds interesting perhaps we should do that. He being a

Brenda, Janet and Gorden Creer in Milford Sound

member of Air New Zeeland's board got on the phone and called Air New Zeeland and arranged a 50-passenger plane to take the 4 of us to Milford Sound. When we arrived at the Milford Sound airport there were no baggage handlers, etc. We did it all ourselves and got in a taxi that was waiting for us to take us to the hotel. We spent a wonderful weekend touring Milford Sound. This is what Google says about Milford Sound: When one visits the Milford Sound area one must take a cruise around the Fjords. It is not the only place in the world where you are surrounded by tall mountains. **Yet the Milford Sound is unique – many of the mountains surrounding it are more than 1,000 meters high.** Some even are between 1,200 and 1,500 m. The panorama views are hugely impressive but **wait till you approach by a boat an almost vertical wall of one km height.** That is really overwhelming! At the pinnacle of Milford Sound is iconic **Mitre Peak** – standing a proud 1,692 meters above sea level, it is certainly an impressive sight to behold.

In the Milford Sound area there is a unique Kea Alpine parrot that is only found in that area, and it loves to eat the rubber from the wiper's blades, etc. from cars.

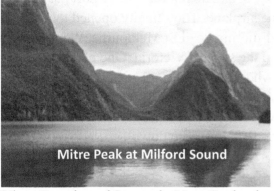
Mitre Peak at Milford Sound

Kea Alpine Parrot

When Brenda and I were in New Zeeland on my last trip there, I was making a call at Mace engineering in Christchurch and Brenda was back in the hotel and then a fire alarm in her hotel went off, so she had to get outside before all her makeup was on.

As Brenda and I were touring New Zeeland it was also pointed out that in addition to New Zeeland having millions of sheep, they also raise lots of red deer. The meat of the red deer is sold mainly to Europe, especially Germany.

Some of the Red Deer they raise in N.Z.

Young man tending his sheep

The following Monday we were off to Sydney, Australia. Met with Kurt Schwotzer, the Hahn & Kolb office manager in Sydney, and spent some time sightseeing in Sydney. One of the sights you must see is the world-famous Sydney opera house.

Sydney Opera House

Leaving our hotel in Sydney, I had an issue with my hotel bill so while I was trying to straighten it out, I told Gordon and Janet to go ahead, and I would catch up with them at the airport. I am now on the plane getting ready to take off to Melbourne where we had a customer call to make later that morning, and there is no Gordon! Gordon and his wife had been taken for a long and scenic drive to the airport to run up the taxi fare. When Gordon arrived at the airport, he left Janet and all the luggage at the curb, and he ran into the airport past the check-in and started to pound on the door of the airplane. They finally opened the door to the aircraft and let him board. We did make our morning call in Melbourne. We obviously did some sightseeing in the Melbourne area and the state of Victoria. One place that is quite famous is Port Campbell National Park, where the twelve apostles are found. However, as you can see from the photo below there are no more twelve apostles. Over time they have been knocked down by the wave action. One time I was there, and it so happened that the formation called the "London Bridge" came down.

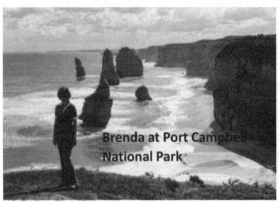
Brenda at Port Campbell National Park

The London Bridge formation

Hong Kong.
After our visit to Australia, we were off to Hong Kong which was mostly a sight-seeing stop on our way to Taiwan. While we were in Hong Kong, we took a ferry across the bay

Typical harbor scene in Hong Kong

Brenda waiting at a floating restaurant

to visit Floyd Patrick's sister who was a missionary there. We saw lots of people doing Tai Chi. Also visiting the harbor is remarkably interesting in that there are thousands of people living and making a living on house boats. Also, you cannot visit Hong Kong without having a meal on a floating restaurant. Thus, we did as you can see above.

After spending a day or two in Hong Kong we were off to Taiwan. I had appointed a distributor there some years before. One of the first things the distributor did on a subsequent visit was to arrange for me to do a slide presentation and a demo of what Compact II was all about. I remember demonstrating our software to the Mining Research & Service Organization. Our distributor had obviously canvased his customer base and had invited many potential customers there to watch my demos.

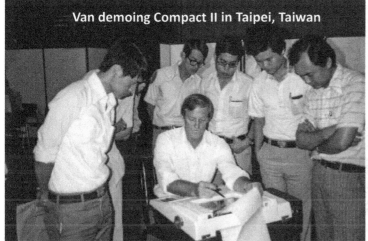
Van demoing Compact II in Taipei, Taiwan

One of the places where I demoed

We boarded a train in Taipei and headed to the other end of the island. What city we wound up in I do not remember. Then we got in a car/taxi and headed to a manufacturing plant of sorts. I got the opportunity to take a few shots along the way. I remember passing a huge duck farm. And there were literally hundreds perhaps thousands of ducks. I know that Peking duck is considered a real delicacy in the Chinese culture. Also got a shot of farmers drying the rice crop right in the middle of the highway.

A large duck farm

Drying the rice crop on a bridge

One day after work we walked the streets and came across what is known as Snake alley. There they have all kinds of weird stuff. Deer horns, dried up fetus, etc. All the stuff to make a man out of you. They have live snakes, and they will kill it and drain the blood into a small cup for you to drink. I guess this too will make a man out of you!

Man selling his wares in snake alley, Taipei

Our Taiwan rep and his son

On this my farewell trip our Taiwan distributor had booked us at a hotel close to his office. When we got to our room, we opened the door and there waiting for Brenda was the largest bouget of roses I have ever seen. There must have been a hundred if there was one. It was also while we were there, I was in our distributor's office and an earthquake hit and rattled the coffee cups and other things on the table in the conference room. Brenda was taking a bath back in the hotel room when the water in the bathtub splashed around a bit. I am not certain whether it dawned on her that she was experiencing an earthquake.

My boss, Steve Imredy told me when in Taipei to book a room at the Grand Hotel. When he was doing lots of travel for the company he worked for before (Cummins Diesel) he always stayed at the Grand Hotel. It certainly was different. I stayed there a few times while we were doing market research and until we appointed a distributor. The Grand Hotel is one of Taipei City's world-renowned landmarks, and the

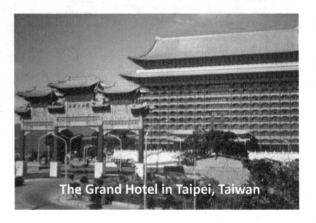

The Grand Hotel in Taipei, Taiwan

premium choice for travel accommodations or business conferences for people worldwide.

Off to Korea April 1984.

Before we left on our extended trip to the Far East, we had arranged for Jeff to meet up with us in Korea as we had scheduled to be there during Jeff's spring break at Calvin College. Thus, when we got to Korea, a day or so later Jeff arrived to join us for the rest of our trip. In addition to meeting with our distributor, we also did some sightseeing. We went to a Korean village where they put on quite a show. It seems that the locals love to play on a teeter tot.

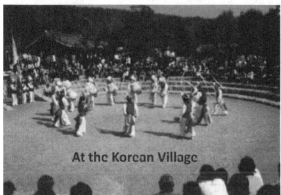
At the Korean Village

Tourist playing on a teeter tot

One of the many temples we visited

View from our Hotel

We also visited a few of the many temples in and around Seoul.

After our short visit to Korea, we flew on to Tokyo and spent a couple of days visiting our MDSI-Japan office in the Shinjuku area of Tokyo. While we were there, the secretary suggested we visit the Kyoto area, which was the former capital. After visiting a few of the many temples/shrines there, Jeff made a comment that the temples all start looking alike, which is absolutely true.

At the Imperial Palace

The Golden Temple in Kyoto

On our way home we stopped off in Honolulu, Hawaii and did some sightseeing on the island. I remember that when we got to our hotel it was Happy Hour and I got happy drinking all that sweet rum. I was glad that Brenda and Jeff were there to help me get back to my room safe and sound. One of the money-saving tips that I got from a local on one of my trips was that if I had a stopover in Honolulu a cheap way to view the island was to go to the bus transfer station at the main shopping center to get a 50-cent bus ticket to view the east side of the island and another 50-cent ticket to view the west side of the island. One could get off and on wherever you wanted. Thus, that is what we did and for $1 we got a pretty good idea what the whole island was all about.

Being entertained at our hotel in Honolulu

After visiting Honolulu, we were on our way back to Detroit. Jeff had a once in a lifetime wonderful spring break. I must say that after spending weeks in the Far East, Brenda was ready to come back home. I was happy and glad that Jeff got to see some of the world where I had been spending a lot of time.

Back in the USA

Aug 1987. Brenda and I went on a boat trip with brother Ike and Jennie to Mackinac Island. What he usually did was to pull his boat up north to the Indian River and drop his boat in (on the western side of the lower peninsular) and take it across the lower peninsular to Cheboygan. From there we went on to Mackinac. One of the main attractions is the Grand Hotel. It supposedly has the largest porch in the world. It should be noted that there are no cars on the island.

Docking Ike's boat at Mackinac Island

Van and Brenda sitting on the front porch of the Grand Hotel

Van and Brenda on Mackinac Island

This is what **Google** has to say about the Grand Hotel.

The **Grand Hotel** is a historic hotel and coastal resort on Mackinac Island, Michigan, a small island located at the eastern end of the Straits of Mackinac within Lake Huron between the state's Upper and Lower peninsulas. Constructed in the late 19th century, the facility advertises itself as having the world's largest porch. Mackinac Island National Park became the second National Park in the United States in 1875.

1988. Feb 1988, Schlumberger had a national service manager meeting in Orlando, Florida and we got to play golf at the Cypress Creek country club. I had played golf one other time in my life; thus, I was not particularly good at it. But that did not make a whole lot of difference because we were there just to get to know each other, etc. They had a beer cart driving around the place. I do not think there was a whole lot of serious golf being played. It does look like Van is ready for the PGA tour.

Van at Golf

Van and other Applicon Mgr.

Van celebrating his 20th anniversary with the Company.

On June 3, 1988, Schlumberger organized a party to honor my twentieth anniversary with the company. It was twenty years that month since Chuck Hutchins had hired me for his small team at Comshare. I was now the only founding employee still with the company. A small crowd gathered in the glass domed cafeteria to salute me, and the company managers presented me with a plaque and a Rolex watch.

VP of HR awarded me my 20-year pin

John Wallace presenting me with a 20-year plaque

Van is awarded a Rolex watch

Van looks like one happy guy!

Mid-summer (July) we had a District 121 informal MDSI/Applicon party at our house on Indianola. Mike Hartke was the district manager, Al Larkin the district sales manager, and I was the district technical manager. It was informal as you can see from the photo, and everyone had a good time. In the photo is Frank Rose, Billy Bishop, Bob Guy, Wes Russell, Terry Myers, Chuck Cooper, Al Larkin, and Mike Hartke relaxing in my back yard.

District 121 informal mtg at Van's house

Pacific Northwest trip. Summer of 1988

Brenda and I took a much needed vacation to the Pacific Northwest. We flew into Seattle and rented a car. Our first trip was to drive around the Olympic peninsula which was quite a trip. There I witnessed for the first time what clearcutting the forest meant. It looked at times like a war was fought there. We eventually met Wes Russell an MDSI AE, who had now moved from Ann Arbor back to Seattle. He showed us around the various sights. One of the sights and places you must visit is the Public Market Center, and while your there you must watch them tossing large fish around. It is remarkably interesting to watch. We caught a ferry and stayed overnight on one of the islands in Puget Sound. While we were in /Seattle, I believe I had salmon for dinner 4 out of the 5 nights. I love salmon. We eventually made our way to British Colombia. We really enjoyed our time in British Columbia, and specially Vancouver. They get a lot of rain and thus everything was very green. It is quite British like in that they even have double decker buses. While we were in the area we visited the famous Butchart Gardens, a lush, 55-acre property, It has **five main gardens**, stunning fountains, intriguing sculptures, trickling streams and explodes with wave upon wave of color for much of the year. Vancouver has a large Chinatown area which is also interesting to visit. After our tour when I turned in the rental car a $400 bill was staring me in the face. I thought I had asked for unlimited miles, but I had not. I wrote a 4-page letter trying to explain the situation but to no avail. An expensive lesson!

The double decker buses lining up for tourist   Brenda at Butchart Garden

Wes Russell told us where the Snoqualmie waterfall was located and thus, we went there.

This particular trip we took one of the many ferries that travel between the from Seattle to one of the many islands in Puget Sound and stayed on one of the San Juan Islands.

Van and Brenda at Snoqualmie falls

The Public Market Center in Seattle

A typical ferry boat travelling the Puget Sound

Celebrating my 50th birthday

Oct of 1988, I celebrated my 50th birthday. Some of my family from Grand Rapids drove

Cora, Jeff, Sandy Guy, Dave Marsman and Ike

Van being teased by Shari Guy

to our house at strawberry Lake to help me celebrate. Our next-door neighbors, the Guys also came over. Shari Guy was quite the tease calling me an old man.

March 24, 1989. Bing.com: The Exxon Valdez, a 987-foot tanker grounded on Alaska's Bligh Reef at midnight on March 24, 1989, spewing nearly 11 million gallons of oil into the rich fishing waters of Prince William Sound. Currents and storms carried the crude over 1200 miles of Alaska coastline. The Exxon Valdez Oil Spill Trustee Council estimates the spill killed a quarter million seabirds, 2,800 sea otters, 300 harbor seals, 250 bald eagles, up to 22 killer whales and billions of fish eggs. It took years for the fish to rebound following the spill, and oil can still be found under the surface of some beaches in Prince William Sound. COS Gazette 9/14/2022. Cleanup alone cost in the region of **US $2.5 billion** and total costs (including fines, penalties, and claims settlements) have at times been estimated at as much as US $7 billion.

Hung up in Paris-July 1989

On one of my overseas trips, I was travelling with a relatively new employee, Rod Nehring (a BYU graduate from one of the best CAD/CAM programs in the nation). He was hired as an Applicon employee (but the Schlumberger people had not yet merged MDSI and Applicon into one company). I was travelling to **MDSI-Germany** in preparation for several MDSI people (Pete Campbell, Gordon Sweet, etc.) to follow me later the following week. Well, Rod and I got to the **Frankfurt am Main Airport** in Frankfurt, Germany Saturday afternoon and checked into the nearby hotel close to our office. When we got to the hotel it was quite common upon check in to hand over your passport to the desk clerk. What they did with it I do not really know. Thus, Rod and I handed over our passports upon checking in and went to our rooms. After unpacking a bit, Rod called me, and he mentioned that he wanted to go sightseeing in **Heidelberg**. I said OK let us meet downstairs and we'll walk over to the office and pick up the company car. When we got downstairs the desk clerk kind of slid our passports to each of us as we walked to the front desk. We got into the company car and drove to Heidelberg. Well, our meetings at MDSI-Germany went off as scheduled and I was on the way to Vienna, Austria. Rod was to deliver a paper he had written to some kind of CAD society in Munich as well as the Applicon office in Munich. After Rod Nehring delivered his paper, he would simply fly back home to Detroit. After my meetings in Vienna, I and the MDSI people who were travelling with me went on to our office in Zurich, Switzerland. After our Zurich meetings we traveled on to our office in Paris, France. All the meetings went off as scheduled and now it is Saturday morning and all of the Ann Arbor based personnel are now on the way to **Charles DE Gaulle** airport ready to go home. Well, here is Van, an experienced International Seasoned Traveler, leading the gang to the Security area and I handed over my passport. I am standing there waiting what seemed like 10 minutes (but it was only a minute or two) and I asked the Security person what is the problem or something to that effect. He turned the passport around to show me and he said, **THIS IS NOT YOU!** Obviously, I knew what had happened when he showed me the passport that I had given him. When Rod and I went downstairs in the hotel and the desk clerk handed our passports back to us they were switched then and there and we never looked at them, we simply stuck them into our pockets. What is kind of puzzling about all of this is that Rod never called the various MDSI offices that I was visiting, thus I was not aware of the potential problem that was waiting for me when I got ready to go home. When Rod got ready to go home it was in the middle of the week and he had time to go to the U.S. Consulate in Munich to explain what happened and get a temporary passport. Why he did not let me know that I had his passport is a mystery to this day.

Well back to me on a Saturday morning at Charles De Gaulle airport. All the MDSI personnel that were travelling with me saw me standing there and they had no problem going thru security. They were getting their boarding pass, checking-in, etc., and **I AM NOT**! They took me down to the main security/custom office and there I tried to explain what had happened. I called Brenda back in Ann Arbor, I think it was about 4 or 5 in the morning to explain the fact that I might not be coming home today. I had her give me the number on my old, expired passport and asked her to bring it to the Detroit airport. If I had known that I had the wrong passport I could have gone to the U.S. Consulate in Vienna, Zurich, or Paris, but here it was now Sat afternoon and it is closed until Monday morning. I then called **Dick Wood**, MDSI legal attorney and he talked to

Custom/Security people to try to convince them that I was an **A OK fellow**. We also talked to the **NW Airline** people, and they finally got me on the plane back to Detroit. When I got to Detroit, I went to the baggage claim and got my baggage. In the baggage claim area, there was a steel roll-up curtain that I could force a small opening by pulling the curtain apart and Brenda being on the other side passed me my expired passport. When I got to the customs area, they did not like what they saw, and I tried to explain to them what had happened, and they wrote me up for travelling without a valid U.S. passport and fined me $80. I tried writing it off on my expense report, but my boss would not let me.

1989.

The summer of 1989 Brenda's mother came up to Michigan and spent some time with us. We traveled up north and eventually wound up taking the ferry across to Mackinac Island. The place to visit and relax is the Grand Hotel. Mackinac Island is also known for its saltwater taffy. We always enjoyed going up North as we would say even if it was only in the lower peninsular. If possible, we would stop off at Charlevoix and walk around the harbor which always had lots of interesting yachts, etc.

Brenda and her mother

A "Cigar Boat" in Charlevoix harbor

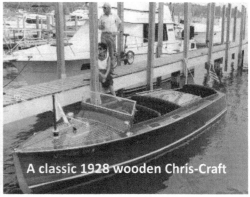
A classic 1928 wooden Chris-Craft

We would also try to stop off at the Bluebird Inn in Leland. We kind of discovered this restaurant accidentally and found it enjoyable. The Bluebird is a family owned and operated Restaurant and Tavern, founded in 1927 at this same location along the banks of the Leland River. They specialize in fresh Lake Michigan Whitefish, Perch, Walleye, and Smelt, as well as the finest Prime Rib, steaks, etc.

Oct 1989. Hurricane Andrew hit Florida in 1990. Up till then it was the worst hurricane ever to hit Florida. Perhaps still is. It left one million people homeless. Most of these problems were blamed on the El Nina effect, which was caused by the warming of the water in the Pacific Ocean.

Technical Conference at Schlumberger world HQ in Paris.
Oct 1989. Robin Kerr asked me and Rod Nehring to schedule a Technical Conference to be held at the world headquarters of Schlumberger in Paris with the MDSI and Applicon Application Engineers presenting their unique technical application that they developed for one of their customers. Rod and I got to play "God" to select the best among the best. Most of the AE's that were chosen to present their papers also took their wives. The company did not pay for the airfare for their wives. I put together the agenda and a package or what to do in Paris on your free time, etc. The women were pretty much on their own as to how to spend their time. Brenda having been there a few times showed a lot of the women how to work the metro system, how to go to the Louvre Museum, Notre Dame, etc. One of the nights we were there we had arranged to take the entire group to a dinner river cruise on the Seine River. I also celebrated my 51st birthday during the cruise.

The whole purpose of the trip to Schlumberger world headquarters was to reward both the Applicon AE's as well as the MDSI AE's for all their hard work and dedication. Below you see some of the AE's present and discussing their unique and customized application that they put together to solve customer problems.

Schlumberger World HQs in Paris

Van being presented with a B-day cake on the Seine R. in Paris

One of the German AE's demoing his program

All of the folks that were there obviously did as much sightseeing as they could. Some went to the Louvre Museum, etc. One of the things you have to watch out for is all the Nigerian street

Illegal street vendors are everywhere in Paris

hawkers selling their merchandise. They are not allowed to do this so when policemen are present, they roll up the towel and get the heck out of there.

Brenda and Van's visit to Holland Oct 1989.

Later that same trip Brenda and I went to visit some of my relatives in Holland. One was Case Slager who owns a butcher shop in St. Anneland. St. Anneland is where my dad was born and raised. When we visited with Case Slager, he was about to retire and the business being a family operated business would be turned over to the son on the left of the photo. We really enjoyed our Sunday night dinner. Stein Slager, Case's wife, baked me a cake for my 51st birthday.

Stein Slager baked a 51st B-day

Having dinner at Case Slagers in St. Anneland

As you can see in the photo below they still sell wooden shoes. These are some of the fancier ones in that they are painted. For everyday use they are not necessarily painted. The photo in the middle is of a couple of houses in St. Anneland that were built in 1694 and 1695. The windmill photo is of a scaled model of a windmill in the area. I think it is quite nice. I had a windmill in our yard on Indianola that my dad built for me. I did not take it with me when we moved to Colorado Springs, but when Brenda and I went back to visit the Ann arbor area and we stopped in at our old house, the windmill was still in the yard.

Lots of wooden shoes

Old houses

Scale model windmill

Colorado 1989.

The summer of 1989, we wound up going to Colorado to see Jeff and his family and Brenda's mother must have been in Colorado too, because the three of us took the steam driven narrow-gauge R.R. out of Durango and took it to Silverton.

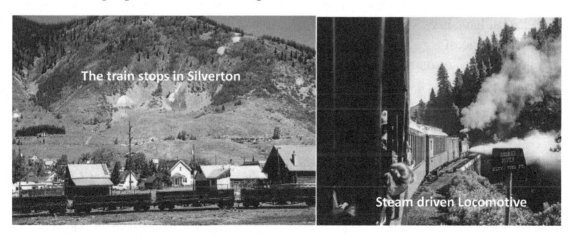

The train stops in Silverton

Steam driven Locomotive

Four Generations of Van Bemdens Dec 1989.

Around Christmas in 1989, Jeff and Karen came back to Michigan to spend time with both families and show off their firstborn daughter, Stephanie. They came over to our house on Indianola and it so happened that my mother and dad were also over. Thus, I have a photo of 4 generations of Van Bemdens.

Dad, Van, Jeff and Stephanie

Three Van Bemden couples

Brenda, Van and Stephanie

Brenda and Stephanie

It looks very much like Brenda and I were very proud grandparents.

That same Christmas all the DeJongs that were in town were invited to come over to our house. I must have been showing some of my slides because I noticed in the photo that there are a couple of trays of slides sitting on the floor. The Guys who lived next door also came over to see our first grandchild.

The DeJongs came to see Stephanie

The Guys looking Stephanie over

That Christmas I must have been ambitious, since there were a lot of Christmas lights outdoors. I strung a few luminaries along the driveway that we had bought in Texas a year or so earlier. That Christmas was kind of special and everyone enjoyed Jeff and Karen's visit back to Ann Arbor.

The Christmas lights at the Van Bemdens

Brenda and Karen opening Christmas presents

Jeff, Stephanie and Karen

One of the things I did whenever I traveled overseas was to send a postcard from where I was to Brenda, my mother and Brenda's mother. She then posted it on the Frig in the kitchen. Years later, my mother gave all the postcards that I had sent her over the years back to me. I have several shoe boxes full of postcards. I believe Brenda's mother did the same thing. Another project that I had undertaken was to remodel the kitchen and put an island in the center. I also hung some wallpaper, because it was "Hospital White" and I had to dull it down a bit.

Frig full of postcards

Our remodeled kitchen

This family photo was taken by Karl Van Oost. Karl worked with Ike and my dad at Imperial Metal Products. He also attended the same church as we did. One of Karl's hobbies was photography, and he had a studio in his basement where he did his photography work. Unfortunately, I do not know the year it was taken.

The Van Bemden clan in G.R.

Several times when I was over in Europe, I had the opportunity to spend the weekend in The Netherlands visiting my relatives and doing some sightseeing. One time when I was staying with my cousin Joe in Muiden, I had the opportunity to visit the Muiderslot Castle. The Muiderslot Castle has guarded the mouth of the river Vecht since 1280. The castle still looks pretty much the same today as it did when they first

The harbor at Muiden and the Muiden Castle in the background

built it. Today the Muiderslot Castle is a much-visited

Duomo Cathedral

national museum. The Muiderslot castle, is one of the oldest in The Netherlands, a true medieval castle surrounded by a moat with the only entrance being a liftable bridge. The building was commissioned by Count Floris V in 1280, then restored to its former glory from 1370 and named an official Rijksmuseum since 1878. The Muiderslot castle has also been placed on the UNESCO World Heritage List.

In the spring of 1990, I was asked to go to Milan, Italy to work with our newly appointed sales engineer to do some demos in Northern Italy. I had been in northern Italy several times before, but I never had a free weekend. This time I did, and the sales engineer showed me around. I remember going to see the huge Duomo Cathedral in Milan where you actually get to walk on the roof, which I did. Google.com: The Milano's Duomo is the largest and most elaborate Gothic building in Italy made of pink-hued white marble from a dedicated quarry, it is 157 meters in length and 108.5 meters high at the top of the main spire, where rests the glistening

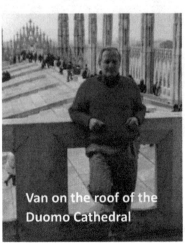
Van on the roof of the Duomo Cathedral

golden statue of the Madonnina, an evocative symbol much-loved both by all Milanese. Incredibly detailed!

This same trip management back in Ann Arbor asked if I would go on to Austria since I was already in Europe. So, after I finished my Italy demos, I was off to Vienna, Austria. Again, I had an opportunity to do some sight-seeing. Spring was in the air. I cannot get over the fact that in lots of European it seems the people love flowers. The green house structure reminds me of a similar structure in England.

Botanical Gardens at the Palace grounds

Lots of flowers at the open-air market

Dick Campbell from UCC, who was one of our main competitors in the Texas came to work for us when Ronnie Barnes was hired. Dick wrote numerous routines for UCC APT based systems when they were competing against us. He was a very smart individual, and noticeably quiet. He had a rudimentary understanding of about a dozen languages.

One time I remember arriving in Melbourne Australia and I overheard someone say something to the effect that person (meaning me) has more leather on him then a cow. I had a leather jacket, a leather briefcase, and one of my suitcases was leather.

One time when Brenda and I were waiting for our luggage to arrive at the DFW airport we ran into our new District manager for the Dallas area and his wife. They were also waiting for luggage to arrive on the same carousel as we were. She had more expensive luggage then you could shake a stick at. That was back in the day when the company was making lots of money and I guess we must have been paying Dick very well.

March 16, 1991 Dad passed away.

Brenda and I were in Grand Rapids because Dad was in the hospital and he was close to dying. I was holding his hand, Brenda and Mom were sitting down next to his bed when he passed away.

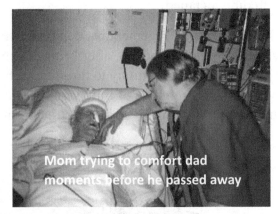

Mom trying to comfort dad moments before he passed away

Back to Ann Arbor and the salt mines. Pierre Boderau must have been in the states and whenever an international person is in Ann Arbor chances are particularly good that he/she would wind up at our house either to relax and or be taken out to dinner. Maybe Pierre came to Ann Arbor because he heard that Van's yard was in bloom.

Lots of flowers in bloom in our backyard

Brenda and Pierre Boderau

Brenda held a shower for Shari Guy at our house. I took a few pictures just to show anyone that a good time was had by all.

Shari and her grandmother

Shari Guy's shower at our house

Oct 1991

Paul and Van

The fall of 1991 I found myself in the New England area. My friend Paul Breniser who lived in that area invited me to stay for the weekend, which I did. Paul and I visited Mt. Washington, rode the cog railroad to the top of Mt. Washington and visited the White National Forest.

The Mt. Washington cog R.R.

White Mtn Nat'l forest

The Mount Washington Hotel

We also drove past the largest wooden hotel in the world. Mt. Washington Hotel. It is one of the last surviving grand hotels in the White Mountains in New Hampshire.

1991 Dec. The Van Bemden clan had a Christmas party at my sister Wilma's house. Most of the local Grand Rapids people were there and I noticed in one of the photos that my brother Adrian and Linda as well as Butch (The Florida gang) were also in attendance.

Scott, Dave, Joe, Carol, Wilma and Mom

Mike, Sally, Brenda and Carol

Adrian, Barb, Wilma, Butch, Eric and Harry

Joe, Ike with one of his grandkids and Carol

Mom and Lena DeJagger

Lots of trilliums!

1992 – 4.

The spring of 1992, my folks must have visited us since I have a photo of Mom and Lena DeJagger (my cousin from the Nederlands) looking into the courtyard in front of my house. My mother loved flowers almost as much as Brenda and I do.

Our first Grandson was born. Aug 5, 1992.
Aug 5, 1992, our first and only grandson Paul Isaac Van Bemden was born.

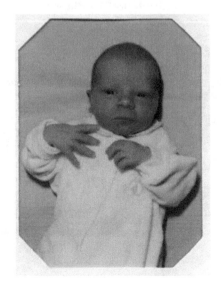

Christmas that year (1992) we wound up going to Colorado Springs to visit Jeff and Karen and see the 2 grand kids. The house that Jeff lived in at that time had an indoor hot tub, which we enjoyed using.

Van and Brenda with Stephanie and Paul

Stephanie and Paul

April 17, 1993, Brenda and I decided that we should be baptized, thus that Sunday morning at the Wesleyan Church in Brighton MI where we attended, we were baptized by full immersion. The Dieblers were Bible translators with the Wycliff organization and stationed mostly in New Guinea. We know the Dieblers from our days in the Ann Arbor CRC. Ellis was getting his PHD at the UM and attended the CRC church in Ann Arbor. Ellis made a presentation at the Wesleyan church about his work in New Guinea.

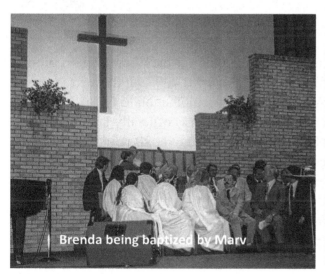

Brenda being baptized by Marv

Ellis and Catherine Diebler

The summer of 1993, Yoshi Taguchi, his wife, and daughter came over to the USA. He spent some time at our house where he had been many times before. I even took the time to teach Yoshi how to waterski on Strawberry Lake.

Yoshi Taguchi, his wife and daughter

Yoshi waterskiing for the very first time

The summer of 1993 we once again found ourselves in Colorado Springs visiting Jeff. This was when he was living on Galway. Note his Jensen-Healey car in the garage. Karen calls it "his silly car." The other photo shows Brenda watching (probably babysitting) grandkids on the swing set that Jeff built.

Van, Brenda, Stephanie and Paul

Stephanie, Paul and Brenda

Van is terminated Dec 1993.

In the fall of 1992, there were still 300 employees working for the "Applicon division of Schlumberger at the Plymouth Road offices of the former MDSI". But the next year, Schlumberger sold what was left of its MDSI/Applicon combination to Gores Enterprise. This led to another round of layoffs, which included me. I was officially laid off on December 1, 1993. I was one of the blessed one in that I had over 20 years of seniority and could tap in on Schlumberger retirement benefits and retirees' health insurance. Many that were let go obviously could not. It was my understanding that one of the conditions that Schlumberger enforced in the Gores Enterprise termination process was that the personnel that were getting terminated were to be terminated with Schlumberger terms and conditions. That also meant that the terminated employees got a month's pay for every year they were employed and that they supplied computers and printers to help the laid off employees work on their resumes. It was rumored that Gores Enterprise paid pennies on the dollar to acquire MDSI/Applicon. I really do not know whether that was true or not. All I know is that they spun it down and MDSI no longer existed.

I knew that this was coming because Schlumberger had no idea how to run a computer software company. They never made a dime on buying us and started to lose money from day one. Bruce Nourse said a few years earlier the painful changes in upper management, with Chuck Hutchins and Mike Long gone and new VPs from outside the company ushered in a new era at MDSI. Says Bruce," A whole bunch of people came in who had not been there from the beginning. They are now the top management, but they did not know the history of the company, they did not know the culture of the company."

Thus, I now had to start looking for a job. I had always thought that I would work until I was 62 and call it a day. However, I was only 55 when this happened, so I had a few years to go. The first place I thought of was Brighton NC and Jack Clausnitzer. Brighton NC was customer #2 because Ken Stephanz was a good friend of the man who signed our contract at Naval Ordinance in Louisville, Kentucky and Ken assigned them as customer #1. Jack offered me a job and I immediately started programming his NC machines.

1994

The summer of 1994 the family had a reunion at Cora's house. The photo on the left has the 3 oldest Van Bemden boys along with Dave Marsman. Maria must have been in G.R. also since the photo on the right has little Cameron in it.

Dave Marsman, Ike, Van and Joe

Lena, Cameron, Cora, Carol and Jennie is standing in doorway

September of 1994 my cousin Izaak Boot and his wife Nellie along with Bram and Montje came over to the US and stayed a few days with us. I remember taking them over to the Detroit Zoo and just showing them various interesting places around Ann Arbor.

Montje, Bram, Izaak and Nellie Boot

The gang at the Detroit Zoo

Nov, 1994, Brenda's lady friends at the Ann Arbor CRC church gave Brenda a surprise 50th Birthday party. From the photo above we were still attending the Ann Arbor CRC while living on Indianola. I don't know exactly when we stopped going to the CRC church in Ann Arbor, but somewhere around this time frame we started to attend the Wesleyan church in Brighton.

Ruth Mieras, Donna Van Kirk and Brenda

Brenda, Chloris Patrick, Jo Ludema and Norma Verhey

Stephanie and Paul

Stephanie and Brenda

1994. Jeff must have been back in town because I have photos of Stephanie and Paul at our house on Indianola celebrating Stephanie birthday.

Stephanie, Paul, Bill and Marilyn DeJong

Paul, Stephanie, Karen and Brenda

The DeJongs were also at our house to participate in celebrating Stephanie birthday. After celebrating Stephanie birthday and the partying was over and everything was said and done, it appears that there were a couple of happy kids. Stephanie and Paul loved sitting in Grandpa's favorite chair.

Stephanie and Paul

July 1995. The summer of 1995 we again must have traveled to Colorado. Brenda's mother was also in Colorado Springs. How she got there I do not remember, maybe Brenda and I went to pick her up and brought her to Colorado Springs. I think she was coming to Colorado with here church group, and they generally stayed in South Fork, CO for a week or more. She made it to Jeff's house and played with her great grand kids.

Paul getting ready to go down the slide

Stephanie, Susan and Great Grandma Lillian Parker

1995

The fall of 1995, Brenda and Diane Zerby flew out to Irvine, California to help setup an office for one small firm that she did the accounting for in Ann Arbor. Diane was a very hard worker and she and Brenda were good friends. Brenda saw Tom and Sandy Ingraham and Sharon Weeden during her time in CA.

Brenda and one of the California people

Dianne Derby, Brenda

1995

The winter of 1995, I was at Jeff's house in Colorado Springs. My brother Pete was also there, and we went skiing with Jeff at I believe Keystone Ski Resort.

Pete, Susan, Van, Karen and Paul

Jeff, Pete and Van Skiing at Keystone

Stephanie driving the toy car

We spent Christmas there and obviously we had to spoil the grand kids. While we were there, Brenda, Stephanie and I walked down to the local park. There I taught Stephanie

Stephanie learning how to ride her bike

how to ride her bike that she got for Christmas.

Paul with his new train. Quite a layout!

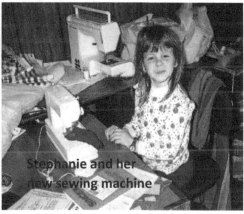
Stephanie and her new sewing machine

1996 – 2.

The winter of 95-96, Jeff was teaching Stephanie and Paul how to snow ski. I do not remember exactly where we were, but I believe it might have been Copper Mountain. Jeff taught his kids early in life how to snow ski. I think he actually taught Stephanie the previous winter.

Stephanie skiing

Paul and Stephanie

That same year in early spring I remember that I along with Paul's help made a spool hanger for Karen to hang all of her different spools of thread on. I believe she still has it. You can really see Paul's red hair in this photo.

Van and Paul making a spool rack

Stephanie and Susan caulking up the driveway

Michael and Denise Parker's wedding June, 1996.

June of 1996 we (meaning Van, Brenda, Jeff, Karen, Stephanie, Paul, and Susan) all drove down to Round Rock, Texas to attend Micheal's wedding. We bedded down in one of the hotels along the highway that had a swimming pool so the grandkids could go swimming. I remember that it was ridiculously hot! Everyone enjoyed a dip in the pool at our motel the afternoon before the wedding. If I am not mistaken, I believe Brenda and I also went swimming but I didn't take any photos of us.

Jeff and all of our grandkids in the motel swimming pool

I think the kids really liked being dressed up to attend Michael and Denise Parker's wedding. After the ceremony we all went down to the reception and watched Michael and his new bride cut the cake, etc. There was even a little bit of dancing going on. Michael came along to say hello to his nieces and nephew.

226

Drinking the Champagne

Cutting the cake

Michael saying hello to our grandkids

As you can see from the photos below a fun time was had by all. Even the Great Grandparents (Brenda's mother and Romelle's mother) were enjoying themselves.

Brenda and the grandkids

Paul, Brenda, Stephanie, Lillian Parker and Romelle's mother

Our visit to Sea World in San Antonio, TX.

The following day or so we must have gone on to Sea World in San Antonio, TX. which again everyone thoroughly enjoyed, especially the killer whale act. The killer whale beached himself to get a fish treat. In the following act we saw a walrus and a seal on the platform waiting to be fed a fish or two. I don't know how long it takes for the trainers to get the animals to do the various acts, but I know that the audience loved it.

A killer whale getting a fish treat

A Walrus and a seal being fed a fish

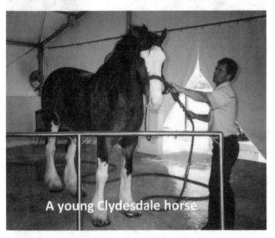
A young Clydesdale horse

While we were at Sea World, we also saw a worker washing down one of the Clydesdale horses. This one being washed is a young one, but it's a Clydesdale. The mature and full-grown ones are the ones that are used in the Budweiser's super bowl commercials. You cannot really realize how big these horses are until you see one in person.

After attending Michael and Denise Parker's wedding in Round Rock, TX and our day at Sea World in San Antonio, we drove back to Colorado Springs and enjoyed a nice dinner at one of the local restaurants.

Enjoying a nice dinner

Went to work at Brighton NC. Dec 1994.

After I got laid off at MDSI/Applicon, I drove over to Brighton NC and talked to Jack Clausnitzer the owner, and discussed what had just happened. He hired me on to not only do his programming of the NC machines, but also to bid on various jobs. Jack (MDSI customer #2) in Brighton, MI, had worked with Chuck at Buhr Machine tool and left to start Brighton NC with one NC lathe. (I believe it was an American 3220 Lathe) in an old run-down barn near Pickney. I remember doing the **Compact** demo there with Chuck when we were still part of **Comshare**. We had the ASR33 in the bathroom where we wrote the program and processed it there because the bathroom had a telephone installed. When I went to work for Brighton NC I was the primary programmer there and supplied programs for all of the NC Machines via a **Series I** programming system that they purchased from MDSI. One of the competitive advantages that Brighton NC had was the fact that we did the entire job in that we did the product development, fixtures, and tooling.

In order for me to program the part shown below, I wound up purchasing a software package (because Compact II was not particularly good for this type of machining) from one of Autodesk's subsidiaries were Jeff Sannes who at one time had work for me at MDSI, but later on he went back to this subsidiary. This particular S/W package that I purchased had excellent 3D machining capabilities

A huge Clevis that I programed on the OM4 at Brighton NC

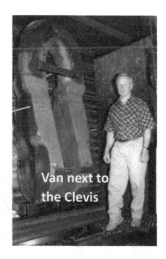

Van next to the Clevis

As a point of interest, after Chuck left MDSI, he and Bruce developed a software package that could be dropped in a generic personal computer called Open CNC. One of the first potential customers they called on was Brighton NC. Jack was willing to install their system but was not one for signing his life away on various forms; to him a handshake was as good as or better than a written contract. Chuck would have none of it; he wanted a written contract. Thus, it was a no-go for Chuck and Bruce's new CNC control business with Brighton NC machine shop.

I worked there for several years and then one Thanksgiving I went off to Grand Rapids to spend Thanksgiving with my family and decided to stay there for the rest of the weekend.

When I got back to work the following Monday, Jack asked me where I was Friday. I told him I was in Grand Rapids spending Thanksgiving with my family. He said that they worked last Friday. I told him that I had discussed the fact that I wanted to stay in Grand Rapids for the weekend with Art (the shop foreman) and that I had my tracks covered in that Art had proven tapes for all the jobs that were scheduled to run. That apparently was not good enough for Jack. (Having worked at MDSI for over 20 years I was used to a lot of vacation time). I decided that we should probably call it a day and left Brighton NC.

Focus Hope in Detroit. 1995

Shortly after leaving **Brighton NC,** I went to work for **Focus Hope** in the inner city of Detroit. Google.com: **Focus Hope** is a nationally recognized civil and human rights organization founded in 1968, after the Detroit riots, by Father William T. Cunningham and Eleanor M. Josaitis. Together, they adopted the following mission: "recognizing the dignity and beauty of every person, we pledge intelligent and practical action to overcome racism, poverty, and injustice." Focus Hope has dramatically transformed thousands of lives through its three key areas of focus: food, careers, and community. **Focus Hope** has an extraordinary record of success in working with underserved and marginalized members of the Detroit/southeast Michigan community. They offer accessible, high-quality work readiness, pre-apprenticeship, and apprenticeship programs in a range of in-demand career fields.

When I went to work for them as the first shift **NC Dept. Supervisor**, they had a large NC machine department which did work mostly for the Big Three auto manufacturers. The big three auto manufacturers also provided a plant manager on a rolling basis; every 6 months or so another plant manager from one of the big three would take over. Many of the larger NC Machine Tool Manufacturers had their latest NC machines in our plant. The machines were operated by a number of trainees from the inner city. They would operate the assigned NC machine for 6 hours and then they would go to the classroom for a couple of hours and learn how to read a blueprint, read a micrometer or a dial indicator,

The Plymouth Acclaim that I totaled

learn some shop math, shop theory, communications, etc.

One morning as I was driving to work, I hit a patch of "black ice" and Brenda's Plymouth Acclaim went into a spin. Just nicked the guardrail and went down backwards into the ditch. Saw my whole life pass in front of me in a matter of seconds. All I could think of was me hitting the guardrail and the guardrail going in one side of the car and coming out the other. Which is exactly what happened to my brother Joe when he was taking his daughter Diane to piano lessons Nov 21,1978. Since the whole body was torqued, I decided that I would sell it. We sold it to my nephew Scott Marsman's mother-in-law. She drove it for quite some time before she finally got rid of it.

This was a remarkably interesting job in that I was working with the latest NC Machines and also helping young African Americans learn a trade. I would normally come in early to see what lay in store for the day and I would always overlap with the 2nd shift foreman. One day one of my machine operators left without notifying me and did not come back for several hours. When he returned, I asked him where he had been, and he told me that he had to go home to see his mother about something. Well, I told him that the next time this happens, and he does not notify me (after all we had production to get out!) I would deduct him for the time that he was missing. He mentioned that you can deduct the whole day and he took a roll of money out of his pocket. He had taken off to what I believe to this day was a drug drop off.

Anyway, that afternoon he hung around while all the rest of the operators went off to class. I did my usual overlap with the 2nd shift foreman and I was ready to drive home. I walked out the front door of the plant and to my surprise here was this operator sitting on the trunk of a brand-new **Chevy Impala** in front of the plant waiting for me to come out. I knew we were paying him $5.00/hr. and here he was driving around in a brand-new Chevy Impala. I continued to walk to the fenced-in parking lot and told the guard that I believed I was being stalked and I did not like it! I told him I want to be taken to the head of security. After I relayed what had transpired, the head of security took me over to the plant manager's office where we discussed the situation. After some discussion, the plant manager called the **Michigan State Police**. The Michigan State Police came to our plant and escorted me to I94. I never returned to Focus Hope in spite of the fact that the plant manager wanted me to return since they were going to terminate this person. It turned out that this person was dealing drugs! They attempted to talk me into staying on, but I told them that life is too precious and short to be threatened by some intercity gangster to whom life is worthless.

Back to Applicon as a Consultant. 1996

Shortly after leaving **Focus Hope**, **Applicon** was running **HELP WANTED ads** in the Ann Arbor Newspaper looking for someone that knew a little bit about tools (end mills, drills, taps, etc.). I called the number and got an interview and a job offer as a consultant working with **Ove Schuett.** Thus, after an absence of several years, I came back to work at Applicon after they picked up an Inventory/Tool Assembly package that was developed in Germany. Ove Schuet (a former German salesman who had immigrated to the US) was selling this tooling package and hired me as a consultant to demo it, train customers in the use of it, etc.

It was a neat tooling assembly package and Ove sold it to a number of clients. He and I were the only ones that knew anything about it and how it worked, the benefit of using it, etc. I put in lots of hours training the customers, making demo programs, etc.

Mazda 929

One time when Ove came to our house on Indianola to pick me up to go do a demo, he noticed my Mazda 929 in the garage. However, I had taken the 929 badges off the trunk so one really had to be into cars to determine what kind of car it was. He really liked the looks of it, etc. When I told him it was a Mazda 929, he was kind of surprised. Mazda builds a good car but their marketing was not up to snuff. Toyota had built a luxury model but broke the model off and created a separate brand, namely Lexus. Mazda should have done the same thing. They had a 323, 626, 929.

By this time Rusty Wigal, who at one time had worked for me, was the technical manager. I was working as a contractor and putting in lots of hours. Then they decided to hire me back but the offer they made me was kind of low. I told him I would have to go home and think about it and discuss it with Brenda and I would come back Monday and let him know whether I would accept it or not. I knew I was not, but I did not want to give him the satisfaction of letting him know then and there. That day was the end of my PAID work career. I finally threw in the towel and retired for good and decided to move to Colorado Springs to spoil the grand kids!

Jeff's visit the Summer of 1997

Jeff and his family came to visit us the summer of 1997. I believe he had borrowed his friends RV (a small Toyota RV). He must have thrown some of the kid's bikes in because I taught Paul how to ride his bike in the front yard of our house on Indianola. He went round and round the windmill island in the front yard and eventually got the hang of it. All of them had a good time at Strawberry Lake swimming and tubing behind the boat.

Paul riding his bike

Stephanie and Paul enjoying the water

Karen and Paul on the tube

While they were in town, I took them fishing at the lake where Dave Taylor lived. The lake was an old gravel pit that was converted to a lake and Dave Taylor had a permanent ski course set up there. That is where Billy Bishop and I went many times to run the ski course. At this stage in the grandkid's lives, it really did not matter how big the fish were. It was just exciting to catch one.

Stephanie caught one

Susan caught one

Paul caught one

Grandkids in front of the fireplace

Van teaching Paul how to ride a bike

While Jeff and his family were there the girls got to play dress up with Brenda and posed

Brenda and the girls playing dress up

for the photo that I took. I believe that Stephanie has Aunt LePearl's fox or mink stole on. These stoles used to be quite popular, but that was many years ago. I think everyone had high heels shoes on. You can see that they were a little big for Susan. Stephanie even had a fan that I believe I got in Japan on one of my trips there.

The fall of 1997 Brenda and I went to Colorado Springs to spend some time with Jeff's family. While we were there, we looked for a house in the northwest part of Colorado Springs. We did not want to look at houses in the other part of town because we would be defeating the purpose of moving to COS. After working with a real estate firm, we still had not found what we were looking for. Then one Sunday afternoon Jeff took us around the Peregrine neighborhood, and we actually found a house that might do. Thus, we contacted the real estate people that we had been working with and they set up an appointment for us to look at the house we were now interested in. We actually looked at it three times. The third time the real estate people did not know about. We drove to the neighborhood where the house that we were interested in and sat alongside of the road to see what kind of traffic, noise, etc. we would be subject to. We actually met the owner of the house, Mrs. Hall, who was moving back to California. During our trip to Colorado Springs, we bought the house on Edgerton Court that we looked at 3 times. Moving to Colorado Springs was an easy move since Jeff was already living there and he had all of the grand kids which was our duty/task to spoil them.

Our new house at 8025 Edgerton Ct. COS

Back view of our new house

234

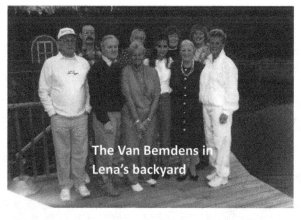

The Van Bemdens in Lena's backyard

Saturday, Nov 22, 1997, I must have been in Grand Rapids since this is a photo of all of the Van Bemdens that were in GR taken in Lena's backyard. L to R: Joe, Butch, Van, Lena, Ike, Jaci, Cora, Mom, Jeni and Wilma.

Visited Holland with my Mother.

Back in Ann Arbor we started to work on selling our house on Indianola. Later that fall, I traveled with my mother and Aunt Connie back to Holland. We enjoyed our time there. While I was in the Nederlands, Brenda, and Debbie Barker (a friend who was also a real estate agent) tried to sell our house on Indianola by owner. They were not successful and subsequently we turned it over to a realtor in the church we were attending.

Izaak and Nellie Boot, Aunt Connie, Izaak Boot and Van

Here are a couple of photos that were taken when Aunt Connie, Mom, and I were in the old country. The first one is taken at Izaak Boot's house; it so happened that my one of my other cousins who is also named Izaak Boot was there. While we were in Kortgene, my mother and I visited the cemetery where mom's last child Willem is buried. We also went to see her parent's grave marker which is shown below.

Mom looking at her parents' grave marker in Kortgene

On moving day back in Ann Arbor, Brenda also retired! Our last day in Ann Arbor when we were supposed to close on the house, the people that bought the house ran into some kind of a problem. We had our vehicles loaded and ready to hit the road, since we had booked a room in Omaha which was many miles down the road, we wanted to get going! We had gotten some pills for the cat to keep her calm, etc. We waited and waited and finally decided to leave and let the real estate people take care of it. We got to Omaha late that evening. Got up early the next morning and continued our journey to Colorado Springs, CO.

These vehicles were loaded with enough of our personal stuff to tide us over until the moving van arrived at 8025 Edgerton Ct.

The Chrysler Sebring

The Dodge minivan that I bought from Schlumberger

Moved to Colorado Springs, Dec 1, 1997

We moved to Colorado Springs after we sold our house on Indianola. The actual move took place Dec 1, 1997.

Paul behind the wheel of the moving van

A vey empty house!

In the process of looking for a suitable house we kept going past Woodmen Valley Chapel, a non-denominational congregation. Brenda and I both agreed that we would not interfere with Jeff and Karen who attended the CRC church. Thus, the first Sunday we lived in COS we went to WVC and have attended there ever since. The first Sunday we were there, when we went to the visitor center downstairs, we were invited to a neighborhood small group that was being led by Paul Bechter.

After we got settled in and following Christmas time roll around, we had Jeff and Karen and the grand kids over to help us celebrate our first real Christmas in Colorado.

Unwrapping the presents

Van, Susan, Stephanie, Paul and Brenda

I become quite involved in volunteer work at our church which was building houses for **Habitat for Humanity.** I enjoyed that type of work, and spent a lot of time helping there, since I did not have much else to do except unpack. Earl Bailey an elder, headed up our church group of helpers. While working on one of the houses I met Don Harper. He tells the story, which gets embellished more and more each time it's told, that the first question I asked him was, "Are you a skier?" Then the next question I apparently asked was, "Do you have a place in Breckenridge?" I might have asked him those types of questions, but I do not believe that I was that direct!

The early summer of 1998 my mother came to visit us. I remember us taking her for a drive to Salida to give here an idea of what Colorado looks like. She was amazed at the mountains and to hear and see the Air Force Thunderbirds flying over our house. While she was here, she got to see some of her great grandkids that she does not get to see that often.

Mom, Paul, Stephanie, Brenda and Susan

Paul racking leaves

That fall, Paul had to help his grandpa (me) rake up all of the leaves that had fallen off of our scrub oaks.

Paul hiding in a pile of leaves

Stephanie and Van on the extreme right

Stephanie

That fall our grandkids got all dressed up for Halloween. Paul as a pumpkin, Susan as the person with the magic wand, and Stephanie as a clown. The spring of 1999, Stephanie had a special occasion at their church and she and I dressed up like fishermen. I do not recall what the occasion was, but I was there.

Stephanie. Look at that form!

That winter Jeff and Karen were teaching Paul how to ski. Now they may have tried to teach them a year or two earlier, but the photos below show Paul without poles. Thus, Paul has not graduated to the point where he was using ski poles. Stephanie has ski poles.

I remember writing a Christmas letter the second Christmas we were in Colorado Springs and bragging about the fact that I got in 15 days of skiing the previous winter. Now I get 60-70 days of skiing. Of course, 15 days of skiing for someone from the Midwest is lots of skiing.

After the 1998-1999 ski season was over my brother-in-law Dave Marsman and my sister Lena came to visit us. We took them to the Royal Gorge Bridge; Lena was so scared that she would not walk across the bridge. To be honest about it, it is somewhat scary. It is the highest suspension bridge in the world. Dave actually drove their RV across it. At

Van skiing

Paul, Jeff and Karen

the very time that we were there, there was a guy from one of the local TV stations making

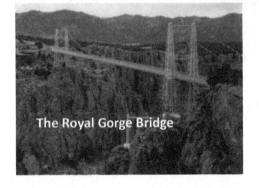

The Royal Gorge Bridge

The Arkansas River 1,053 feet below!

videos of people walking/driving across the bridge. Lena was interviewed and thought she was going to be on the news that night. Lena's interview was not shown; however, we did see Dave driving their RV across the bridge on the news that evening.

Travelling back home along the Arkansas River (Hwy50) they spotted some bighorn sheep that had come down from higher up to get a drink as well as to eat some grass. We also took them to visit Cripple Creek. Cripple creek is an old mining town that now has mostly casinos. There are some donkeys that are descendants from the donkeys from the mining days of long ago that roam the street and the area around Cripple creek at will.

Bighorn Sheep along the Arkansas River

Dave enjoying his Cripple Creek visit

While Dave and Lena were in Colorado, we took them to the mountains and visited Breckenridge. It so happened that there were still remnants of the snow sculptures there. They thought that was genuinely nice. We obviously took them to the Garden of the Gods.

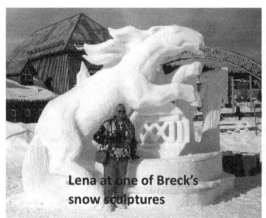

Lena at one of Breck's snow sculptures

GOG in COS

One of the biggest surprises to us when we moved to Colorado Springs and into the Peregrine neighborhood was the number of mule deer roaming the neighborhood. Whenever we had out of town visitors they always commented about the deer. They are everywhere! By now we had made friends with one of the bucks and gave him the name Prancer. Most of the time the visitors would want to feed it. This is not encouraged! It is against the law! The photo on the right shows my sister Lena feeding Prancer a carrot.

Lena feeding Prancer

A week after Lena and Dave left town we were hit by a pretty strong hail storm. It blew several tiles off the roof of our house. It also smashed the glass top table on the deck into a thousand pieces.

Broken tiles from the storm

Glass top table no more!

The winter of 1998-1999, I started to finish the lower level of our house, which was completely unfinished. After applying for various permits, I laid out on the cement floor the various walls and rooms that I planned on building. I even marked where the 2x4s were going to be to get a rough estimate of how many I needed. After having a rough idea of the supplies that I would need, I went to the big box stores, Home Depot and 84 Lumber. My brother Casey who lived in Florida and was in the construction business sent me a pneumatic nail gun. Roughing in the various walls for the 2 bedrooms, a bathroom, wet bar, and a Y2K pantry kept me busy for some time. After I had the walls up and the bathroom roughed out, I got one of my friends from church who was a licensed electrician to come over and install a mini electrical panel in the lower level. After that was done Jeff and I ran the electric wiring and switches to the various rooms, etc. At this time High Mountain Inc. was building houses in what became known as The Village in Peregrine," just down the hill from where we lived. I would go down there to see how they were doing things such as floating walls which I never heard of let alone how that was accomplished. By now Brenda and I were part of a small Bible study group that included Lee Bolen the president and owner of Saddle Tree. I asked him to come over and look at the project that I had going on. I was about to rough in the sofit above the wet bar with 2x2 lumber and he suggested that I go to the lumber yard and get an I-beam the length of the wet bar area and do it that way. It saved me a lot of work. After Jeff and I finished running the electrical wires, I was ready to do the drywalling. Thus, I went to Home Depot and ordered the number of 4 x 10 ft sheets of drywall that I thought I needed. They delivered them and placed them on the street by the mailbox. Unfortunately, it started to rain soon after they were delivered. I called Jeff and he came over and we carried 76 sheets into the downstairs family room. They were heavy and that was a lot of work carrying them and moving them inside. I had an idea that I would go down the hill and find out if the guys that were doing the drywalling there would be interested in doing the drywalling at my place. Well, they were, and they came the following weekend and completely roughed in the lower level. It was either the following day or the following weekend that they taped the joints, etc. Then they sprayed all of the walls and ceilings and finished it in a texture they called knockdown. They did all this work for what I believe was around $1,0000. I would still be sanding the joints, etc. today!

240

The downstairs Bathroom

The wet bar area

The Y2K pantry

I finally completed the lower-level project and had the carpet laid. Not long afterwards, a week or two, it started to rain, and it rain and rained. I went downstair to get something and I was walking across the carpet, and it was soaked. I immediately, called Jeff and we raised all the furniture and put it on blocks to get it off the carpet. The next thing I did was to try to figure out what was causing this to happen. Several of the neighbors were complaining that water was running inside the house through the window wells. Our neighborhood was very rocky, and rocks do not absorb much water. I knew that we had a French drain around the house, and it was running into a large 12" diameter rubber tube just off of the lower patio. However, it did not have a sump-pump installed. Thus, I got on the phone and started to call every place I could think of to try to get a sump-pump. There were not any to be had in all of Colorado Springs. I finally got a lead that this place in Castle Rock might have one. I called them and they had some and I told them I would be right there to pick one up. I installed it and it pumped water out of the tube for days on end. We lifted the carpet up and rented some large fans to dry it out.

I have a photo of us going out to dinner, but I do not recall the reason why. According to the time stamp on the photo a day later the grandkids were at our house and again I do not know why.

Out to dinner

Brenda, Stephanie, Van, Susan and Paul

That summer we were visited by one of my cousins from Holland who had visited us when we lived in Ann Arbor. He and his wife were going to spend some time in Denver, and he knew that we had moved to Colorado Springs. We enjoyed their visit and had a chance to catch up on news of relatives in Holland.

My cousin Jan Boot and wife Anne-Marie

1999-05-22
Dear Uncle Bani and Aunt Brenda,

You might remember me as the cousin that visited you in the summer of '91. I happened to be in the US on a summer vacation. I learned water-skiing in just 1 day, thanks to the excellent teaching. Since you moved to Colorado, we have a possibility to meet again this summer, if you would like so. We (my wife Anne-Marie and I) are spending our vacation this summer in Denver. We would very much like to meet you in your new residence, if that is ok with you. Please let us know what you think about it.

Kind regards,

Jan ("John") Boot
Het Hooge Land 3
NL-4213DA Dalem
Netherlands
Tel.nr. (+31)-(0)183 632247
E-mail: jaboot@hetnet.nl

Our MI trip and visit with my H.S. friends.

Van with some of his High School friends

Later that same summer (June – July) we must have driven back to MI and unbeknown to me my sister Lena had arranged for some of my high school friends/buddies to meet me at my sister Cora's house for a get together. I believe every one that was there really enjoyed themselves. There were a couple of buddies that I really had not seen since high school graduation and several I had seen at a couple of the 1957 class reunions that I attended.

Front row, left to right: Fred Koetsier, Adrian Gilder, Chuck Dykhuizen, Urbanes Van Bemden, Gary DeArmond, Gary's wife. Back Row, left to right: Adrian's wife, Judy Allen (Potter), Brenda Van Bemden, Margaret Videan (Backstrom), Don Videan, Allen Baird.

Below are a couple of more informal photos taken during the evening get together.

The Guys!

Adrian Gilder and his wife with Chuck Dykhuizen

Later that summer Rose Phillips, who was an exceptionally good friend of ours back when we lived in MI, came to visit us in Colorado Springs. She had been to Colorado Springs several times before when she was married to Larry Cameron. Larry was Rose's first husband and worked for GM at the Milford, MI proving grounds. In fact, one time she and Larry drove their motorcycle out to Colorado Springs. GM also had a garage in Manitou Springs to tune the various GM cars that drove up Pikes Peak, and that is what brought her and Larry out to Colorado several times. Larry Cameron died of Lou Gehrig's disease also known as ALS.

This is what **Google** has to say about Milford proving grounds. It is located in **Milford, Michigan** and covers 4,000 acres (1,600 ha). 4,800 staff work in its 142 buildings today. The proving ground includes the equivalent of 132 miles (212 km) of roads representative of conditions found on public roadways and other specialty surfaces for vehicle testing.

A horse being shoed along Hwy 24

While Rose was here, we drove around to show her some of our favorite Colorado sights. We passed a couple that were shoeing horses along Hwy 24. Rose wanted to stop and talk to them, which we did. They gave her a couple of worn horseshoes as souvenirs.

What is the Y2K bug!

The reason we built a Y2K pantry downstairs when we finished the lower level of our house on Edgerton Ct was because some people thought the world was going to stop spinning, computers were going to stop working, etc. Companies spent millions of dollars reprogramming to work around this potential bug that was going to happen when the clock struck 12 o'clock midnight Dec 31, 2000. This is what **Google** said about the Y2K bug.

Millions of dollars were spent in the lead-up to Y2K in IT and software development to create patches and workarounds to squash the bug. While there were a few minor issues once Jan. 1, 2000, arrived, **there were no massive malfunctions**.

How much money was wasted on Y2K?

Federal estimates set the cost of year 2000 preparations in the U.S. at $100 billion, with 8.4% of that amount spent by the government. But observers' estimates put the figure much higher -- from $150 billion to **$225 billion** in U.S. government and business expenditures, as estimated by Stamford, Conn.

Summer of 1999.

The summer of 1999, Brenda's mother came to visit us, and we drove to Durango. There we took the narrow gage R.R. to Silverton. When you are in that part of Colorado, it is the thing to do. On the way back home, we saw an authentic cattle drive along Hwy 160 which was kind of unique. We actually had to wait along Hwy 160 and let the cowboys round them up and move them to a new pasture.

Downtown Silverton, CO

Cattle drive along Hwy 160

My Mother's 85th birthday, Nov 7, 1999.
Nov 7, 1999, we once again found ourselves in Grand Rapids to celebrate my mother's 85th birthday.

Mom with some of the grandkids

Mom with some of her kids. Except me, I took the photo

Later in the month we celebrated Stephanie's 10th and Brenda's 55th birthdays. Since they are only a week apart, we generally have been celebrating them together.

Stephanie 10th B-day

Stephanie in the girl's room

In the photos above you can see Stephanie blowing out candles on her cake. You can also tell that Brenda is very happy with the clothes that I bought her. Stephanie is in the girl's room at Grandma and Grandpa's house.

2000 – 2. The winter of 2000 we took the grandkids to Woodmen Roberts school to do some sledding. Here is Paul pulling Susan on their toboggan, and it does look like they are enjoying playing in the Snow.

Paul pulling Susan on the toboggan

Jeff and the kids skiing at Breck

Ruth, Rod Porter, Van and Brenda

We took a trip with Rod and Ruth Porter to Snowmass Village and stayed overnight at the Pokolodi Inn where Rod had his timeshare unit. The following morning while we were having coffee, we noticed some bear paws in the mud just outside of our door.

Christmas time. 2000

Members of our WVC small group at Christmas

Louise, Brenda, Sharon and Ron McWhirter

Wednesday Dec 20th, 2000, the WVC small group that we belonged to held a Christmas party at our house on Edgerton Ct. Most of the members lived in our neighborhood so it was easy to gather, and no one had to drive far, etc. Members of our group included: John and Linda Taylor, Paul and Sharon Bechter, Ron and Joyce McWhirter, Don and Louise Monohon, Frank and Shirley Irwin. In the photo L to R. John, Linda, Sharon, Frank, Ron, Joyce, Paul, Brenda.

Ron McWhirter showing Louise Monohon how to play Jenga. With Jenga you stack all of the pieces on top of each other and then you take turns pulling them out and stacking them back on the top of stack without the stack collapsing. It quite challenging! You must have steady nerves.

the photos below Karen and the grand girls are enjoying Christmas at the Cragmor CRC.

Susan singing a song

All dressed alike. Karen made these dresses

Our trip to Florida. Feb 15th 2001.

Feb 15th, 2001, Brenda and I took a trip to Florida. We visited Naples, Ft. Myers, the Florida Keys, etc. We eventually wound up spending a few nights with Casey and Dee in New Port Richey, FL. To our surprise half of the Van Bemden clan from Grand Rapids were there. Lots of the Van Bemden clan from Grand Rapids like to go down to Florida in the winter. My mother happened to be there also.

Photo on the left and starting in the Back row on the left: Casey, Dee, Pete, Van, Brenda, Lena, Dave, Butch and Debbie. Sitting: Adrian, Mom and Maria. Sitting on the floor: Barb and Tracy.

The photo on the right is a photo of Mom and **HER** kids that were in Florida Feb 2001. L to R is Casey, Van, Butch, Pete and Adrian. Sitting is Lena, Mom and Mary.

Back in Colorado, Mon June 25, 2001, Randy Davis (our neighbor) and I climbed 3 of the Colorado 14ers: Mt. Democrat, Mt. Lincoln and Mt. Bross. These are near Alma and relatively easy.

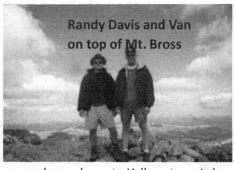

Randy Davis and Van on top of Mt. Bross

July 15, 2001, I was invited to go fishing at Yellowstone National Park with Rod Porter, John Kwiatkowski (Big John), Bill LeBarron, and Tom Williams. So, Rod and I drove to Bill LeBarron's home in Wyoming and stayed overnight. The following morning we drove down to Yellowstone Lake

Loading the canoes

Van caught one

Getting our food out of reach of bears

and put the canoes into the water and boated over to the camp site that Big John had reserved.

After unloading all of our supplies and hanging them far enough off the ground so the bears could not get them, we were off to catch some cut-throat trout. This was all catch and release, but it was fun since I had never fly fished in my life.

Our Vancouver to Calgary train trip July 28th, 2001.

July 28th, 20001, Brenda and I decided that we should take a train trip from Vancouver to Calgary, Canada. Thus, we flew into Vancouver and did a quick tour of the city. The next morning, we boarded the train that would take us to Calgary. Along the way there was some narration as to what we were looking at and where we were. Lumber is big business in Canada, and we saw quite a bit of lumbering activity along the Frazer River. We saw huge barges of logs floating down the river to the various sawmills.

Sawmill along the Frazer River

Floating logs down to the sawmills.

We also saw the neatest tree cutting machine I ever saw. It wraps itself around the tree cuts it off, then pulls it in and trims all of the branches off and cuts it into whatever length you want. Super-efficient!

11 Mountain goats looking for minerals

Bighorn sheep and lambs

Once we got to Calgary, we rented a car and went to visit Jasper Park and traveled up and down the highway between Banff and Jasper. Saw lots of waterfalls along the way. We also got to see a mother black bear with 3 cubs. I guess the mother bear was fatting up eating berries. We saw Bighorn Sheep, Elk, and quite a few Mountain Goats. In other words, we saw quite a bit of wildlife during our tour. Specially around Banff and Jasper Park.

We took the snow mobile up to one of the glaciers and really enjoyed that. When we were in Calgary, we noticed the remnants of the 1988 winter Olympics.

Our snow coach to the glacier

Remnants of the 1988 Winter Olympics

One of the more beautiful sights was when we were at the overlook at Peyto Lake. You might ask: Why is the water so green? This is what **Google** says. The water in Peyto Lake **comes from the Peyto Glacier**. Many glacier-fed lakes take on this incredible color due to "rock flour" or fine rock particles that the movement of the glacier grinds like flour. The way the sunlight reflects off of these particles suspended in the water gives the lake its stunning color.

Peyto Lake

Another glacier fed lake along the Ice field

The events of Sept 11, 2001.

On September 11, 2001, 2,977 people were killed in the deadliest terrorist attacks in American history. The following is from the Millercenter.org web site but it sums of the events of 9/11.

The World Trade Center in March 2001 *Wikimedia Commons*

The moment shocked the nation. Two planes, hijacked by Islamic jihadists vowing death to all Americans, plowed into both towers at the World Trade Center in New York. Another plane was flown into the Pentagon in Washington, DC. A fourth

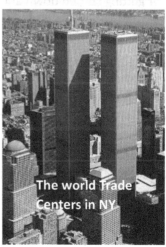

The world Trade Centers in NY

plane, presumably headed for the White House or the U.S. Capitol, was heroically diverted by passengers and ended up crashing in an empty field in Pennsylvania. After reports of the first plane hitting the North Tower, millions watched the second plane hit the South Tower on live television.

It was a terrifying, startling, and humbling event for the country. The 9/11 attacks were the deadliest on American soil since the shock attack at Pearl Harbor 60 years before, and the sense of outrage was reminiscent of that moment. The attacks in New York occurred in the country's busiest city on a busy workday. And the staggered nature of the attacks meant that news footage captured almost everything as it happened, ensuring that millions of Americans saw the events precisely as they unfolded.

In the fall of 2001 Brenda and I went to Aspen to visit at the Maroon Bells. I did not know at that time that I would be back many times and that I would actually climb to the top of both of them twice years later when climbing the Colorado 14ers bug got to me. This certainly was the start of my love affair with the Maroon Bells.

Brenda and Van at the Maroon Bells

A neat reflection of the Maroon Bells

After getting settled down and after we had been in Colorado Springs a year or two, Brenda and I were co-leaders in a class at our church, "Welcome to our Town". The main purpose of the class was for new comers to the church, as well as the town to familiarize themselves as to where various things were in town such as hospitals, groceries stores, as well as who was responsible (and introduce them to that person) for various functions of the church. The class was only 6-8 weeks long. You could not repeat this class. We would have 8-10 couples attend each class. It gave newcomers an immediate access and friendship with people who attended the class. We would have several potluck dinners during the class duration, mostly at our house! This is where I met one couple namely Duane and Linda Jensen. Linda told me about climbing Pikes Peak which is a 14er. I said to myself, if she can do it, I ought to be able to do it. What Linda did not tell me when she first mentioned that she had climbed Pikes Peak was that she spent the night at the Barr Trail camp. Thus, when Jeff asked me if I wanted to climb a 14'er with him, I said yes. We climbed Mt. Sherman and that was the start of my climbing 14ers journey. We climbed several others, namely Gray and Torreys together. I kept climbing but Jeff stopped climbing. Of course, he was working, and I was retired!

Another couple that we met in "Welcome to our Town," was Gary and Jerri Zimmerman who were the directors of a mission organization named Love in Action International Ministries LIAIM. It was meeting them that got me involved in mission work.

Another WVC potluck

Gary and Jerri Zimmerman, Brenda, Rod and Ruth Porter

The evolution in my skies

I also spent a lot of time skiing in the winters. I often said that if I was not working at **Habitat for Humanity** or **skiing**, I was probably hiking one of the **Colorado 14ers.** For you do not know what a 14'er is, it is a mountain peak that's over 14,000 feet high. I hiked all 55 of the 14ers and I did not hike my first one until I was 63 years old. The summer of 2004 I hiked 19 of them and spent a lot of time in the mountains. In the summer as well as the winter.

In the early 2000's one started to see a real evolution in skis. Trend is toward shorter and fatter. I started out with skinny 205mm and now I am down to using 160mm. Lots of all mountain skis.

Living on Edgerton CT. we had Prancer as our own pet and very tame mule deer. Even the grand kids wanted to feed it. In the photo Paul is feeding Prancer some bread. Prancer was by far the tamest of all of the deer in the neighborhood.

Paul feeding Prancer

Christmas of 2001, our grandson Paul apparently was asked to play Santa Claus at Lincoln elementary school. When we celebrated Christmas at our house a few days later, Paul got a new bicycle that had been hidden in our garage.

Paul playing Santa Claus at Lincoln School

Paul found his new bicycle

2002

Jim with the Elk he hit on his way home

Jan 22nd, 2002, Jim Gilman on his way home from visiting Aspen and skiing with us a couple of days hit a large Elk and did quite a lot of damage to his Chevy Suburban. Jim Gilman is the man who is responsible for us skiing in Aspen and staying at Paul Wagner's condo.

Our trip to Blythe, CA to see the Gillilands.

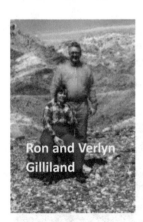
Ron and Verlyn Gilliland

Tuesday March 19, 2002, Brenda and I decided that we would take a trip to California to visit with Ron and Verlyn Gilliland. We got to know the Gillilands at the time we were helping with

One of the 3 Blythe Intaglios

"Welcome to our Town ". They knew Gary and Jerri Zimmerman since they went to the same college and they were members of the same denomination. For a time, Ron sold Pontiacs at the local dealer in Colorado Springs. However, after living in Colorado Springs for a few years they moved to Blythe, California. When we visited them, they took us to see the Blythe Intaglios. You might ask what are the Blythe Intaglios? Bing.com: The *Blythe Intaglios* or Blythe Geoglyphs are a group of gigantic figures incised on the ground near Blythe, California, in the Colorado Desert. Who made them, no one is sure, but they supposedly are over 1000 years old.

The Blythe, CA area is mostly agricultural with hay being the primary crop. Mostly because the Colorado River runs thru this area and they use the water for irrigation. Note the green hay field.

The Colorado R. at Blythe, CA

Lots of interesting rock formations at Joshua Tree Nat'l Park

After visiting Ron and Verlyn, Brenda and I decided that we should visit Joshua Tree National Park. The photo shows our car in the shade of the Joshua tree. This is probably the biggest Joshua tree in the world! Joshua Tree National Park is obviously known for its distinct trees, but it is also known for its amazing rock formations as well as glorious sunrises and sunsets.

A very large Joshua tree

One of the many large windmill farms

Brenda and I could not get over the number of windmills in the area. There were literally hundreds. However they were mostly smaller than the ones you see today.

On the way back from CA we stopped off at Norm and Gloria Hawk's house in Rio Verde, AZ. Norm and Gloria Hawk were one of our neighbors when we lived on Indianola. They had retired

Some of the numerous varieties of barrel cactus

Norm and Gloria Hawk with Brenda

and moved to a warmer climate. While we were there, we visited a cactus garden and saw some interesting desert plants. One of the more interesting things that we saw while we were sitting on their patio were the Javelinas also known as collared peccary. They are medium-sized animals that look similar to a wild boar. They have mainly short coarse salt and pepper colored hair, short legs, and a pig-like nose. We also saw several Gambel's quail. We do not see these in Colorado! Thus, we found them quite interesting.

Sunday, May 12th, 2002 the grandkids and Karen were over to our house on Edgerton Ct. to celebrate Karen's 39th birthday. I believe the grandkids helped Grandma Van Bemden with baking a birthday cake with the appropriate number of candles.

Brenda, Karen and the Grandkids

Blowing out the candles

Van and Brenda at the waterfall

May 19,2002 we again were hiking in Queens Canyon at Glyn Erie. This is a genuinely nice hike and it is not very strenuous. It is mostly pretty flat at least up to the waterfall. This time Mike Bode and Ellis Diebler were with us. Right after 9 11 they basically shut down access to the canyon. However, we found out a little trick to hike the canyon and that was to tell the guard that we want to visit the book store.

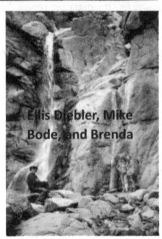
Ellis Diebler, Mike Bode, and Brenda

Longview, Texas here we come. Just before the end of the month, we all headed to Longview,

The Van Bemden grandkids enjoying the pool

Even Grandpa and Grandma are enjoying the pool

TX to celebrate Memorial Day at Brenda's mother place. Not only the Van Bemdens were there but the entire Parker clan was also there. The community (HOA) where Lillian Parker lived had a community swimming pool which most everyone enjoyed. You can see Paul doing a cannon ball trying to make a big splash. Susan has already completed her big splash.

Here is a photo of Great Grandma Parker and Grandma Van Bemden playing games with the grandkids.

Great Grandma Parker playing games

Lillian Parker's Great Grandkids

Lillian Parker's three grandsons

Now a photo of Lillian Parker's grandsons. From left to right: We have Jimmy Parkers two sons, Paul and Michael Parker and Van and Brenda's son, Jeffrey Van Bemden.

We also have a photo of Lillian Parker's granddaughters in-law. From left to right: we have Paul Parker's wife Angela, Jeff Van Bemden's wife Karen, and Michael Parker's wife Denise.

Lillian Parker's three granddaughters

Below is the photo of the Parker family and the Van Bemden family that got together in Longview on Memorial Day 2002.

The family get together in Longview, TX on Memorial Day 2002.

June 23, 2002, I, Ron McWhirter and his daughter drove to Georgetown, CO and then drove up to the top of Guanella pass and parked the car. We put on our backpacks and started to climb up to Mt. Bierstadt. Once we got to the top of Mt. Bierstadt, we decided that we would go on to Mt. Evans via the famous saw tooth route. Ron McWhirter and his wife were members of our small neighborhood Bible study group. Ron's daughter was an Air Force Academy graduate and was now a pilot in the U S Air Force and was home on leave and she had never climbed a 14er so this was her chance.

The 3 of us on top of Mt. Bierstadt

The 3 of us on top of Mt. Evans

Now I had ticked off another two of Colorado's 14ers.

June 4th, 2002, I came back home from some outing and Brenda informed me that there was a newborn fawn hiding among the rocks along the pathway to our lower patio. She had accidentally watered it when she was watering the plants along the walk to the patio. We had never experienced such an event. Thus, I had to take a picture of it.

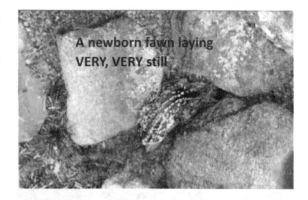
A newborn fawn laying VERY, VERY still

Saturday, June 8th, 2002, the Hayman fire started. At that time, it was not immediately known how serious this would become. Wikipedia has this to say about the Hayman fire: The **Hayman Fire** was a forest fire started on June 8, 2002, 35 miles (56 km) northwest of Colorado Springs, Colorado and 22 miles (35 km) southwest of Denver, Colorado and was, for 18 years, the largest wildfire in the state's recorded history at over 138,114 acres.

Firefighter's tent city along Hwy 24 in Lake George

Hundreds of firefighters fought the fast-moving fire, which caused nearly $40 million in firefighting costs, burned 133 homes, 138,114 acres, and forced the evacuation of 5,340 people.

The Hayman Fire burned from June 8, 2002, until it was classified as contained on July 18, 2002.[2] The cause of the wildfire was found to be arson.[3]

Colorado Springs Airshow. Wed June 19th, 2002 there was an Air show at the Colorado Springs Airport, and we took the grandkids there. I believe they really enjoyed it and wanted their picture taken while they were looking over the various airplanes. I do not know where Paul got his hat and whether or not he got to keep it.

The three grandkids in front of a homemade airplane

Paul at one of the Army Helicopters

Friday July 7th, 2002, we took the kids on a hike up Queens Canyon at Glen Eyrie going as far as the waterfall at the end of the canyon. They seemed to enjoy that. Many times, when we would take the grandkids for a hike, we would take along some treats as well as water.

Brenda and the grandkids along the Queen Canyon trail

Taking a break

That same summer I also hiked the Queens Canyon with Don and Mike Bode. One of the things about hiking the Queens Canyon at Glen Eyrie is that it's mostly in the shade because it's so deep and narrow.

A small herd of Bighorn Sheep

One of the things you will notice is that there are a lot of bighorn sheep in and around Queens Canyon and Glen Eyrie. In fact, it's been stated that it's one of the largest Bighorn

Don Bode at the waterfall

Sheep herds in the front range. They have captured many of them and moved them on to other places such as Pikes Peak. This is the same herd that is in and out of the Garden of the Gods. They don't understand fence barriers.

We heard via the grapevine that there is a nice hiking trail along Hwy 67 about halfway between Divide and Cripple Creek which one can take to the rock formation which is known as Pancake Rocks. Thus, we had to check it out which we did with Bill and Mary McCollum.

The Rock formation known as the pancakes

Mary McMullen on top of the Pancakes

My Brother Ike's family visit. July 23, 2002.

Ike, Jennie, Van and Brenda

Tuesday, July 23, 2002 my brother Ike and his wife Jennie came to visit us in Colorado Springs. We tried to show them some of the interesting sights around Colorado. We showed them the large open pit gold mine at Victor, the highest suspension bridge in the world at the Royal Gorge, took them to Breckenridge, the Llama farm near Florissant, etc. On the way to Breckenridge, we stopped at the Mc Donalds in Idaho Springs. After ordering a cup of coffee, Ike went outside to smoke a cigarette, and someone told him that smoking was prohibited because there was a wildfire in that area. I noticed that as we were driving around Lake Dillion, I had never seen the water level that low. It was obvious that all of Colorado was in a severe drought.

Lake Dillion is INCREDIBLY low!

As we were driving south on the road between Florissant and Cripple Creek, we spotted a herd of elk. We did not stop but I took a shot of them since this was something that Ike and Jennie had never seen. This herd's homebase is Mueller State Park but is certainly not confined to that large state park. They roam where they want to.

A large herd of Elk

The Royal Gorge

It so happened that Ike's son Mike and his family were also in Colorado Springs. Since we had a 5-bedroom house, they all stayed at our house. Mike's family members are, his wife Cheryl, his son Zachary, and his daughter Kelsey.

Ike, Jennie, Mike, Cheryl, Zachary and Kelsey

Monday, Aug 5, 2002, we helped our grandson Paul celebrate his 10th birthday. Here he seems to be incredibly happy with the soccer game cake that his mother baked for him.

Paul's 10th birthday cake

Celebrating Jeff's 39th birthday.

Jeff celebrating his 39th Birthday

We celebrated Jeff's 39th birthday at our house on Edgerton court. I do not remember the reason Jeff and Karen are laughing. It might have something to do with what we bought him for his birthday which was a can of paint to paint his Jenson-Healey sports car which was in bad need of a paint job.

Sunday, Sept 15th, 2002, Jeff and I drove up to Denver to watch a Grand Prix race in person. After the race we asked one of the garages to give us a worn-out tire. We took it home and Jeff was eventually going to make a coffee table stand out of it. It is now 2023 and Jeff still has the tire but has not had the time to make it into a coffee table. He had many other higher priorities in remodeling and updating his house.

One of the many Grand Prix race cars

Stephanie, Brenda and Susan

Dec 18, 2002, we attended Stephanie's orchestra performance at Holmes Middle School on Mesa Rd. Here she got to play her violin.

Skiing in Colorado

Actually, I have to tell this story if the photo below is going to make any sense. Shortly after we moved to Colorado Springs, we met Rod and Ruth Porter. We became good friends, and we visited back and forth quite a few times. Rod was an Optometrist and he was also a snow skier. He also had a timeshare at Pokolodi Lodge in Snowmass Village. Rod and Ruth had lived in Wyoming and while he lived there, he became good friends with Jim Gilman, John Kwiatkowski, and some other folks. While Rod lived in Wyoming, he owned a cabin up in the woods and that group would go hunting in that area. Rod also had a friend who was also an Optometrist who also had a timeshare at Pokolodi Lodge. Rod and I would go skiing at the various Summit County ski resorts and finally we went to Snowmass during his timeshare week. Well, Big John had contacted Rod's friend, and he also was there in Rod's friend's timeshare unit. They would always try to get the units next to each other. We did this arrangement for several years. We always went in for lunch in the unit that Big John was in. Now Jim Gilman enters the picture. One of Jim's daughters was playing basketball and hurt one of her knees. Jim knew that doctors in Aspen know how to repair damaged knees. Thus, Jim and his daughter traveled to the Aspen area to repair his daughter's knee. While his daughter was in the hospital, Jim elected to go skiing at Aspen Mountain. Jim was skiing at Ruth's run and not being familiar with Aspen Mountain did not really know where the run would take him. He saw a couple of guys standing there and asked them where this run led. Those two guys happened to be Paul Wagner and Roger Boyer. While he was getting information, they talked about other things like what he was doing in Aspen and where he was staying while his daughter was in the hospital. Jim mentioned that he was staying in Carbondale and was driving back and forth. Paul suggested that Jim stay at his place at the Gant since he had a 3-bedroom condo and was only using 2 of the bedrooms. I do not know how long Jim stayed at Paul's condo, but it was the beginning of a friendship that has lasted more than 25 years. After Jim and his daughter returned to Wyoming, Jim talked to Big John and others and suggested that they do something in exchange for Paul Wagner. Thus, they put together a river cruise down the Missouri river on a float/pontoon boat. I was not there but I heard that Paul really enjoyed that. Now, Snowmass Village was going thru a major building boom, and they were going to tear down the Pokolodi Lodge to make room for high rise condos. Thus, Rod's timeshare vacations had come to an end. Eventually Paul started to invite Big John, Rod, and me to stay at his condo. Once ski season started, I was off to Aspen, Paul would invite several of the Aspen ski group of which I was a member to stay at his condo at the Gant. This is the first known photo of us staying at Paul's place. Big John did most of the cooking; once Brenda started to go to Aspen with me, she and John took turns cooking.

The photo of the guys skiing at Snowmass was pretty much our group for quite some time. Every once in a while, Jim Gilman would join us for a long weekend. However, that was a lot of driving for Jim just to ski 2-3 days.

Paul Wagner, Roger Boyer, Big John and Bruce Smith

Big John, Bruce Smith, Rod Porter, Roger Boyer and Paul Wagner

Bruce Smith also had a timeshare unit at Pokolodi Lodge and for several years we would see him and his wife Kathy in the lobby eating breakfast. We finally asked him if he wanted to ski with us. He said sure and that was the beginning of him joining our group. Bruce also had a condo in Avon. He sold that and was lucky enough to get his name drawn for a condo in the first Condo complex at Snowmass Village.

Big John, Jan K, Van, Jim Gilman and Paul Wagner

For several years when Paul would invite Rod Porter and me to stay in his condo, we would take turns driving to Aspen. However, it got to the point where after a few days at Paul's condo Rod wanted to go back to Colorado Springs. Thus, I drove there by myself and stayed for the entire time Paul invited us. Eventually Rod was no longer invited.

When I am in Aspen with the rest of the gang, we ski mostly at Snowmass; however, we do ski at the other resorts from time to

Pyramid on far left and the Maroon Bells on the right

Van at the ski patrol hut at Aspen Highlands

time. When we ski at Aspen Highlands, I generally take my camera with me, because one cannot get a better winter photo of the Maroon Bells and Pyramid than from the ski patrol hut at the top of Aspen Highlands Ski Resort. As my friend Rob Parham a professional photographer put it, "My favorite view of Pyramid Peak is from the ski patrol hut at the top of Aspen Highlands ski area. That view is about as dramatic as any winter scene in Colorado."

There are five bighorn sheep in this photo! Can you spot all of them?

One time when I was on travelling on I70 on my way to ski at Keystone, I caught a glimpse of some bighorn sheep along the road at the last exit before the Eisenhower tunnel. I immediately stopped and backed up and got a shot of them. It is amazing how they blend in with their surroundings. Can you spot all five of them?

The spring of 2003 Jeff must have bought a trampoline set for the kids because this shows Paul and Stephanie in their backyard on Galway really enjoying the bouncing. For a while every time we went to Jeff's house the kids would be playing on the trampoline.

Paul and Stephanie playing on their trampoline

By the summer of 2003 Brenda and I were hiking in some of the more popular local trails, such as the Garden of the Gods, Waldo Canyon, Palmer Park, the Peregrine Hoodoos, etc. Certainly, one of our favorite places was Waldo Canyon. There were several lengthy loops that we really enjoyed. Here we are stopping for a break, and it so happens that this is a photo of us on one of the Waldo Canyon trails with Pikes Peak in the distance.

Brenda at the Siamese Twins in the GOG

Van and Brenda hiking in Waldo Canyon

The Grandkids on the Peregrine Hoodoos

The Grandkids on top of the arch in Ute Park

Sometimes we would hike with our grandkids. One of their favorite hikes was Ute park. They all had their favorite hiding place in Ute Park. Also, in the summertime we had to watch the grandkids as they participated in their favorite sport's activities. Paul and Susan both participated in soccer.

Paul kicking the soccer ball

Susan chasing the soccer ball

Dutch Presentation. Aug 2003.

At the beginning of the school year in 2003, I was asked by Karen to make a Dutch presentation to Susan's kindergarten class for Susan's show and tell. So, I hustled over to a Costume store in Colorado Springs to rent a Dutch costume. I got all of my very Dutch stuff together such as wooden shoes, scaled windmill, Dutch alphabet poster, Dutch book with photos, and a poster from the area I was born in. I made a presentation to Susan's class and then they talked me into doing the same thing for Paul's class. That was held in the library. That is Susan with her overall outfit 2nd from the right. And Paul is the most left person in the photo in the library.

Van in Paul's class in the library

Van in Susan K-class

While I had the Dutch Costume, the grand kids wanted their picture taken with me. Of course, while I had this neat suit, I thought that I should take a photo of myself before I returned the rental suit. Now, I would say that was a rather good looking dutchmen all dressed up in his knicker pants and a neat cap as well as a nice pair of wooden shoes.

Van in Dutch costume

The weekend of Sept 7, 2003, Labor Day weekend, Chuck Ferrari and I drove the very nasty four-mile, four-wheel Colfax Lane that would take us to the trail head that led to Colony Lake where we would set up camp. The next couple of days we would climb Crestone Needle and Crestone Peak. I sure was glad that we were in Chuck's Ford Ranger pickup, because had we been in my Olds, we would have had to walk an extra 4 miles to get to the trail head. Colfax Lane is a very, very rough road.

The Crestones from Colony Lake side

Sept 9 Chuck and I climbed Crestone Needle. This is an exceedingly difficult class 3-4 climb, depending on which route you take. Chuck Ferrari is a former Air Force guy who used to smoke 1-2 packs/day and got winded really fast. When we got to the top we rested up from our climb and had a little snack; however, he wanted to stay up there a lot longer than I did. Thus, we soon were on our way down. The

Van and Chuck Ferrari soaking wet!

next day we climbed Humboldt Peak which is a walk in the park so to speak. Later that day we had Jim Keen and Jerry Funk join us. After pitching tents, they proceeded to climb Humboldt. Later that afternoon it started to rain. It rained and rained. It so happened that Jerry Funk's tent leaked and he eventually upon an invitation from Jim Keen crawled into Jim's tent. The rest of the weekend was basically awash. The photo above is looking at Creston Needle and Creston Peak from our camp site. These 2 mountains are some of the hardest 14ers to climb. Chuck and I finally packed it up and headed back to our vehicle. By time we got back there, both of us were soaking wet!

Visit to Michigan in the fall of 2003.

Van, Brenda and Aunt Connie

Jennie, Arla, Rob, Brenda, Van's empty chair and Ike

September of 2003, we went back to Michigan to visit our family and friends. We visited my Aunt Connie Boot who was still driving her car. I just noticed that she had a picture of my grandpa and grandma Boot hanging up above the lamp. We also went with Ike and Jennie to visit my cousin Rob and Arla Boot.

Back in Grand Rapids at mom's house I took some photos of the Van Bemdens that were there.

Wilma, Brenda and Cora

Wilma, Mom, Brenda and Cora

Wilma, Mom, Jeni, Cora and Van

Ike, Jennie, Carol, Joe, Brenda and Van

The summer of 2003 while we were living on Edgerton Ct. we witnessed the demolition of the St. Francis barn along Woodmen Rd. The property was slated to be converted to a strip mall and a neighborhood swimming pool. However, in opposition from the neighborhood, the strip mall idea was rejected and voted down. Later it was made into the La Bellezza Italian style village.

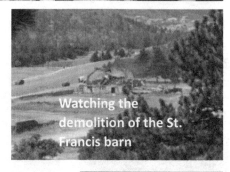

Watching the demolition of the St. Francis barn

Paul's team getting ready to make a touchdown

Back in Colorado that fall of 2003 our grandson Paul went out for football in the various sport programs sponsored by Colorado Springs recreation dept. Paul was the team's center. They practiced and played at Memorial Park. It might not look like it, but that is one proud Grandpa standing next to Paul.

Paul in his football uniform.

Stephanie's photo of her violin. Fall of 2003.

Playing the violin made eight-grader Stephanie Van Bemden happy. Taking pictures of it makes her even happier. Stephanie photographed her violin for the PTA Reflections contest, and the photo made it to the national level of competition after taking first place in the state. The theme for the arts contest- including categories for literature, dance, art, and photography is "I am really happy when . . ." Considering the theme, Stephanie thought first of her violin and how she feels when she plays. Stephanie took about 75 pictures using my digital camera. The hardest part was picking one she said. Stephanie's photo shows her violin, with piano music scattered behind. She played the violin for about five years and the piano longer. The other photo of Stephanie on the right was taken when she was in the nineth grade at Coronado High School. She was first chair.

The photo of Stephanie's violin that won 1st place in the state

Stephanie was first chair

March 2004.

Jeff's family and I went skiing at A-Basin. The photo shows Jeff and Karen watching the 3 kids going thru the moguls. Our grandson Paul at our house on 8025 Edgerton court playing and bouncing around on his pogo stick. He got to the point where he could really bounce.

Jeff watching the kids do the moguls at A-Basin

Paul on his Pogo stick

Susan singing in the school choir

Later in March, Brenda and I went to Lincoln elementary school to watch Susan sing in the school choir.

Our grandson Paul is quite musically talented in that he plays trumpet, drums, and piano.

Paul playing his trumpet

Paul playing the drums

Paul playing the piano

At the end of the school year, we got to watch Paul participating in the various track activities.

Paul throwing the shotput

Paul running on the track

April 25, 2004, the WVC 9 AM Usher team had a get together at Frank and Joe Simmons's house in University Village. I believe this was just before Frank turned the job of being the Head Usher over to me. The head users' job is to make out the monthly Sunday schedule as well as assigning the row for serving Communion. In the photo below from L to R: Eline Lardie, Sharon Summers, Jane Bennett, Frank Simmons, Guy Bennett, Don Monohon.

Some of the 9 O'clock ushers at Frank's house

WVC "Launch your Faith" campaign May 2004.

In May of 2004 WVC had a "Launch Your Faith" campaign at newly acquired Woodmen Heights property. It consisted of cleaning a lot of rocks and gluing on a "Launch Your Faith" metal tag on each rock. I believe the Aluminum tags were made by Duane Jensen, since he owned a labeling plant along Centennial drive near the Garden of the Gods Road. The weekend services were also held at the future home of WVC Woodmen Heights grounds.

Brenda washing and gluing tags on the rocks

At the weekend service at the future home of WVC Woodmen Heights

Summer of 2004.

The summer of 2004 we took a drive down to North Cheyenne Canyon Park. Just before you enter the park you come to the Starsmore Nature Center. If you turn left and drive another hundred ft or so up the hill you come to Starr Kempf house where in his yard are a half dozen or so huge aluminum sculptures that are incredibly detailed. Most of them are wind direction indicators. He had to move them because it was causing traffic problems in the neighborhood. You can find some of them in the Ute Fine Arts Center along North Nevada Ave.

This same summer, Brenda and I drove to Crested Butte to see the wildflowers. Crested Butte is Colorado's Wildflower Capital. We saw a lot of wildflowers; however, we were not there at the peak blooming time. That varies from year to year depending on the severity of the winter and the snow fall. While we were in Crested Butte, I noticed this dog wearing a pair of sunglasses.

Brenda among the Lupines at Crested Butte

Dog wearing sunglasses

On the way home after climbing a Colorado 14er on the western side of the state I was travelling along Hwy 50 when I passed a farm that had some Yaks. That was the first time that I have ever seen real live Yaks in my life. Of course, I had to stop and take a photo of it.

A Yak along Hwy 50

Brenda's mother spent some time with us and the Grandkids (Her Great Grandkids). I believe she may have been on a bus tour that happened to pass thru Colorado Springs on the way to Rocky Mtn National Park.

Lillian Parker and her Great Grandkids

Llamas and their young cria

The spring of 2004 we took the grandkids to see the Llamas at the Llama farm that is located halfway between Cripple Creek and Florissant Fossil Bed National Monument. At the time of our visit, I believe they had over 100 Llamas. There were many baby llamas. A baby Llama is called a "Cria." Cria is a Spanish word for baby.

Summer of 2004 Steve and Carol Meyer (my niece) came to visit us. When we went over to Jeff's house, the grandkids had to play their instruments. Steve had a rather low voice and can really sing bass. So here we have Karen playing the piano and Stephanie on her violin. Then Paul had to play the piano and we were singing songs.

Stephanie playing her violin, Karen on the piano

Steve Meyer getting ready to sing

That same trip Steve wanted to climb Pikes Peak; thus, the following morning Jeff, Steve, and I drove to Manitou Springs and left our car there and started to hike. When we got to the top, Brenda and Carol Meyer had driven up to the top of Pikes Peak to meet us. Steve did not need to hike back down to Manitou Springs. I believe we all had enough hiking for one day.

Steve, Van and Jeff on top of Pikes Peak

The Fall of 2004.

The bull elks are keeping watch over their harem

The fall of 2004, Brenda, and I spent a week or so in Steamboat Springs. Our good friends Don and Pat Harper were

Riding in a 1900 Locomotion

with us. We drove to Rocky Mtn National Park to watch and witness the Elk bugling. We took photos of waterfalls, etc. I also got a ride in a 1900 Locomotion mobile.

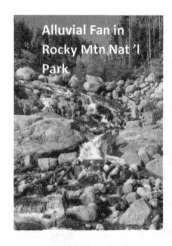
Alluvial Fan in Rocky Mtn Nat'l Park

Looking out the window of our condo I noticed that it really was starting to snow. I said I think I will go to Fish Creek Falls and take a photo or two.

While we were there, we said we all ought to go soak ourselves at the famous Strawberry Park hot springs. Thus, the four of us went to Strawberry Park.

Fish Creek Falls

Van and Brenda at the Strawberry Park hot springs

We also saw a sheep herder riding his horse and with help from his specially trained sheep dogs was moving hundreds of sheep to a new pasture. That was the first time that we saw so many sheep since we visited New Zeeland!

Sheep Herder and his dogs

Hundreds of sheep

Celebrating my Mother's 90th birthday in Grand Rapids.

November of 2004 we found ourselves in Grand Rapids. We were there to celebrate my mother's 90th birthday. It was celebrated at Plymouth Christian school which is a school that was founded years ago by the Nederlands Reformed Congregation in America which is the church that the Van Bemdens grew up in. Lots of Mom and Dad's friends were there to greet her. Some of the Florida Van Bemdens were also in town.

Mom waiting to be taken to her Birthday party

Aunt Connie, Len DeWaal, Audrey DeWaal and Mom

Van and Brenda at Mom's house

Joe, Pete, Adriaan and Van

The picture of the men was of all the Van Bemden boys that happened to be in town. The photo with Mom and ALL of the girls, they are lined up age wise from left to right. Lena, Cora, Wilma, Mom, Maria, Jaci and Jeni.

Mom with all the girls

Mom with all of the Van Bemdens present

On the way over to mom's 90th birthday party, Carol Meyer (Ike's oldest daughter) called me on my cell phone to tell me that her dad (Ike) was in the hospital with an acute case of Leukemia and would not be there. My brothers Casey and Gerard (Butch) stayed in Florida. I should include some of my siblings family photos, since about the only time we have this kind of gathering is an occasion such as this.

Fred and Cora Roelofs family

Eric and Jeni Pannill family

Harry and Jaci Lucas family

Julie Koning (Van Bemden) and her 3 kids

Dave and Lena Marsman

Cora, Gerard Boot, Elaine Boot, Rob Boot, Lena and Cameron

Maria, Cameron and Traci

Additional shots of the Van Bemden clan. I have also included the 3 sets of twins in the family. There is Valerie & Mitchell Van Bemden, Landon & Logan De Meester, and Jonas & Ava Bont. Valerie and Mitchell are Butch and Julie's kids. Jonas & Ava are Lisa (Roelof) Bont's kids. Landon & Logan are Dan and Kathy DeMeester's kids. The Photo with Maria is: Maria (Van Bemden) Gingrich, Traci Anderson (Maria's daughter), Traci's son Cameron Anderson.

3 sets of twins in the family

Ike Van Bemden passed away Dec 4, 2004.

Dec 4, 2004 my brother Ike passed away. He was 67 years old. He was the first of all of my brothers and sisters to pass away.

The Fall of 2004 we also attended the grandkids' piano recital. All of the students that were taking piano lessons got to play their piece on this grand piano. The photo is of Susan playing her selection on a grand piano.

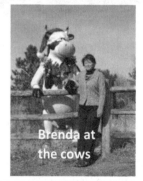

Susan at her piano recital

2004 – 12.

The grandkids at the cows

Driving along Woodmen Rd. just before you enter the Peregrine Subdivision, at the intersection of Westwood Rd. and Wooden Rd. lived an artist that had 2 life sized fiberglass cows standing up on their hind legs leaning against a split rail fence. It was

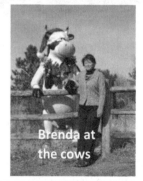

Brenda at the cows

quite unique. Well, I thought it would be nice if I took the grandkids there and posed them in front of the cows. The 2 cows were stolen at one time, and she put out a reward for info leading to return of the cows. They were found and put back up.

Grandkids tobogganing

The photo of the kids on the toboggan was taken during their Christmas break and we happened to have a little bit of snow.

One day I was looking out of the living room window, I could not believe my eyes. I saw a dozen or so deer in our front yard. I could not go out the front door because I would scare them away. Thus, I went down to the lower level and snuck out the sliding glass door, walked across the street and took this picture looking back at our house. This photo has become known as Van's deer farm! There are 11 deer in this picture.

11 deer in our front yard at 8025 Edgerton Ct

2005 – 3.

Brenda and I had bought a timeshare week at Grand Timber Lodge in Breckenridge. The unit at Grand Timber lodge included day use which in essence means you have the opportunity to park your car in underground parking, plus you have the opportunity to use the lockers to change clothes and also use the hot tubs. March 25, 2005, we were skiing at Breckenridge Ski Resort and after we got done skiing, we all went to soak in the hot tub.

Our grandson Paul getting a little air

Stephanie, Brenda and Van and Susan in the hot tub at GTL

April of 2005, Rose Phillips our good friend from Brighton, Mi came down to visit us. We took her around some of our favorite places in Colorado. Here she is with Brenda at the Ski trooper Statue in Vail.

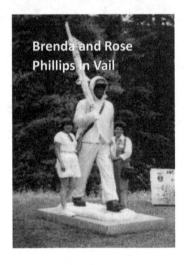

Brenda and Rose Phillips in Vail

2005 – 4.

April of 2005 we drove down to Texas to spend some time with Brenda's mother and then went on to visit Jimmy and Romelle Parker. Jimmy was still living in Round Rock, TX. On the way there we saw lots of wildflowers along the road. Indian paint brushes were everywhere, the same goes for Texas Blue Bonnets.

Indian Paint Brush along a highway in Texas

Texas Blue Bonnets

I also got a nice shot of a Chameleon in Jimmy's backyard. It blended in very nicely with the plant foliage. Of course, when you are in Texas, you will probably see a Texas Longhorn or two.

A green chameleon on green leaves

A large Texas Longhorn

We got back to Colorado Springs just in time to see the crab apple trees in bloom. Fairview Circle in COS is one street that has very mature crab apple trees.

Apple blossom time in COS

My Florida visit. May 10th, 2005.

Tuesday, May 10th, 2005, I flew down to Florida to visit my 5 siblings there. Casey and Butch were building houses and Pete was driving big Kenworth dump trucks hauling dirt, asphalt, cement, etc. He had several other drivers driving some of his Kenworth dump trucks. I believe he had 4 of these big dump trucks.

Casey, Butch and Pete

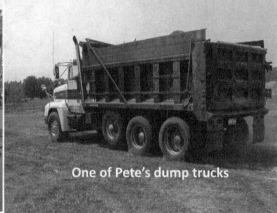
One of Pete's dump trucks

Adriaan and little Adrian (Adriaan's son) were both working at the U.S. Post Office. Little Adrian was apparently building a covered patio. Anyway, Casey drove me over to little Adrian's house so I could say hello to them. Pete had an interesting pet goat that he kept behind his garage. I believe it eventually got loose and he never found it.

Adriaan, Little Adrian and Casey

Pete's pet goat

Van and Brenda in one of the models

The house we purchased

Later that month, Brenda and I took a tour of the new houses that Classic Homes was building along Orchard Valley Rd. The house on the corner is the house that we purchased.

Lowell Thomas Museum in Victor, CO. Aug 2005.
August 2005, we visited the Lowell Thomas Museum in Victor CO. The place is loaded with old artifacts from the great Cripple Creek/ Victor gold rush of 1891.

An old washing machine

An old vacuum cleaner

Mine drilling machine

From there we went on to the overview of the large open pit Victor gold mine. At the overview one can see some of the actual machinery that was in place when they looked for gold deep down inside a mine shaft.

A winch to raise and lower carts

A large mining dump truck

Zion National Park. Sept 2005.
Sept 2005, Jeff asked me if I would be interested in going with him and Hilmar Wiesner to Zion National Park. Never having been there I said I would. I also invited Johnny Wilson who is a professional photographer who lived across the street when we lived just off of Orchard Valley to come along. Hilmar had apparently made a reservation to camp in Zion.

Jeff and Hilmar working on breakfast

We hiked the Hidden Valley trail and looked down into some of the slot canyons. Unfortunately, they had water in the bottom and thus they were not hike able.

Wind created holes

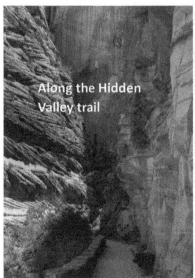

Along the Hidden Valley trail

Looking down the Virgin River Valley

Looking down the valley

Jeff overlooking one of the many slot canyons

After some hiking down the valley, we decided that we should climb up to **Angels Landing**. Now Angels Landing is one of the world's most renowned hikes and is an unforgettable adventure worthy of all bucket lists. The Angels Landing Trail is a total of 5 miles round-trip, from the trailhead to the summit and back. Depending on how much time you take once your there to admire the stunning view of Zion Canyon, but the hike takes about **4 or 5 hours**. Angels Landing trail is **strenuous and challenging for both the mind and body**. We would not recommend it for anyone with vertigo, a fear of heights. For the final climb, you traverse a narrow ridge with anxiety-inducing drop-offs on either side. If it is any relief, when you are at the narrow ridge, they do have a metal chain that you should hang on to and for guidance as you work your way to the very top.

Some of the hairpins on the trail

Start of the chain section

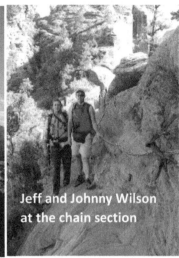

Jeff and Johnny Wilson at the chain section

Once we got to the top, we had to take in the view as well as take a little rest.

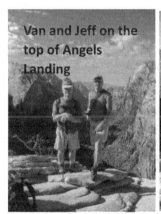

Van and Jeff on the top of Angels Landing

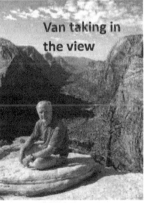

Van taking in the view

Looking down the valley from the trail of Angels Landing

We wanted to hike up the Narrows of the Virgin River the next day so that afternoon we went to a local store and rented some rubber shoes/sandals and a broom stick handle which was the recommended gear to do what we wanted to do. Here I am about ready to start my hike. The other photo is looking back to Jeff and Johnny trying to keep their gear from getting wet.

ALL NARROW CANYONS ARE POTENTIALLY HAZARDOUS. FLASH FLOODS, COLD WATER, AND STRONG CURRENTS PRESENT REAL DANGERS THAT CAN BE LIFE-THREATENING. YOUR SAFETY DEPENDS ON YOUR OWN GOOD JUDGEMENT, ADEQUATE PREPARATION, AND CONSTANT ATTENTION. BY ENTERING A NARROW CANYON, YOU ARE ASSUMING A RISK.
YOUR SAFETY IS YOUR RESPONSIBILITY.

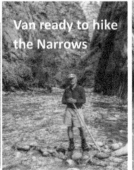

Van ready to hike the Narrows

Trying to keep our equipment dry!

A typical view along the Virgin River in the Narrows. There are actually people in the lower middle next to the green tree. That should give you an idea of the height of the sheer walls along the river.

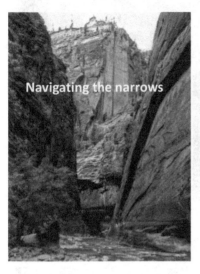
Navigating the narrows

Jeff along the Virgin River

Jeff, Johnny and Hilmar

Off to Bryce Canyon Sept 5, 2005.

After hiking the narrows, we left Zion National Park and headed for Bryce Canyon. Once you start getting close to Bryce you start seeing the colorful hoodoos.

Colorful Hoodoos

More colorful Hoodoos

There are trails thru the hoodoos, however we did not take the time to hike any of them on this trip.

Lots of trail thru the Hoodoos

Bryce Canyon taken from Inspiration Point

Joe Van Bemden's visit to COS, Sept 29th, 2005.

Thursday, Sept 29th, 2005 my brother Joe and his wife Carol came to visit us. One of the first trips we took them on was to visit Breckenridge. One of the shops that we went into had all kinds of silly hats. Joe is always up for a laugh or two. Thus, he had to try a few on. The following day we took a trip to Cripple Creek and Victor to see the fall colors and the old mining sites in and around that area.

Joe and Carol trying on hats

Colorful Aspens along Hwy 67 on the way to Cripple Creek

We must have stopped in Woodland Park to eat. After finishing our lunch and while we were in Woodland Park, I needed to get a shot of the arch that is made up of deer and elk horns.

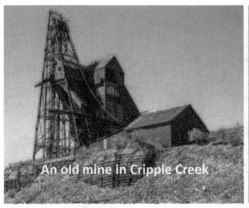

An old mine in Cripple Creek

Having lunch with Joe and Carol

The Arch in Woodland Park that is made up of deer and elk antlers. While they were here, we also drove over Independence pass and on to Aspen.

The Arch in Woodland Park

INDEPENDENCE PASS
Elevation 12,095 feet
CONTINENTAL DIVIDE

Joe and Carol at the top of Independence Pass

We had to visit the historical Jerome Hotel in Aspen. We even took them to my favorite place in the Aspen area, that being the Maroon Bells.

Joe, Carol, Van and Brenda at the Jerome Hotel in Aspen

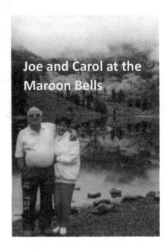

Joe and Carol at the Maroon Bells

While we were in Aspen some of the local ski shops had sales on and so I had to check them out to see if there was something that I could not live without.

Van checking ski equipment

Rose Phillips visit to COS, Oct 7th, 2005.

Oct 7th, 2005 Rose Phillips came down to visit us. We went to breakfast and stayed at GTL. While we were there, we invited Mike and Becky Wolfe over for dinner. Since they were from Houston we started watching the Houston Astors playing the Atlanta Braves in the last of the

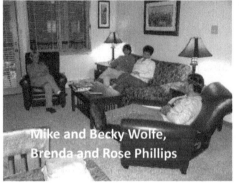
Mike and Becky Wolfe, Brenda and Rose Phillips

playoff games. Brenda had never watched a baseball game and wound up watching the longest playoff game ever played. It lasted 18 innings and was won by Houston. Houston then went on to play the St. Louis Cardinals who won the world series in 5 games. It lasted 5 hrs. and 50 minutes. That Sunday it snowed 22 inches in Breck. Unfortunately, Breck ski resort was not yet open for the season.

Mike Wolfe was a ski buddy that Rod and I met while we were skiing at Keystone. Mike lived in Houston and had a condo right along the shores of Lake Dillon when I first met him. He and I had this skiing arrangement where he would call me from Houston and ask me what I was doing such and such a day. If I did not have a commitment, he would say well I will fly down to Denver, and I would pick him up at DIA and we would drive to his condo and the next week or so we would ski.

One of the many foxes ones sees around GTL

This went on for years and years. We also saw this fox outside of the condo and he looked like he was looking for something to eat. Thus, we did what we were not supposed to do and that is feed it.

After our short stay in the condo at Breck we returned to COS and took Rose on a hike in the GOG. I took her picture at the fence on the trail to the Siamese Twins Rock Formation. Then I

Rose Phillips

took Brenda and Rose's picture at the hole in the Siamese Twins Rock with Pike Peak in the distance with snow on it.

Rose Phillips and Brenda at the Siamese Twins

Christmas time 2005.

Christmas time in 2005 we once again found ourselves in Longview, Texas. While we were there, I would usually go and visit the Letourneau Campus. Additionally, I would go past the plant and see if there were any large new earth moving equipment. As I drove down to the plant, I couldn't help but recall the purpose of the cement house that was built many years ago. It was a poured cement small house that R. G. Letourneau

A small entirely poured cement house

was going to build in the jungles of Africa and South America. Certainly, it was way before the 3D printed houses that some house builders and research teams (2020-2023) are playing around with today.

On the way back home driving thru northern New Mexico we decided to stop off at the Raton-Clayton Volcanic field. We had driven past it many, many times on the way to Texas and finally we stopped.

The Raton-Clayton Volcano

View of the surrounding country side

Back home in Colorado Springs at 2554 Sierra Oak Dr. we were all set up to enjoy Christmas which we did but it was now Jan 1, 2006. Jeff's family had to wait till we got back from Texas to get their Christmas presents.

Christmas tree at 2554 Sierra Oak

Karen, Paul, Susan, Stephanie and Jeff

Sunday, Jan 15th, 2006 we had our WVC small group over for lunch. The photo on the left and going from left to right: Ray Walkowski, Shirley Irwin, Don Monohon, Frank Irwin, Don Harper, Lynn Walkowski, Bill McCollum.

The WVC small group having lunch

The girl's chatting about something

Since Shirley Irwin has a birthday in January, Brenda baked her a carrot cake. Why it only has 3 candles on it, I really do not know and neither does Brenda. Shirley was pretty lucky in that later that month she again celebrated her birthday at our house with some of her girlfriends.

Shirley Irwin blowing out her 3 candles

Shirley and her lady friends

Shortly after celebrating Shirley's birthday, I got ready to go to Aspen for a short 2-week ski vacation. The photo represents our ski group for many, many years. The only one missing is Jim Gilman who is responsible for starting this group. He generally did not come except for a short weekend. We apparently had some fresh powder at Snowmass that morning. I am somewhat amazed that I could get the group to stop long enough for me to take this photo. Going from left to right we have: Paul

Our ski group skiing at Snowmass Ski resort

Wagner, Roger Boyer, Bruce Smith, Rod Porter, Urbanes Van Bemden and John Kwiatkowski (Big John).

Early Feb 2006 I was looking out the window and I could not help but notice all of the deer in our back yard when we lived on Sierra Oak. I quickly got my

16 mule deer going thru our backyard on Sierra Oak

camera and went on to our deck and took the shot below. There are 16 Mule Deer going thru our backyard. I have said it once and I will say it again, Peregrine has a deer problem!

My brother Adriaan's son whom we call Little Adrian was in Colorado in Feb 2006 and he called me because he wanted to go skiing with me. So, Wed, Feb 18th, 2006 we went to Keystone, and I had to show him that his Uncle Van knew how to ski pretty well. However, in fairness to little Adrian,

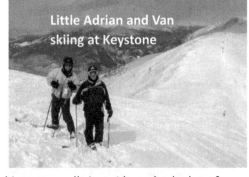
Little Adrian and Van skiing at Keystone

I should know how to ski pretty well since I have had a lot of practice. He was amazed at how different the skiing in Colorado was compared to the skiing he was used to in the Carolinas.

In March 2006 we attended Stephanie's concert at the Air Force Academy.

Stephanie playing her violin at AFA

Sunday, May 14th, 2006, I talked the grandkids into posing with the cow sculptures along Woodmen Rd. one more time since it was not going to be too long before the cows would be gone since the people that they belonged too were moving. The summer of 2006 my brother Joe was once again in Colorado. While he was here, we took him past my hiking friend Ray Butler's house who lived in Evergreen a suburb outside of Denver.

Stephanie, Susan and Paul at the cows

When we were at Ray's house, I could not get over the number of hummingbirds that were dining at the 3-4 hummingbird feeders that Ray had hanging. There were multiple hummingbirds at each feeder. At our house we hardly ever see 2 at the same feeder. After leaving Ray's house we continued

Hummingbirds

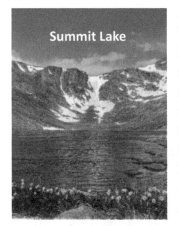

Summit Lake

up the road that takes you to Mt. Evans. We stopped at the Summit Lake Visitor Center, and I had to take a photo of Summit Lake. The Summit Lake visitor center is where there are lots of Bristlecone Pines. These Bristlecone pines are among the oldest living things on earth. There supposedly is one in this area that is over 1500 years old. Mt. Evans is known for the fact that it's one of the 2 Colorado 14ers that one can drive to the top of. The other is Pikes

Bristlecone Pine

Peak. It is also known for one being able to see lots of Mountain goats. Brenda even followed me the last hundred ft or so to get to the very top of Mt. Evans. I do not recall the temp but according to this photo of Brenda it must have been cold.

Mountain goats near the top of Mt Evans

Brenda on the top of Mt Evans

A brilliant rainbow

Mon July 10th, 2006, we visited the Denver Botanic Gardens with Don and Pat Harper. We love visiting the various gardens around the country whenever we are in the vicinity of one. The Denver Botanic Garden has many interesting flowers. One of my most favorite shots is of a yellow swallowtail butterfly on a daylily.

Yellow Swallowtail on Daylily

On the way home and just before we got to the Monument hill there was a very brilliant partial rainbow. Of course, I had to stop along I25 and take a photo (see previous page) of it.

We visited St. Elmo, July 13th, 2006.

Thursday July 13th, 2006 Brenda and I took a drive to visit St. Elmo which is one of Colorado's ghost towns near Buena Vista. **Google** has this to say about Elmo. Elmo, one of the most well-preserved ghost towns in Colorado, was founded in 1880. Built around mining, the town hit its prime in 1890. With over 150 mine claims, a telegraph office, general store, five hotels, dance halls, a newspaper office and a schoolhouse, the population peaked at about 2,000 people. One of the things you will notice as you first drive up is the number of Chipmucks waiting to be fed some sun flower seeds.

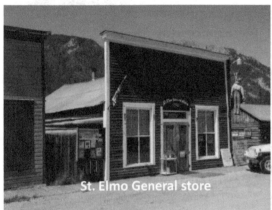
St. Elmo General store

The Stark Bros. store and the Post Office

Driving to St. Elmo one cannot help but notice the White Chalk cliffs. The white cliffs in Colorado

The White Chalk Cliffs on the way to St. Elmo

are not actually chalk but a soft clay mineral called kaolinite. The mineral is formed by deposits from the many surrounding hot springs.

Feeding the Chipmucks

Don Harper driving a bus

After visiting St. Elmo, we went on to see what Don Harper's day of driving old school buses for Noah's Ark White Water Rafting Co. looks like. Don's stepdaughter and her husband own Noah's

Noah's employees loading rubber rafts

Ark in B.V. and employ about 125 young college age students in the

summertime. Many of them are sons and daughters of Don and Pat's kids. Don does the payroll for them. He also has a commercial driver's license so he can drive the buses.

Conquered Wilson Pk, my last Colorado 14er.

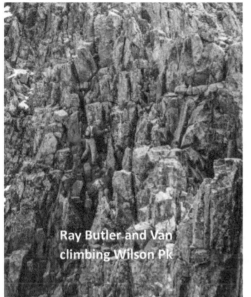
Ray Butler and Van climbing Wilson Pk

Thursday, July 20, 2006, I finally climbed my 55th 14er. I climbed it with Ray Butler, and he had one of his son-in-law's with him who took this photo of Ray and me climbing toward the summit of Wilson Pk. I really like this photo since it really shows the lichen on some of the rocks as well as the ruggedness of the climb. Ray had taken a small bottle of Champagne along that we would drink on the top to celebrate the fact that I had now climbed all of the 14'ers in the state. An intere sting fact is

Van and Ray celebrating with Champagne

that this is the 2nd attempt to climb this mountain. The first time we were here in 2004, Ray backed out since there was too much snow in the dip/notch. I had already started to go thru the dip; however, Ray said he was not going to do it. Thus, I said I am not continuing if you are not, so I turned around and we headed back to our campsite to live another day.

My visit to the Cripple Creek and Victor open pit Gold Mine.

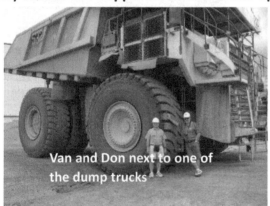
Van and Don next to one of the dump trucks

The tour guide

Thursday, August 17th, 2006, I had read in the local paper that one could get a free tour of the Cripple Creek & Victor open pit Gold Mine operation. Thus, I called Don Harper and asked him if he was interested in joining me on a free tour of the Víctor Gold mine. He said yes, I would love to join you and so we were off. The first thing that you notice is the size of the equipment used. Above is a photo of the lady that was conducting the tour by one of the dump trucks.

Here is a photo of a large backhoe filling one of the large dump trucks. Looking into the Fuller-Traylor NT Gyratory Crusher, which reduces the ore/rocks to fragments of 3/4 of an inch or less.

Loading a dump truck

The Fuller-Traylor rock crusher.

Wikipedia says: The gold is recovered from the ore by heap leaching.

CC&V's heap leach pad is one of the biggest in the world. We also got to tour the plant; however, it was fairly dark in there and subsequently I do not have any good photos. Whether that were gold flecks in the bottom of this tank I do not remember.

Google says that: Once we reach the ore, it takes 20 tons of rock to produce one ounce of gold. Yes, 20 tons. The gold bearing ore from the mine pits is processed by crushing, grinding, concentrating, and recovering the gold and then smelting it into Doré bars. These bars are a semi-pure alloy of gold, usually about 90% gold.

There is gold in this container

Climbing the Maroon Bells again.
Tuesday, August 29th, 2006, Ray Butler as well as Jerry Funk asked me if I would guide them at the Maroon Bells as well as Pyramid since I had already climbed them and I knew the way. Well, I agreed that I would do that and so here we are off for some more camping and climbing.

Looking at the Maroon Bells

John Reynolds, Jerry Funk, Ray Butler and Van on top of one of the Maroon Bells

March 6, 2007, David Marsman, my sister Lena's husband, passed away at the age of 67. He will be lovingly remembered by his wife of 47 years and his 3 sons. Auto racing was one of Dave's passions in life.

Dave and Lena Marsman

Registration building

Sunday, March 18th, 2007, I attended the WVC Men's retreat at the YMCA camp with Don Bode. I do not recall how many men were present, however we had a large crowd. Rich Griffith spearheaded the retreat. Matt Heard is about to give the blessing for the men's breakfast.

Matt Heard is about to bless the gathering

Brian Head Ski Resort in Utah.

April 19th, 2007, Brenda and I checked in at Brians Head resort in Utah. We used this as our base of operation. From there we made trips to the Arches National Park, Escalante National Park, Zion, and St. George. Some of the more famous and well-known rock formations as you enter into the Arches National Park are: The 3 Gossips, Sheep Rock, The Court house Towers.

The 3 Gossips   Sheep Rock   The Courthouse Towers

As you continue your drive the next rock formation that you should see is Balanced Rock. You cannot really appreciate how large that boulder is; the best way to appreciate how big it is if you have a shot with people around it. There are a number of people on the right side of the photo of Balanced Rock. After stopping off at Balanced Rock we drove down to "The Windows Section" of the park. One of my favorites rock formations in that area is the Double Arch. Again, to get an idea of the largeness of this arch one needs a photo with people in it. If you look closely, you will see dozens of people in the arch.

Balanced Rock, estimated to weight 3600 tons

Double Arch

Another must see and/or hike is Delicate Arch. This is the arch that you see on the Utah State license plate. It is shown here with the snow covered La Sal mountains in the background. If you look closely, you will notice that there is a man sitting on the left base of the arch. He would not move and people including me were hollering at him to move. The only good thing about him sitting there is it gives one an idea how big this arch is and also perhaps how delicate it is. Please note the small thickness on the left. Keeping your eyes open while you are walking around, you will see the Mormon Tea Plant, which is a shrub.

Mormon Tea Plant

Next, we traveled on to Escalante National Park.

Driving along Hwy 12 which seems like an endless desert and waste land you come to Calf Creek Falls. Looking carefully as you drive along the dirt roads you might come across some petroglyphs which are always interesting.

Lower Calf Creek Falls

Petroglyphs along the road

It is remarkably interesting to me the different colored rock layers that you see as you travel along. We came across some nice red Claret Cup Hedgehog blooming cactus. An interesting fact about this particular cactus is that they are pollinated by hummingbirds instead of insects. Another flower that we saw quite a few of is Red Penstemon.

Colorful rock layers

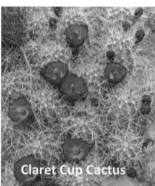

Claret Cup Cactus

Red Penstemon

Below is Brenda checking out some more wildflowers next to a large boulder slide. Driving down this dirt road we came across lots of narrow canyons.

Brenda looking for more flowers

Narrow Canyons

Our next hike was in Kolob Canyons which is part of the greater Zion National Park. A five-mile scenic drive along the Kolob Canyon Rd allows one to view the crimson canyons and provides access to various trails. One of our favorite hikes was along the Taylor Creek trail. Hiking along this trail we came across this old pioneer cabin.

An old pioneer cabin

Brenda under a large rockslide

Along the way we were intrigued by the number of what is known as seep lines along the various cliffs. These seep lines are formed by water seeping out of the rock and leaving behind minerals that create a dark line on the rock surface. The steep walls and cliffs really stand out when you can capture them when you have a blue sky with some white clouds.

Lots of seep lines

Beautiful red cliffs with blue sky

After hiking at Kolob Canyons, one of the following days we drove over to Bryce National Park. The roads across the mountains were at times snow covered and dangerous. Once we got there it was cold and very overcast. There are some formations that are famous, such as Thor's Hammer and Silent City.

Silent City taken from Inspiration Point

Thor's Hammer

After driving around, we parked the car and went for a hike down in the hoodoos.

Hiking down in the Hoodoos

Typical scenery down in the canyon

Later that morning it started to snow. Once back in the car we drove to the Natural Bridge Arch. The photo on the right is one of my favorite shots where the light was exactly right, and the oranges were incredibly brilliant. Straight out of the camera and it's not photoshopped!

The Natural Bridge Arch

Not Photoshopped!

Zion National Park-April 21, 2007.

The next day we drove to Zion National Park. Leaving our condo driving north on Hwy14 toward Parowan we saw a mountain lion cross the road a short distance in front of us. I tried to see if I could get a shot of him, but he was long gone in the woods. When we got to Zion, it was still raining and there was quite a bit of fog. However, it soon cleared up and off we went to see the sights. On our hike to the Lower Emerald falls we passed an extremely healthy clump of shooting stars.

Rainy and foggy on our arrival

I would have liked to have gotten a time exposure of the Lower Emerald Falls; however, I did not have my tripod with me. In that same area of the park, I saw what appeared to be a waterfall coming out of a solid rock wall. The water had found a crack in the rock wall.

A large clump of shooting stars

Water Fall out of a solid rock wall

Lower Emerald Falls

Driving thru the park we came to what is known as Checkerboard Mountain. Taking a close look at it, you can see why it is named Checkerboard Mountain. Also, it is hard to not appreciate the colorful orange, yellow, and red rocks formations throughout the park.

Checkerboard Mountain

Colorful rocks

We hiked as many short trails as we could. But some of them were somewhat dangerous. I was happy that the sandstone wasn't wet because it can become slippery when its wet. Brenda was certainly being very careful.

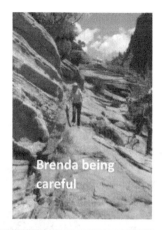
Brenda being careful

If one comes into the park from the east side eventually you will have to go thru a fairly lengthy tunnel. The tunnel has several large openings to let the exhaust fumes out. There are several places within the park where one can get a fairly good idea of how curvy the road thru the park is. One would say thank God for switchbacks.

Exhaust outlet

Lots of curves and switchbacks

We also hiked up to Angels Landing which is a pretty strenuous hike for anyone. Angels Landing is a 5.4 mile round trip hike, with 1500 ft of elevation gain with most all of it all at once. When we got to the place where the notorious chain section begins that is where Brenda said enough is enough. She had enough of the sheer drops on both sides of the trail. I asked her to wait for me as I am going to continue. I think Brenda did EXCEPTIONALLY well!

Looking down at the switchbacks of the trail

Brenda coming down from Angels Landing

Another interesting thing we saw was the number of rock climbers; it seemed like they were everywhere. Of course, there are lots of sheer cliff walls within the park. There are several rather famous and/or well-known towering figures in the park. Rather than insert 3 different photos, I will insert a photo of the plaque that shows these biblical towering figures. That is Abraham Peak on the left, Isaac Peak in the middle, and Jacob Peak on the right.

One of the many rock climbers

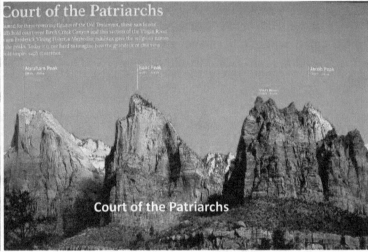
Court of the Patriarchs

Antelope Slot Canyon in Page, Arizona.

Leaving our Brian Head Ski Resort condo we headed toward Page, Arizona. The reason we headed toward Page was the fact that over the years I had been reading about the slot canyons found in that area. You might ask, What is a Slot Canyon? Well, a slot canyon is a narrow canyon that is formed from water (and wind) rushing through rock. What starts off as a tiny crack steadily grows larger from repeated flash floods and erosion over millions of years. The end result is a narrow canyon with high walls. The narrower canyons usually feature twists

The entrance to Antelope Canyon

Once inside its beautiful!

and turns and beautifully scalloped walls. Because slot canyons are formed from rushing water, the danger of flash floods still exist today. Before hiking through any of these slot canyons, it is important to check the weather. In the one we are hiking, back on Aug 12, 1997, 11 international hikers drowned. They now have installed a ladder to get out in case of a flash flood. The flooding was caused by a sudden storm some 15 miles away.

The slot canyon Antelope, is considered to be the Cadillac of the slot canyons. There are two Antelope Slot Canyons, the upper and the lower, they are basically across the street from each

Brenda finding her way thru the narrows

other. We chose the Northern one and we were not disappointed. We paid our $20.00/pp, and we could take as much time as we wanted. It was not terribly busy, and if my memory serves me correctly there was only one other couple in the slot canyon when we

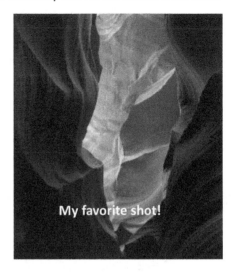

My favorite shot!

dropped down into it. I do remember that he had his camera set up on a tripod in the area where he was waiting for the sun to shine directly overhead so he could get a photo of a shaft of sunlight inside of the canyon. I found out later how one gets that classic shot of a shaft of sunlight and that is when the sun is shining down into the canyon, you throw up a hand full of sand. Basically, you have dust in the air and that is what creates the shaft of sunlight. I did not do that. Once inside there is no end to picture taking. You move 6 ft and it is completely different. We really enjoyed visiting this slot canyon. I am also glad that we did it back in 2007 because it had become extremely popular and busy and more expensive.

Monument Valley.

Leaving Page, Arizona we traveled on to and through Monument Valley. Monument Valley is a region of the Colorado Plateau characterized by a cluster of sandstone buttes, the largest reaching 1,000 ft above the valley floor. It is located on the Utah–Arizona state line, near the Four Corners area. Monument Valley is located on Navajo lands and is actually a tribal park operated by the Navajo people, who consider it a very sacred place. As a result, access is restricted within the park. One can drive a 17-mile section through the park on your own, however, you will need a Navajo guide to do anything more than that. For Landscape photography which is my primary interest this is prime country.

A panoramic photo of Monument Valley

There are just tons of famous and well-known rock formations in Monument Valley. Just as you are about to leave Monument Valley going east to 4 corners, you will come to what is known as the Mexican Hat rock formation. The Mexican Hat is a caprock of Cedar Mesa sandstone atop a pedestal and talus cone of the Halgaito Formation, a bed of red shale and siltstone. It is quite big and can easily be seen from the highway.

A large rock formation in Monument Valley

Mexican Hat

Our visit to Mesa Verde National Park.
Heading to 4 Corners, and on to Cortez, we soon arrived at Mesa Verde National Park. Mesa Verde is best known for a large number of well-preserved cliff dwellings. One of our favorites and must see is Cliff Palace. In the photo I happened to catch it when nobody was there.

Cliff Palace

Treasure Falls near Wolf Creek Pass

Leaving Mesa Verde and heading home over Wolf Creek Pass, we stopped to take a photo of Treasure Falls. I have never gotten a good photo of this fall, and I am not sure this one is either. Continuing on to Lake City because I have a photo of North Clear Creek Falls taken on the same day and the waterfall is on the way to Lake City.

North Clear Creek Falls

May 2007. Brenda and I must have taken a hike in the Garden of the Gods, since I have a nice photo of the Siamese Twins rock formation and looking through the opening, one sees Pikes Peak with snow in the distance. Going to the Siamese Twins is one of our favorite hikes in the Garden of the Gods specially if Pikes Peak has snow on it.

Siamese Twins

My visit to India June 2007.
June of 2007, I went to India again Global Action. See my more detailed Mission's report elsewhere in this book.

Life Changers Conference
Sept 21-23, 2007, Global Action held a "Life Changers Conference" at Cheyenne Mountain Resort in Colorado Springs where I made a presentation on my designs for buildings in Motipur. Various groups from all over the world where Global Action has ministries made their presentations and reports to the attendees.

Sheeba Subhan introducing a group

Looking into the conference room

Lars Dunberg at the closing

Van and Brenda with the Egyptian leaders

Lars Dunberg, CEO of Global Actions knows how to ask for the order (i.e., your commitment!).

The day after the conference was over, Rose Phillips, Brenda and I were on our way to Cripple Creek to shoot some fall foliage photos and when we passed Jeff's house there in the sky was a hot air balloon that caught on fire and was coming down. I cannot say it crash landed in the field by Jeff's house, it could have been much worse than what it turned out to be. In the photo you can see some of the damage the fire did to the canvas. After seeing that everyone was OK we were off to Cripple Creek and Victor.

The Hot Air balloon that caught fire

Rose and Brenda along Hwy 67

On the way to Victor, one passes the Victor gold mine. You can see in the photo below that they are knocking down whole mountains to get to the gold.

Van checking out the best vantage point

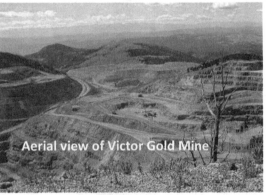

Aerial view of Victor Gold Mine

Off to India once again. Oct 2007.

Oct 2007, I found myself once again back in India. See my Global Actions writeup for more details.

Oklahoma City April 2008.

April 2008, Brenda and I visited the Oklahoma City National Memorial Site where Timothy McVeigh bombed the Federal building killing 168 people. Next to the reflective pool there is a somewhat different memorial in that there is an area called the Field of Empty Chairs where there are 168 empty chairs. Among the empty chairs are nineteen shorter chairs to represent the children killed on the day of the bombing. I've included a couple of plaques that are worth noting that were found in this same general area.

The reflective pool

A field of empty chairs

My sister Wilma McCarty passed away. Nov 12, 2007.

My sister Wilhelmina "Wilma" McCarty, aged 58, was called to her heavenly home after a courageous 17-month battle with cancer (brain tumor). She left behind her son, Jordon.

Our trip to Sante Fe, New Mexico May 2008.

We happened to be in Sante Fe when many of the spring flowers were blooming. I got a particularly good shot of Wisteria and a Red Bud tree.

Wisteria

A Red Bud tree

Off to Bolivia for LIAIM. May 2008

Later on, in May 2008 Don Houghton and I flew to Bolivia to get ready for LIAIM's open house. Don had brought a paint gun with him from Colorado Springs. His main objective was to paint all of the buildings. My job was to help Don move the scaffoldings and keep his paint gun supplied with paint. Then I would run off and do whatever was necessary such as hooking up the plumbing, running electrical wires, etc. This was the same trip when a large green anaconda snake crawled past our orphanage during the night. Don and I wondered why we heard lots of noise while we were trying to sleep. The next morning, we knew!

Van installing a sink

Don Houghton painting one of the buildings

Van and a large snake

A photo of LIAIM's foreman Guillermo at Guayaramerin, Bolivia. He was a genuinely nice man. If I recall correctly, we paid him $4/d because he was the foreman. How he fed his family of 6 kids is beyond me. The other photo is of most of the workers in one of the casas who were working tirelessly getting the place looking good for open house enjoying lunch.

Our LIAIM foreman and his family

Having lunch in one of the casas

Coming home late one night after we went out for dinner got to the main gate and there was this most interesting moth clinging to the gate. I had never seen one this interesting. The other photo is of Gary Zimmerman, LIAIM's director and founder, putting the finishing touches on the sign at the main gate of the orphanage at Guayaramerin, Bolivia.

A very interesting moth

Gary working on the sign

July 17, 2008, I was back in the USA. Jerry Funk and I decided that we would climb Conundrum Peak. I have to tell you why we decided to climb Conundrum Peak (2nd time for me). I had climbed it when Chuck Ferrari and I climbed Castle Peak. It is because of Conundrum Peak proximity to Castle Peak, and because Conundrum rises less than 300ft above its connecting saddle with Castle, it has not qualified as an official fourteener on most peak lists. There are rules that one must follow! Anyway, Jerry and I climbed it all by itself so thus it counts. On the way down Jerry decided that he would sit on his shovel and just kind of toboggan down.

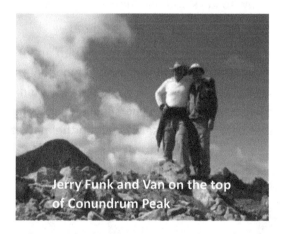
Jerry Funk and Van on the top of Conundrum Peak

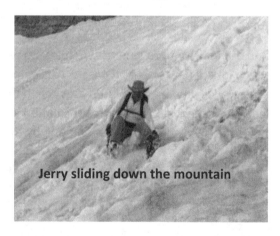
Jerry sliding down the mountain

Coming back from a hike in the Garden of the Gods, I happened to see that there was a small herd of Bighorn Sheep down at the entrance to Glen Eyrie. Thus, I drove down there and took a few shots. The following day I was in our front yard on Sierra Oak Dr. and a good sized black bear came walking across the street and went in between our house and the neighbors. It so happened that Brenda was in the back yard watering the grass and almost got run over by this bear.

Black Bear crossing Sierra Oak

Bighorn Sheep at Glen Eyrie

Taking a look at our future home at 1835 Sand Rock Pt.

Van's arms are black and blue

A few days later we took a tour of the house at 1835 Sand Rock Pt. the house where we now live. A month or so later we were in the process of moving in. We hired a U-Haul truck and Jeff and I moved our stuff from Sierra Oak Drive to 1835 Sand Rock Pt. In the process of being on the heavy end of the dolly my arms turned black and blue. I had worked for Allied Van Lines in Grand Rapids for 2 summers when I was going to college. Thus, I knew how to pack and load household furniture, etc.

One of the first improvements we made to our new house was to finish the garage. Jeff and I added lots of new electrical outlets cause one can never have to many outlets in a functional garage. We even put a light and a switch in the attic so if I ever needed to go up there, I could see something. I also blew some insulation above the garage ceiling. My personal feeling is that all of what I did should have been done by the builder before the house was put on the market.

Finishing the garage

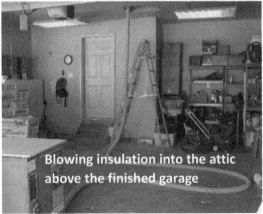

Blowing insulation into the attic above the finished garage

310

Back in Grand Rapids Michigan. Fall of 2008.

Brenda and Stephanie

The fall of 2008 we were back in the Grand Rapids area. We met our oldest granddaughter Stephanie and her new boyfriend Ryan Church, who helped her move into her room at Calvin College. She apparently met Ryan at a dorm mixer and thus the romance began. We took them out to dinner to try to get to know Ryan. Once back on Campus Grandma had to check things out in Stephanie's

Stephanie and her roommate

room. Also got to meet her roommate Karin Diener. Took a photo of the lovely couple upon our return to the campus. While we were in the Grand Rapids area, we had a small get together at Cora's house to celebrate MY birthday. We also happened to be there when the autumn foliage was at it prime.

Stephanie and Ryan Church

Brenda, Mom and Van

Fall foliage in Joe's backyard

Back home in Colorado Springs, it was rutting season and the male mule deer were taking their frustration out on everyone's trees and shrubs. Mid Nov we had our first measurable snow, and the finches were certainly looking for something to eat at our thistle seed feeder. Well, it is now

A big buck taking it out on my tree!

Lots of finches trying to get to the feeder

Dec 2008 and Brenda and I are in Aspen for our first of two seasonal skiing outings. Every year our friend Paul Wagner invites us out to go skiing in Aspen. Generally, our first trip is in early Dec and the second trip is late Jan early Feb. One day after I got home from skiing, Brenda and I went down to visit the John Denver Park in Aspen. In the park they have several of John Denver's songs etched into huge boulders. Christmas time in Aspen is always a fun time to be there. Lots of decorations all over town. At the Gant, where Paul has his condo, there are two huge/tall spruce trees that have lights all the way to the top. They do not take them down after Christmas.

Large boulders at John Denver Park

Christmas lights in downtown Aspen

Lights at the entrance to the Gant

Christmas 2008 in COS.

Christmas 2008 was spent at Jeff's house. If we are in town and not in Texas at Christmas time we would generally be at Jeff's place. Brenda seems incredibly happy with the Christmas present that I got her.

Stephanie, Susan and Paul playing with a puzzle

Stephanie and Brenda

Brenda relaxing

A very decorated yard

New Years Eve, I drove up the hill on Woodmen Rd. to take a picture of the most decorated house in our neighborhood. It seems it gets more elaborate each year. Out of our kitchen

Deer are waiting to be feed!

window we see all these deer looking for a handout.

The year 2009.

Doing the finishing touch

Every winter generally late Jan-early Feb the town of Breckenridge has a snow sculpture contest. Teams of sculptors from around the world will

The Dutch entry

descend on Breckenridge to carve 12-foot-tall, 25-ton blocks of pristine man-made snow into intricate works of art.

Off to Aspen once again.

Pyramid and the Maroon Bells

Bruce, Paul and Big John

After our ski trip to Breck we were home for a few days then off to Aspen for our 2nd annual ski trip. Generally we like skiing at Snowmass, however I generally try to go to Aspen Highlands because the view of the Maroon Bells and Pyramid are much better. Even though I have dozens of shots of these mountains I keep trying to get better shots. The photo of the 3 skiers is what is left of my ski friends. I must say that Big John is the best tree skier that ever lived.

Celebrating Pat Harper's 73rd Birthday.

Pat and Shirley

Shortly after we got home from our Aspen ski trip, we had Pat and Don Harper as well as Shirley and Frank Irwin over to celebrate Pat's 73rd birthday.

Don and Frank

In March 2009, we attended our granddaughter Susan's High School concert. Susan loved singing and she has a beautiful voice.

Off to Texas to see the Azaleas in Nacogdoches.

A couple of weeks after attending Susan's concert we were off to Texas to visit Brenda's mother in Longview.

Susan in the middle

Azaleas at Steven F Austin Gardens

Jimmy and Romelle were also in Longview. While we were there, we decided we would drive to Nacogdoches to see the Azaleas and Dogwoods in bloom. This is what the chamber of commerce says about the Azalea season in Nacogdoches. You really must see this to believe it.

Designated "The Garden Capital of Texas,"
Nacogdoches is home to the largest azalea garden
in Texas. The Ruby M. Mize Azalea Garden boasts
one of the most diverse azalea collections in the
United States. Encompassing eight forested acres
along the historic Lanana Creek on the campus of
Stephen F. Austin State University, the
impressionistic style garden features more than
7,000 evergreen and native azaleas accented with
vibrant Japanese maples, camellias, and other
unique collections.

Azaleas in Nacogdoches, TX

Azaleas, White and Pink
Dogwoods. What a garden!

The tulips were also in bloom at Steven F Austin College in Nacogdoches, TX.

Leaving Longview and on the way back to Colorado, I was able to get some photos of the Texas
Blue Bonnets blooming along the road.

Tulips at Steven F Austin College

Texas Blue Bonnets

Van and Don Harper's visit to the Denver Auto Show. April 2009.

April 2009, Don Harper called me and asked if I was interested into going to Denver to see the Auto Show. Being an old car buff and having spent 25-30 years in the Detroit area going to an Auto show was almost an annual thing. I remember my brother Joe who sold cars in Grand Rapids at the Highland Plymouth & Chrysler dealer for what seemed like 50 years, every year he would go to Cobo Arena downtown Detroit to see the latest models. Sure, I was interested in going to see the latest models. They even had some classic old cars and hot rods there. One that I really enjoyed was the 57 Chevy Bel Air hardtop.

Don Harper checking out a new Chevy Camaro

A 57 Chevy Bel Air Hardtop

There were also some concept cars on display. Below are two Jeep concept cars and now as I am

typing this in 2023 neither of these have hit the market. I guess the Jeep Renegade was their version of a modern dune buggy.

A Jeep Renegade concept

April 2009 Brenda and I were hiking in Ute park and at the pond by the parking lot, we noticed a Canadian Goose in the cattails sitting on a nest. It

A Canadian goose sitting on her nest

seemed quite alert as to what was going on. We also keep our eyes open this time of the year for wild Pasque flowers which will be blooming along the trails. These Pasque

Wild Pasque

flowers remind me a lot of crocuses, except they are a lot fuzzier.

Visit to the GOG in COS.

We also hike a lot in the GOG park. Here are a couple of photos where I snuck up a trail where I was not supposed to be. However, I was looking for some particular shots and those are off the beaten path!

Red and white rocks at GOG.
Pikes Peak in the background

Kissing Camels

Young Magpies ready to take flight

May 2009, we discovered that we had a Magpie nest in our big Blue Spruce tree. Now nobody wants young mag pies near any window of their house. They are

Finally down on the ground

the noisiest birds that ever lived. They seem to cry out Feed Me, Feed Me, …. After they left the nest, I tried to destroy their nest so they would not use it again next year.

May 2009, Brenda and I attended Paul and Susan's jazz band concert at Coronado High School. Paul played his trumpet and Susan played the piano.

Our Grandson Paul playing his trumpet

Our granddaughter Susan playing the piano

317

A week later we went to see her choir group sing in a church along Cascade Ave. in COS.

Susan singing in the choir
Susan playing the piano

Paul playing his trumpet

Birds visiting our feeders.

Brenda and I really enjoy watching all of the different species of birds coming to our bird feeders. We had Evening Grosbeaks raising their young. We had Black-headed Grosbeaks, Gold Finch, House Finches, Eurasian Doves, etc. At the Ute Park pond we witnessed Redwing

Black-headed Grosbeak, and Gold Finch

Eurasian Doves

Blackbirds doing their mating call.

There are several species of birds that we have never seen before, such as the

Red winged Blackbird

Western Tanager and the Lazuli Bunting. I just wish there were more of them around.

Western Tanager

Lazuli Bunting

My Mother takes a serious fall, Sunday, May 31, 2009.

June 1, 2009, I was informed of the fact that my mother had taken a serious fall. My mother had been living alone ever since my dad died in March 16,1991. My sister Jaci had been taking care of her all this time. Jaci came home from church Sunday May 31, 2009 and stopped at mom's house and there she was lying on the floor in the living room. She was taken to the hospital and never came home. The photo taken by Jennie in her hospital room shows what I believe to be a very hurting person and in a lot of pain.

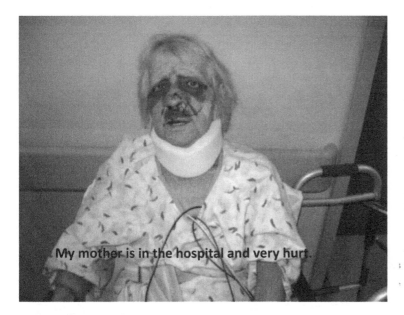

My mother is in the hospital and very hurt.

VAN BEMDEN Pieternella Van Bemden, aged 94, of Grand Rapids, died Thursday, June 11, 2009. She was preceded in death by her husband, Cornelius Van Bemden; her son, Ike Van Bemden; her daughter, Wilma McCarty; her son-in-law, David Marsman; and two grandchildren. She is survived by her children, Joe (Carol) Van Bemden, Urbanes (Brenda) Van Bemden, Lena Marsman, Casey (Dee) Van Bemden, Piet Van Bemden, Cora (Fred) Roelofs, Adrian (Linda) Van Bemden, Mari Gingrich, Jaci (Harry) Lucas, Butch (Deb) Van Bemden, and Jeni (Eric) Pannill; her daughter-in-law, Jennie Van Bemden; 34 grandchildren; 46 great grandchildren; three great great grandchildren; and many other relatives in the Netherlands. Funeral services will be held Wednesday 11:00 a.m. at the Zaagman Memorial Chapel with Rev. J.B. Zippro of the First Netherlands Reformed Congregation officiating. Interment Graceland Memorial Park. Visitation will be held at the funeral chapel Tuesday from 2 to 4 and 7 to 9 p.m. In lieu of flowers, memorial contributions may be given to Plymouth Christian Schools.

My Mother passed away June 11, 2009.

Her obituary reads in part as follows: Pieternella Van Bemden, aged 94, of Grand Rapids, died Thursday, June 11, 2009. She was preceded in death by her husband, Cornelius Van Bemden; her son, Ike Van Bemden; her daughter, Wilma Mc Carty; her son-in-law, David Marsman; and two grandchildren. She is survived by …. She had 34 grandchildren; 46 great grandchildren; three great great grandchildren; and many other relatives in the Netherlands.

While we were in Grand Rapids attending Mom's funeral and at the funeral luncheon, I got a chance to take a few photos of my family and friends of the family. So here it goes!

From left to right: Piet, Cora, Maria, Casey, Van, Butch, Lena, Adrian, Jeni, Jaci and Joe.

Van, Brenda and Jeff

Dee and Casey

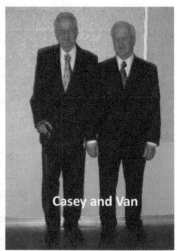

Casey and Van

Eric Pannill's Family

Fred Roelof's family

Piet, Joe, Casey, Butch, Van and Adriaan

Jaci, Maria, Lena, Cora and Jeni

Adriaan and Linda

Butch, Debora, Jesse, Valerie and Mitchell

Brenda, Stephanie and Jeff

Scott Marsman's Family

Jeff, Stephanie, Brenda and Tom Boot

Rob, Arla and Gerard Boot

Since most of the Van Bemdens were in town, we had a little family get together at Cora's house before everyone went their separate ways.

Adriaan, Linda, and Pete chit chatting at the table.

Enjoying each others company

Cora, Harry and Joe in Cora's sunroom

To think that I actually got to be in one of the photos. WOW.

Casey and Eric enjoying a cold one.

Casey and Eric enjoying a cold one

Van, Adriaan, Linda and Pete

On the way home I remember passing some Catalpa trees along I 94 in Michigan and I just had to stop to take a photo of them because our oldest granddaughter, Stephanie was doing a class project, and her project was to gather leaves from various trees. We were still living in Michigan and so I got her some Catalpa tree leaves. One does not see any catalpa tree in Colorado, at least not in Colorado Springs. These trees have large, heart shaped leaves, and produce clusters of large, trumpet-shaded flowers that turn into a long bean like seed pod.

A Large Catalpa tree

A field of Sun flowers along I76

Getting closer to home, coming down I76, I noticed a field of sunflowers and so I stopped to take a photo. As I climbed across the barb wire fence and as I dropped down to the ground there were some snakes sunning themselves and I landed in the middle of them. I just got goose bumps all over. I got out of their real fast, and I never even told anyone about it until now. A few days after we got home from my mother's funeral, Brenda and I went hiking in Waldo Canyon. We loved hiking in Waldo Canyon because there are so many different wildflowers there.

Stemless Evening Primrose

Parry Beardtongue

Milkweed with Lady bugs

Stone crop at Waldo Canyon

A nice stand of Penstemon

Also, one can see many Rocky Mountain Columbine which happens to be the state flower of Colorado. It is also known as the white and lavender columbine. It was adopted as the official state flower of Colorado on April 4, 1899, by an act of the General Assembly, after winning the vote of Colorado's school children. Waldo Canyon is also the first place I ever encountered a wildflower known as "Shooting Star."

Shooting Stars

Bighorn sheep at Glen Eyrie

Coming back from our hike at Waldo Canyon we saw a large herd of Bighorn sheep at Glen Eyrie.

The next day we went hiking at Seven Bridges. In the process of getting to the trail head of Seven Bridges you go past an interesting water fall in Cheyenne Canyon named Helen Hunt Falls. I did not have my tripod with me, so I did not get a photo of nice smooth silky water. I believe it was the first time I saw a Western Tanager. I did not get a good shot of it either.

Helen Hunt Falls

Western Tanager

Our son's front yard was rolled with toilet paper for no apparent reason in that none of the kids were graduating. But I am quite sure our grandson Paul's buddies had something to do with this.

Jeff's front yard being rolled

Hot Rod car show June 2009 in Pueblo.
Don Harper got wind of the fact that there was going to be a Hot Rod car show in Pueblo, so Don and I were off to see the various hot rods. There were many more, but these photos should give one an idea of the kind of Hot Rods that were on display.

Ford Pickup

During the summer of 2009, I finished the lower level (Walkout Basement) at the Taylors.

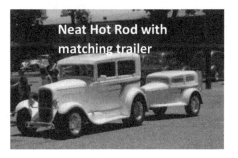
Neat Hot Rod with matching trailer

Dinner at the Irwins.

After church service Aug 10, 2009 we were invited to the Irwin's for lunch. Louise Monohon's daughter Debbie happened to be in town and thus the Monohons were also there. This was toward the end of Loiuse's life.

Brenda, Shirley, Frank, Deb, Louise and Don

Susan checking out her birthday presents

A little later our youngest granddaughter was over at our house to celebrate her 13th birthday.

Walking around the block I saw these 3 crows and a red tail hawk playing chicken. i.e., who is going to move first. The crows did not want the hawk in their territory as they had young ones. Also, around the same time there was quite a bit of bobcat activity around the neighborhood. I was lucky enough to catch this mother bobcat with 3 kittens going thru our backyard. This photo appeared in the Colorado Springs Newspaper, the Gazette as the photo of the day.

3 Crows and a Red Tail Hawk

Mother Bobcat and 3 kittens

Checking in with local goat farmers

Because of my involvement with Global Action in India, and that they were going to get some goats, Lars Dunberg asked me to find out what is involved in housing and milking them. Thus, I checked around the area to find out if there were any goat farms. I found several and I visited them so I could design the proper shelter and milking stalls before my next trip to India.

Lots of Goats

A goat milking stand/stall

This is one of the Global Action India employees Janaman that I would be working with. Janaman happened to be in Colorado Springs getting some training at Global Action Corp

Van and Janaman

Headquarters, so I invited him over to our house and showed him around. I took him to Breckenridge, etc. When I went to India a few months later, Janaman took me to Taj Mahal, in Agra, India.

Janaman at Loveland Pass

Aug 5, 2009, Brenda and I were at Jeff's house celebrating Paul's 17th birthday. Paul likes to let me know that he is considerably taller than me. I just tell him that most people are taller than me.

Paul and his Birthday cake

Van and Paul

Jimmy Parker's visit to COS, Aug 6, 2009.

Shortly after celebrating Paul's birthday all of Jimmy Parker's family came to the Colorado Springs area. Jimmy had rented a house in the Cascade area along Hwy 24.

Visit to Rocky Mountain National Park, Aug 10th, 2009.

Osprey on their nest

Lily Pad Lk

Neat grain pattern

Monday, Aug 10, 2009, Jeff, and Karen was able to rent a condo near Granby called Silver Creek Inn, on the west side of Rocky Mountain National Park. Jeff and Karen were there a few days and then Karen had to come back to Colorado Springs in preparation for the new school year. Jeff stayed there and I drove out there for the rest of the week. Jeff and I went to Rocky Mountain National Park and did quite a bit of hiking. On the way to Grand, before we actually entered the park, we saw quite a few Elk as well as Osprey nests right along the road. I thought the grain pattern in this old pine tree stump was quite interesting.

Alluvial Fan

Long Peak in the distance

This is a shot of the Alluvial Fan area. The Alluvial Fan area is a fan-shaped area of distrubance in Rocky Mountain National Park. It was created on July 15, 1982, when the earthen Lawn Lake Dam above the area gave way, flooding the Park and the nearby town of Estes Park with more than 200 milion gallons of water. We also got a nice shot of Long's Peak in the distance with nice blue sky and puffy white clouds.

Jeff and I hiked to Dream Lake and got several shots of Dream Lake with Hallett Peak and Flattop in the background. At Dream Lake there is a very knurled and twisted pine which is kind of unique.

Dream Lk with Hallett Peak in the distance

A very knurled and twisted pine

On the way back from Dream Lake Jeff and I stopped to rest and eat something. In no time there was a Golden Mantled Ground Squirrel looking for a handout. It finally ran off with my partially eaten apple. Initially I thought it was a chipmunk, however after doing a little research I found out that it was not a chipmunk but a Golden Mantled Ground Squirrel. This ground squirrel is often mistaken for a chipmunk because of its resemblance. However, it is larger and has no

A Golden Mantled Ground Squirrel

stripes on its head. The tail is also shorter. On its neck and shoulders is a russet to golden "mantle." It also has cheek pouches for carrying food. On one of our other hikes, we witnessed a bull elk trying to de-velvet his horns by taking his frustration out on a pine tree. In many cases this process can completely demolishing small trees. As velvet is skin, rubbing it off can look very gruesome as it does in this case. You can see the velvet hanging off of it horns. We also kept our eyes open for moose. Luckily, we saw several. We also hiked into an area where there were quite a few waterfalls. Hiking through the woods we saw evidence of the Pine bark Beetle. This beetle lays eggs into the bark of pines and the larvae tunnels under the bark and eventually kills the tree.

Bull Elk de-velveting his horns

A good size bull moose

Jeff getting ready for a million dollars shot

Pine bark beetle damage

Aug 20, 2009, A few days after I got home from our trip to Rocky Mountain National Park, I went to help Don Monohon repair his RV. Don had an old Ford RV that had a leak or two and the plywood had started to rot. Thus, after disassembling the area that was in dire need of repair, we started to put it back together.

Don Monohon's RV

Looking at what needs to be repaired

Ellis Diebler's daughter's family, the Jacksons, stayed at our house when they were in town to drop their son Peter off at the AFA prep school. One morning while they were getting ready for the day, they noticed a bear family out the sliding glass door on the lower level of our house chopping away on the acorns. They took a few photos of the bears. I wished they had come up stairs to tell me about it before the bears moved further down the hill.

Cubs eating acorns in my backyard
The Bear Family

A week later we were in Breck and on the way back way (via US 24), we passed a large buffalo herd in Hartsel. One time I stopped to take a photo of this herd while the ranch helpers were repairing a fence and they told me that they have about a half dozen or so WHITE buffalo.

A large herd of buffalo near Hartsel

A couple of white buffalo

When we got to Breckenridge, I just had to take a photo of the restaurant on the north end of Main Street that we went to for a steak dinner. I have never seen such a luscious display of flowers.

A luscious display of flowers in Breck

Casey Van Bemden passed away. Aug 12, 2009.

Friday, Aug 28, I flew to Florida to attend my brother Casey's funeral.

Thursday, Aug 13th, 2009, my brother Casey passed away. I flew down to Florida to attend his memorial service. At the memorial service I turned on my camera 90 degrees to video record the service to get a better view of the pastor. Unbeknownst to me I had my camera turn sideways and the entire video recording is sideways. I thought that the system would automatically rotate the video like it does for photos. I was wrong! I do have a photo of Casey's adopted son Greg and his wife Debra and their son Gregory.

Debra, Greg, and Greg Jr. Van Bemden

Socializing after Casey's funeral

After the funeral service, most of the family gathered at my sister Maria's house. I was able to take a photo or two from the part of the family that lives in Florida.

Piet, Lori, Anglie and Char

Adriaan, Maria, Piet and Urbanes

Ryan, Brandie, Aiden and Chase Romeo

Greg, Debra and Katie Van Bemden

Our Beaver Creek Trip, Sept 2009.
Brenda was able to get a condo in Beaver Creek via Interval. Now we would use this condo as a base for doing day trips here and there. We asked Don and Pat Harper if they wanted to join us, since we knew that we would have a 2-bedroom condo. Pat apparently had a hair cutting appointment that she did not want to break. However, after we got there and called Don and Pat and mentioned how nice our 2-bedroom condo was, they decided to join us in a day or two.

Don and Pat Harper looking out of the balcony

Whenever Brenda and I are doing our fall foliage trips we generally wind up going to Steamboat Springs. When we are there, we always wind up going to Yampa River Botanic Garden. This is an extremely nice garden for the size of town that Steamboat Springs is. They generally have many flowers blooming and one that is particularly interesting is the fall crocus. Another interesting scene you do not see everywhere is a Hummingbird Moth also known as Sphinx moth, drinking nectar from the various flowers. As a point of interest, I took a photo of one in our rock garden that was published in the Colorado Gazette as "Photo of the day." These moths can hover like a hummingbird and have an extra-long proboscis to sip nectar. They love Bee Balm flowers.

Fall Crocus

A Hummingbird moth

Lots of color

One of my favorite photos from this particular trip to Yampa River Botanical Garden in Steamboat Springs is the one above taken on a berm. I gave Dr Allan, our dentist, a copy of this photo because he wanted to do his berm similarly.

An interesting fact about this garden is that there is a person by the name of Jeff Morehead who lives in the trailer park at the south end of the garden. He has built a gate that leads into the Yampa Garden where he has a good size garden with many interesting flowers and plants.

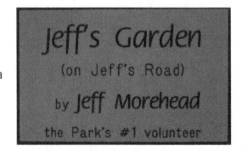

Jeff's Garden
(on Jeff's Road)
by Jeff Morehead
the Park's #1 volunteer

We also try to go to Fish Creek Falls which is one of the larger waterfalls in the area. If you look closely, you will see some people just above the horizontal log. This should give you an idea how high the fall is.

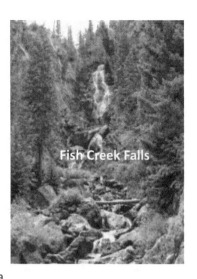
Fish Creek Falls

Colorado National Monument. After visiting Steamboat Springs, the following day we drove to the Colorado National Monument near Grand Junction.

The rock slide

After visiting Colorado National Monument, we drove to Colorado's Grand Mesa. Let's see what Microsoft Bing has to say about Colorado Grand Mesa.

The Grand Mesa is a large mesa in western Colorado in the United States. It is the largest flat-topped mountain in the world. It has an area of

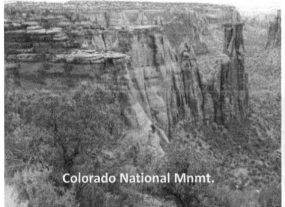
Colorado National Mnmt.

The Coke ovens

about 500 square miles and stretches for about 40 miles east of Grand Junction between the Colorado River and the Gunnison River, its tributary to the south. The mesa rises about 6,000 feet above the surrounding river valleys, including the Grand Valley to the west, reaching an elevation of about 11,000 feet. Much of the mesa is within Grand Mesa National Forest. Over 300 lakes, including many reservoirs created and used for drinking and irrigation water, are scattered along the top of the formation.

Golden Aspens

The Grand Mesa is flat in some areas, but quite rugged in others.

I took a nice photo of a stand of Golden Aspens. This was the first time I actually saw and took a photo of a Green-tailed Towhee.

Green tailed Towhee

333

Silver Saxifrage

The following day we went to visit Betty Ford Garden in Vail. Brenda and I love visiting this garden mainly because they have so many unique plants and flowers. Below is what MS Bing says about Betty Ford Garden.

The Betty Ford Alpine Gardens are the world's highest botanical

Dew on the Blue Bells

garden located in Vail, Colorado at an altitude of 8,200 feet in the Rocky Mountains[1]. The gardens are named after former First Lady Betty Ford who lived in Vail with her husband, President Gerald R. Ford for many years[2]. The gardens focus solely on plants that thrive in harsh alpine environments around the world[2]

Leaving Betty Ford Garden, we drove west and picked up US 24 and crossed over the Tennessee Pass near Minturn. The Aspens here were near their prime. Travelling along US 24 heading toward Leadville one comes to a Colorado ghost town by the name of Gilman. Gilman is an abandoned company owned mining town. At one time lead and zinc were mined there.

Golden Aspens near Tennessee Pass

Gilman the old abandoned mining town

Our next stop was back to our condo in Beaver Creek. In Beaver Creek they have an interesting trail called the five senses trail. There is also a nice church there that President Ford attended. This church has a most interesting front door. It's glass and has a wrought iron shaped tree.

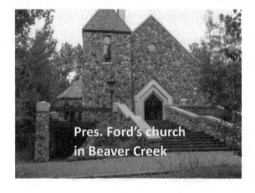

Pres. Ford's church in Beaver Creek

A very interesting front door

A ski rack by the church

Our Smores package

Something which I had never seen before was the lockable ski rack for those that skied to church.

One evening during our stay, they had a Smores roast which was fun. They had given each guest a small package with crackers, chocolate, and marshmallows.

Brenda roasting our marshmallows

The following day we drove to Snowmass Village to visit with Bruce and Kathy Smith. Bruce is one of the fellows in our ski group when I am in Aspen in the wintertime. Bruce owns one of the condos in the new base village. Just as we got to Snowmass Village there were several hot air balloons at the golf course taking people for a hot air balloon ride. After meeting Bruce and Kathy, we decided that we would hike one of the trails that gives one an exceptionally good view of Snowmass Village.

Hot Air Balloons at the golf course

Kathy Smith and Brenda hiking in Snowmass Village

Now being this close to the Maroon Bells, Brenda and I decided that we would go there and see what the state of the fall foliage was. Although it is not my best shot of the Maroon Bells, we were not disappointed.

Kathy and Bruce Smith high above Snowmass

The Maroon Bells across the lake

After we got back to Beaver Creek, Brenda and I walked around downtown Beaver Creek. One of the stores had a glass chandelier hanging that was made by the famous Dale Chihuly.

Chandelier by Dale Chihuly

One day the four of us drove over to Vail to see some of the cars from the "1000-mile Tour of Colorado" that had made a stop at Vail. There were many, many foreign classic older cars as well as some new cars. In the main area where they had the cars, they also had quite a few very colorful flower wagons.

Don and Pat Harper looking over a Lagonda

Brenda likes this Morgan Roadster

A very colorful flower wagon

Attended an AFA Football game, Sept 26, 2009.

Sept 26, 2009 I was invited to attend an AFA football game by Don and Linda Rubin. Don and Linda Rubin are one of the couples in our small Bible study group. AFA played San Diego State and AFA won by a score of 26-14. As you can see it was very sunny and hot. I am trying not to get sunburned.

Van and the Rubin's at AFA

One of the traditions of AFA football is that the cadets do pushups for the total score each time new points are scored. Another tradition is that they usually have fly overs, usually with the AF Thunderbirds, especially when they play one of the other armed forces.

Cadets doing pushups

A huge plane doing a flyover

Oct 19,2009 I was in India. See more details in the section Global Action elsewhere in this book.

Thanksgiving 2009 was spent at Jeff's house. Karen's parents were also in town.

The Oct 19, 2009 team to India

Bill DeJong and Brenda at Jeff's house

Aspen Elk Club

At the Little Nell

Right after Thanksgiving I was back in Aspen skiing with our Aspen Ski group. While I was in Aspen, I took a few photos of the Christmas lights in and around downtown.

Dec 28, 2009, I believe the men, i.e. (meaning Van, Jeff, Paul and Ryan) went skiing at Breckenridge. Jeff and Paul were both boarding, and I was on skis. As you can see, we cannot afford those $15 hamburgers and $20 lunch breaks so when we go skiing, we generally brown bag it.

Christmas Day 2009.

Christmas Day 2009 was spent at Jeff's house. That is where we generally gather to exchange Christmas presents. Stephanie was home from college and brought Ryan along perhaps to see what he might be getting into.

Jeff snowboarding

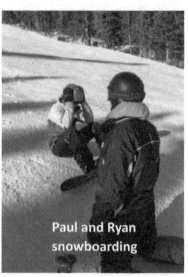

Paul and Ryan snowboarding

Brenda looking down at the Grandkids

Ryan, Stephanie, Paul and Susan.

Brenda has no idea what I got her for Christmas.

Paul seems happy with 2 Michigan sweatshirts.

Love In Action International Ministry—LIAIM
Mission work in Bolivia

A map of Bolivia.

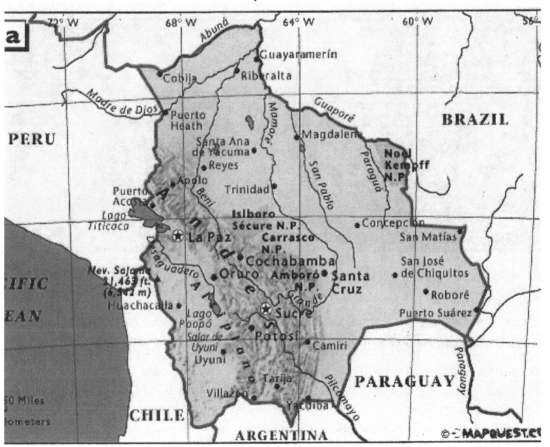

Mission work in Bolivia. 2000-2008.

After Gary and Jerri Zimmerman attended the "Welcome to our Town" class and encouraged me to join them on a mission trip to Bolivia, both Brenda and I decided to do just that. Going back a number of years when we lived in Ann Arbor and were attending the CRC church there, Majia Kaldjian kept after me encouraging me to go on some mission trips. But back then I was busy in my job and did not feel I could take the time to do that. Now, since I was retired, I could not use the excuse of saying I was too busy, etc. Thus, Brenda and I were off to our first ever mission trip. Gary and Jerri Zimmerman are the founders and directors of a mission organization named Love In Action International Ministries (LIAIM). At the time we met them, they had a work project (finishing a church) already underway in Santa Cruz, Bolivia.

The LIAIM team Oct 2000.

Our team of volunteers that went to Santa Cruz, Bolivia with LIAIM Oct 2000. Rod and Ruth Porter, Gary Zimmerman, Larry Krieger, Brian, Van, Brenda, Verlyn, Sandra, Jerri Zimmerman.

Notice the swing and gym set in the background. It's an exact duplicate of our son Jeff's swing and gym set. I created a set of prints from his to take to Bolivia to build a swing and gym set for the kids at the Santa Cruz church. I also bought a slide stateside that I cut in half to take. That is the yellow slide on the right in the photo above.

All the members of the team met in Miami; there we boarded a plane and flew to La Paz, Bolivia. At 13,325 ft La Paz airport is one of the highest commercial airports in the world. At La Paz airport we unloaded some passengers then flew to Santa Cruz. Lucas Antelo, LIAIM's contact person in Bolivia, had arranged for several cars to take us to the church where we would be staying.

Lucas Antelo and his family and parents.

We slept at the church where we put two pews together and they provided us with a small mattress, and everyone was quite comfortable. In the photo below Gary Zimmerman is looking at his camera and I guess he does not know that I take lots of pictures. There is no need for him to take pictures! Ruth and Rod Porter are getting dressed and Brenda is still sleeping as you can see in the lower right of the photo. The other photo is Van (me) cooking breakfast.

In addition to working on the church, Rod Porter and Larry Krieger were both licensed optometrists and they were able to bring along a number of used eyeglasses that were gathered via the Lion's club. Rod and Larry saw hundreds of local people in need of eyeglasses.

Our sleeping quarters

Van cooking Breakfast

Rod and Larry would determine what glasses a given person needed and the helpers would look thru the boxes of eyeglasses to find a good match.

Rod Porter hard at work

Brenda handing out Tootsie rolls

After the bricks were laid, the entire church was stuccoed. Some of the team members were assigned to keep the men who were doing the stucco supplied with stucco (cement). Meanwhile others were digging the foundation for the bathroom addition.

Stuccoing the Church exterior

Bathroom foundation ready to be poured

Van bringing home the lumber

Before we could build the swing and gym set,

Gary, Lucas, Lumber man and Van

Gary, Lucas, and I drove over to the local lumber yard to get the lumber required to build it according to my blueprint. The photo on the shows us wheeling and dealing at the lumberyard.

Brian and I and some of the younger men hanging around the church started to build the swing and gym. Now there was this one particular young man who wanted to test my strength. They had a homemade barbell that he wanted to challenge me with. Thus, I accepted the challenge. We did curls as well as overhead presses. I believe he was somewhat surprised because I always did just a few more reps than he could do on either one.

Brian, Van and our helpers

Van doing some curls. The challenger standing by

Following the regular mission trip, Brenda, Van, and Brian stayed over and joined the Zimmermans and visited a half dozen other places in Bolivia where Gary and Lucas felt that LIAIM could do some work.

Brian, Gary, Jerri, Brenda and Van in front of the small plane we flew around Bolivia in.

Creating mud blocks

Some of the places I remember visiting were Cochabamba, Trinidad, San Borja, La Paz, etc. We also took a boat ride on Lake Titicaca. Notice the large boat made up of reeds. Watched the local women weave rugs, blankets, etc. Brenda purchased a small rug from one of the women. All of the material comes from the Llamas. Another thing you will notice when you are out in the

countryside is that many of the buildings are made out of the mud blocks that we saw being made by a couple of men. Also, the indigenous women wear bowler hats and a long decorative shirt called a pollera. Look at the picture of Brenda below to see the skirt and bowler hat.

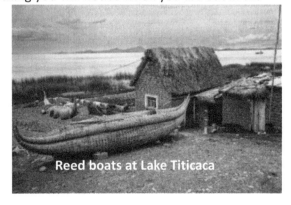
Reed boats at Lake Titicaca

At the church that was partially built the foundation and columns for the bathroom addition were in place; the bathroom layout was not. I remember Gary started to sketch out the bathroom layout on the side of the church with a large carpenter pencil, which would be gone when the outside of the church gets painted. I knew from my CAD/CAM work career that there was a better way and I told Gary that I would develop a set of blueprints to detail the bathroom addition. Thus, when I got home, I purchased a cheap CAD program by the name of PUNCH for about $50 and started developing prints and scale models of the various buildings. This software program had exceptionally good rendering capabilities; one could do a walk through and a fly over.

Brenda watching spinning

2001 – 11. Went back the following year at around Thanksgiving time.

The LIAIM team 2001

This time I was more prepared than my first trip when I did not know what to expect. On this mission trip Rod Porter and Larry Krieger had brought along thousands of pairs of eyeglasses. People came from miles around in the hopes that they would receive a pair of glasses. They started to line up hours before the clinic opened. Thus, the doctors and their supporting folks were quite busy all day long. It is kind of interesting in that some of the folks were kind of fussy as to what eyeglasses they wanted. Some styles they just did not like.

People lining up to get their eyes examined

Looking for the correct eyeglasses

The construction folks were transported via Lucas's pickup truck to the church where the work was taking place. I worked with Harold on the electrical wiring of the church. I guess the details of my electrical drawings allowed him to fully understand what we wanted done. Just like God's love, electrical circuits are somewhat universal. One of the most surprising moments was when Harold was sitting in the front pew at the church the following Sunday with a guitar. I did not realize he was so musically inclined. The reason I say this is because both of us whistled the tune "How Great Thou Art" day in and day out. One would have thought he would have had several tunes in his whistling repertoire. The photo shows Harold climbing to the rafters in the church. The ladder itself wasn't high enough to reach so we started out with a table, then we added a 50-gal drum which had a rusted-out bottom, placed a board on top of the barrel and then put the ladder on top of that. It was BAD NEWS!!!! OSHA would have a field day here! While Harold and I were doing the electrical work in the church, other construction workers were building a septic tank.

Harold going up to the rafters

Laying bricks to build a septic tank

Van up in the rafters

One of the things that I noticed during my first trip to Bolivia was that not much was done for the kids other than conducting Bible school. Thus, while I was back in the states and before I set off on this mission trip, I would try to do something for the kids. Well, it so happened that there was a neighborhood garage sale and I thought that would be a good time to look for some toys for the young boys and girls. So, I went to the neighborhood garage sales and bought many toys, such as trucks and dolls, that would fit in a large box but stay below 50 lbs.

Another fun thing that we did in Bolivia was go to the local market and buy some food for the coming week.

A local meat market

The boys playing with their new toys

We would hop into Lucas's pickup and head for the local market. There we bought bananas, vegetables, spices, etc. The first thing Gary would do is hire a young boy with a wheelbarrow and as we went around we would simply toss our purchase into the wheelbarrow.

Everyone on board!

Lots of Spices

Vegetables galore

Burlap bag full of cocoa leaves

One of the more surprising things I learned was the fact that lots of day laborers chew cocoa leaves which supposedly suppresses hunger. It is readily available at most markets. Another situation that caught my eye was when a young man was pulling a tooth out with a pair of pliers. No anesthesia. The poor guy just sat there, no screams nor hollers.

Dentist

The construction crew poured cement into the night with the help from the lights of Lucas's pickup.

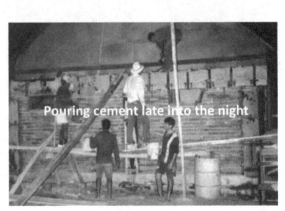
Pouring cement late into the night

June 2003. Went back to Bolivia the summer of 2003 to continue to work on the church that was started a few years back. I think this was the first trip where I had a digital camera. It was an

Break time!

Laying out the plumbing in the church bathroom

Olympus C3100Z, 3 megapixel and it sold for $499. Back in 2002. Anyway, I have several photos that were taken on this trip. In the photos above, I am taking a break with some of the helpers. In the other photo I am laying out the plumbing for the bathroom addition that we just finished with the walls and roof. No inspection to meet.

Below we are unloading a truckload of handmade bricks. The other photo is of me tiling the pulpit area of the church that we've have been working on the last couple of trips.

Unloading the handmade bricks

Van tiling the pulpit area

Below are several CAD models of the bathroom addition, church, and the parsonage. Since I

have several lines that I can type before I go to the next page, I want to insert a line or two from an email that Gary received from Lucas regarding the bathroom addition that I designed, and help build on two separate trips to Bolivia.

A scale model of the bathroom

Hello Van, wanted to share a quote that we got from Lucas regarding the Nuevo Amanecer Church: He said, "The word is that this is one of the nicest looking churches and the best bathroom of any of our churches." Thought you might like to know this. Thanks for all you have done for the church and look forward to having you on another team of your choice. See you soon, Gary.

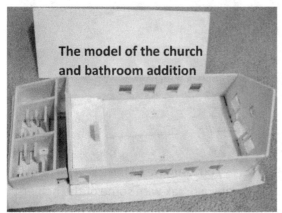 

The model of the church and bathroom addition

We also built a parsonage on this same lot. A scaled CAD model of the parsonage is shown above.

The 2004-2005 time period, Gary and Jerri Zimmerman were incredibly involved with their daughter Andrea who had a rare type of cancer and they thought at one time it was cured but it returned. Thus, as far as LIAIM was concerned, there were not a whole lot of mission trips other than Gary going to Bolivia and meeting with Lucas on various fact-finding trips.

I was a LIAIM board member from 2001-2003 and we held several board meetings at our house on Edgerton Ct. When my term ran out in 2003, I was asked if I would consider being a board member for the years 2004-2006. However, I turned it down.

It happened that a pastor and his church gave LIAIM an entire small city block for the development of an orphanage/school in Guayaramerin. Thus, when Gary got back to Colorado Springs, he came over and discussed how we might go forward. Here we have an empty small city block and how can we best utilize the space we have. Where are the casas (houses/dormitories) to be placed, where are the classrooms to be placed, etc. Thus, I had enough work to keep me busy for a while designing the various buildings using the CAD (Punch) software package I had bought several years earlier. I started out designing the first casa to accommodate 20-25 young children plus house parents to watch over them. While I was designing the various buildings, Gary had rounded up a local work crew to begin building an 8-10 ft brick fence around the entire perimeter of the property. Thus, after several rough designs, Gary and I settled on the design pictured below. Note that it has 6 bedrooms for the orphans and each can easily accommodate 4 single beds. It has 2 bathrooms, 1 for the boys and 1 for the girls. Plus, it has separate accommodations for the house parents, i.e., their own bedroom, bathroom, and sitting area to get away from the 20-25 little kids. Each casa is 3757 sq. ft.

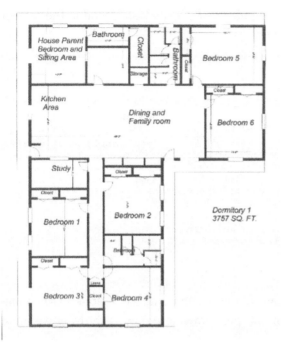

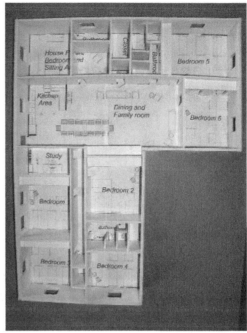

A CAD drawing for Casa 1.   A scale model of Casa 1.

A CAD rendering of Casa 1.

This was to be the design for all of the casas used in Andrea's Home of Hope and Joy.

In the "The Love Letter" a publication that LIAIM published every so often and in the May 2005 issue the following appeared.

Urbanes Van Bemden...

...volunteers to design buildings for LIAIM projects. He is currently designing a two-story Sunday School Classrooms/Dining Hall building for the church in Santa Cruz, Bolivia and an Orphanage/School to be built in northeast Bolivia. These buildings for the orphanage include a dormitory, dining hall and chapel which will be built on the property recently given to LIAIM. Van is a retired engineer and lives in Colorado Springs, Colorado with his wife Brenda and has been a team member on various teams to Bolivia.

After some discussion about how we might want to lay out the entire envisioned Orphanage in Guayaramerin, Bolivia, Gary and I agreed that the plot drawing below is the way we want to proceed.

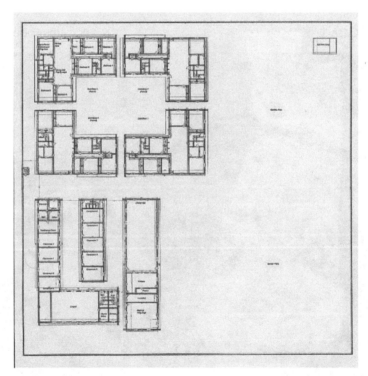

Plot layout of the Guayaramerin Orphanage.

The 4 Casas in the upper corner, Classrooms and Admin building lower left, Chapel in lower left corner. Cafeteria and Maintenance building in the lower middle.

In Bolivia for 6 weeks. On Oct 16, 2006, Gary Zimmerman, LIAIM director and I left to go to Bolivia to spend six weeks working with the Bolivian team. Our main aim was to oversee and continue construction on the orphanage project. I finally got to see the property that was given to LIAIM to build the Orphanage that I was designing.

Sad looking kid doesn't know what to think

On the property there was an old shed like building that a family was living in. Whether they were squatters or what I never found out. They had a young boy and he would look out between the boards to see what was going on. They eventually moved out of the shed which we then used to store our equipment. The young boy looks incredibly sad, and I could not help taking a photo of him.

The crew that Gary had hired to start building the wall around the entire property was busy at work doing just that. It should be pointed out that the need to build the outer wall is because if there was not one, the locals would rob you blind. Gary on previous trips had already started to build the first casa (house). Most of the buildings that one sees around the area are built from bricks if one could afford it because of the millions of termites. Most of these are mound-building termites that one also finds in Africa, Australia.

Building the outer wall

The Sawmill

It so happened that one of the church members owned a sawmill/lumber yard just a few hundred yards down the road from the orphanage. Thus, we had ready access to the lumber that we needed at a particularly good price.

Because we arrived in the rainy season, one of the first things we did was build a canopy over the area where we were going to build trusses. Also, I would like to point out that I had befriended a man by the name of Craig Harrison at Foxworth-Galbraith Lumber Yard Truss Division in Colorado Springs who had a software package that he used to layout trusses for the local builders. He made a set of trusses for me that were needed for the casas as well as some of the other buildings, such as the dining hall the classrooms and the chapel.

Our canopy cover to keep us dry

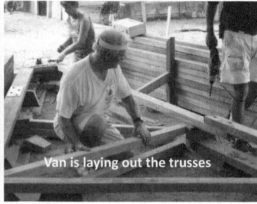
Van is laying out the trusses

After building a number of the trusses they were manually carried by some of the local workers to the first casa and hoisted in place. The lumber that was used was very heavy and not

Carrying the trusses to the casa

Setting the trusses in place

necessarily a standard size like a 2 x 6, etc. But with enough people we got the job done.

Almost the finished product! Now comes the selection of what type of roof tiles we want to use. While we were there we got to see where the bricks that we were using were made by hand.

Casa 1 with most of the trusses in place

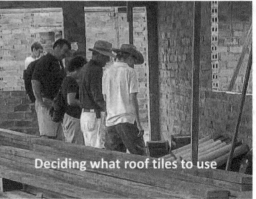
Deciding what roof tiles to use

Making bricks by hand

Oven/Kiln where the bricks are made

Following one of my trips to Bolivia with LIAIM, Gary Zimmerman asked if I could create some **sectional views**. Well, **PUNCH** really did not have that kind of capability. (As we use to say, **"it's all smoke and mirrors!"**). Lying awake at night, thinking "How can I give Gary what he wants and really needs?" I had a thought; I should call **Ken Barker** and find out if he is still in contact with **Jeff Sannes**. A day or two later I called Ken and asked him if he still was in contact with Jeff and he mentioned the fact that he was. They go to the same church, and he would see him that Wed eve. Well, I explained to Ken what I was doing and what I needed. I would send him a package illustrating what I was doing with the **PUNCH** program, and he could grease the skids so to speak with Jeff Sannes. Jeff Sannes had worked for me at MDSI for a short time but went back to the company that I hired him from which was later bought out by Autodesk (Autodesk PowerMill CAM S/W). A week or so later, I called Jeff Sannes and explained what I was doing and what I needed. He went on to tell me that **Autodesk** had just released **Autodesk Architectural Desktop 2007** and Jeff being a semi-wheel in the organization and a strong Christian who believed in mission work could give me a copy of ADT! WOW! I could not believe what I was hearing. So now I have a free copy of the S/W (4 Disc $5-6K) that all of the Architectural firms were using. Now the challenge was to learn how to use it. The Manual is 2100 + pages. Lucky for me, I met a young Christian lady by the name of Sara Hill who was a System Administrator at a local Architectural firm and knew the software in and out. She was willing to help me learn the software. Now I could finally give Gary what he needed. So, in the process of supplying the drawings needed to complete the church in Santa Cruz, I also drew up all of the drawings for the entire Orphanage in Guayaramerin, Bolivia (in the Amazon basin). I have had the good fortune of going to Bolivia 6 times to work and review prints for new buildings, etc. Also, in this same period of time, I was introduced to Ted Locke (Owner/President of a small Architectural firm here in Colorado Springs) who also went to WVC, and he had an **HP DesignJet 800** printer that I could use to print my drawings for the orphanage.

About the time I started to get involved with Global Action, Ted called me and asked me if I was still interested in the HP DesignJet 800. I told him I was, but I could not pay what I thought he wanted since I am retired and trying to get by living on a fixed income. Well, he said that he wanted to give it to me. I said, **"THANK YOU VERY MUCH!"** I was sure I could get one of the mission organizations that I was doing all the drawings for to send him a nice thank you letter.

Now I had the latest and greatest S/W package, namely **Autodesk Architectural Desktop** and a **Hewlett Packard 42" DesignJet 800** printer. I am now in business!

Bolivia team from WVC Spring of 2007

In the spring of 2007, I went back to Bolivia and continued working on the Orphanage. I noticed that Casa 1 was starting to look a lot like the computer rendering. After working there for some time, I returned to Colorado Springs, and I was asked to assemble a mission team from the Colorado Springs area. I had prepared a slide presentation that Dave Wayman, the pastor that was in charge of missions at WVC, allowed me to present to Woodmen Valley Chapel at the 9:00 AM service as well as the 11:00 AM service showing what LIAIM was doing in Bolivia. The presentation went over very well and a number of people wanted to join me in a trip to Bolivia. I did assemble a team from Colorado Springs, most of the people were from Woodmen Valley Chapel, the church that Brenda and I attended from day one after we moved to Colorado Springs. Thus, now I started to hold meetings in my house to inform the volunteers what lay in store for them and what needed to be done before we flew to Bolivia.

Casa 1 roughed in

The 2007 team from WVC

The team that I took Bolivia consisted of: Ashley Musseau, Don Houger, Jean Houger, Paul Kaufer, Bruce Kautz, Katrina Kautz, Glenn Hess and me.

We flew down to Miami, on to La Paz, Bolivia, then on to Santa Cruz where Lucas had arranged transportation to take us to his church for an overnight stay. The following morning, we boarded a small plane and headed to Guayaramerin in the north-east corner of Bolivia, our final destination. Flying from Santa Cruz to Guayaramerin you cross over a lot of the greater Amazon Rainforest. In the photo below you can tell where the real river runs (its muddy) and where the river once ran, but changed its course and is now a captive lake so to speak, cut off from the main river.

Our team on the way to Guayaramerin

A river that had changed its course

Every one of the team members was happy to finally be there and to begin working. Don Houger and I would concentrate on the plumbing and electricity. Bruce Kautz, a doctor, worked at the hospital.

Our team on landing in Guayaramerin

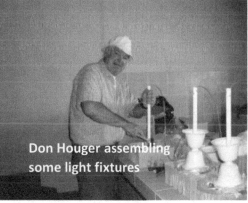
Don Houger assembling some light fixtures

Now that we had a decent system and procedure to build trusses most of the members of the team spent considerable time building trusses. We also took time to see some of the local sights and sounds. We saw locals washing clothes in the river which was remarkably interesting.

Paul Kaufer and Jean Houger assembling trusses

Wash day in one of the local rivers

While their mothers were washing, some of the younger boys caught some small fish and they were eager to show us their catch. The other photo shows the motor bike from the orphanage slightly overloaded.

Showing off their catch

5 is a crowd! Poor bike!

The needed building supplies such as paint, nails, bolts, etc. were mostly purchased across the river in Brazil. It should be pointed out that Guayaramerin is located on the west side of the Mamore River facing the Brazilian city of Guajara-Mirim. It is a port in which there is a permanent port of the Bolivian Navy. Bolivia is a land locked nation, but the river is large enough to support quite large ships. Before we went across the river, we exchanged money.

Don Houger and Paul Kaufer exchanging some money

At the dock ready to go to Brazil

Everyone was extremely interested in going to a local meat market. Most, if not all are open air, no refrigeration, and a fly swatter either in hand or close by. Since a large river was close at hand, there was always fresh fish for-sale.

A typical local meat market

Plenty of fish for-sale

A look inside the local church that donated the small city block in Guayaramerin to LIAIM to build the orphanage.

One of the more common everyday items that is eaten is yucca. The yucca root has a **thick** outer peel that looks similar to the bark of a tree. Yucca has been a staple in the Andean diet for thousands of years. Actually, they are quite good, and we had them most days while we were there.

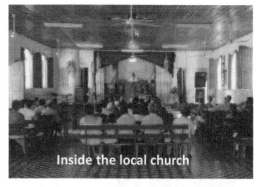
Inside the local church

I personally think they are best when they are fried like French fries. The photo on the right shows a couple out in the jungle grinding a yucca root into a pulp like substance. The man is peddling on a bike turned upside down to turn the grinding wheel where the women is holding the yucca root against the grindstone. Quite clever and ingenious.

Yucca roots/tubers for sale

Grinding yucca roots into a pulp

While the construction crew was busy working on the various phases of the orphanage, Dr. Bruce Kautz was busy at the local hospital doing things only an M.D. can.

Mixing mortar and delivering bricks

Dr. Bruce Kautz examining a small child

Up till now all of the cement for the foundations and the mortar for laying the bricks was mixed by hand. Lucas had ordered a used cement mixer in Santa Cruz, and it was being shipped to Guayaramerin on a boat. This literally took a couple of months to get to its destination. However, it finally arrived. Thus, mixing cement and mortar by hand was a thing of the past. Toward the end of our stay, we had a team photo including most of the local team taken in front of some of the rafters that we had assembled.

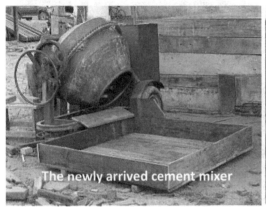
The newly arrived cement mixer

Our team and the local workers

This particular mission trip report would not be complete without pointing out the one particular family that the church was trying to help. The husband of the woman in the photo was killed when a large tree fell on him while harvesting trees in the jungle. Now she had 8 kids to take care of and no husband. Several of the younger kids will wind up at the orphanage when it opens. In the meantime, the church is taking food there, etc. The photo below shows Gary Zimmerman leading our daily morning devotions.

The family that was left behind

Gary leading our morning devotions

A couple more photos of team members hard at work.

Katrina Kautz stenciling

Don Houger and Paul Kaufer cutting the trusses

Jean Houger and Ashley Musseau sawing some lumber

The photo below actually belongs in the following pages but here there was some empty space. To give you an idea of how much paint Don and I used in preparation for Open House in 2008 I've included the photo below.

Empty paint containers

Back in Ann Arbor. 2007 – 9.

The fall of 2007 we wound up going back to Ann Arbor and we stayed with Tim and Char Larsen. We also made a presentation to some of our friends from the Ann Arbor CRC about LIAIM's work in Bolivia. After my presentation I got an email from Vi Kokmeyer stating that she really enjoyed my presentation and would like to send a donation to LIAIM to support the work being done in Bolivia.

Don Houger and Van return to Bolivia to prep for Open House. 2008

May 23, 2008, Don Houger and I flew back to Guayaramerin, Bolivia to work on the orphanage to do what was necessary to get ready for the Open House Ceremony, which was scheduled for Sat, June 14, 2008. We met up with another team in Miami and joined them on the way to Bolivia. That team that we met up with in Miami was only going to be there until June 3. Don and I would remain in Bolivia until Jun18, 2008. Because the classroom buildings were finished, most of the team members stayed in them rather than at the local hotel where we have stayed many times before. This obviously was saving some money that could be better used elsewhere. Since Casa 1 was now finished we would have our meals there. As you can see it had a genuinely nice kitchen area as well as roomy bedrooms.

Casa 1 has a beautiful kitchen

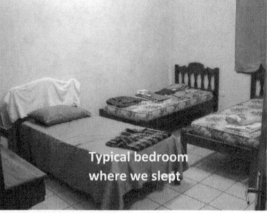
Typical bedroom where we slept

We had our daily devotions led by Gary. The first Sunday we were there we sang the currently popular song, "Amazing Love." at the church. I made a dozen copies before leaving the USA.

Gary leading our daily devotions

The USA team singing "Amazing Love"

Amazing Love

I'm forgiven because you were forsaken
I'm accepted, You were condemned.
I'm alive and well, Your spirit lives within me.
Because You died and rose again

Amazing Love, how can it be?
That You, my King, should die for me.
Amazing Love, I know it's true.
And it's my joy to honor You.
In all I do, I honor You.

A photo of the team members at the start of our trip, as well as all the local workers that were there preparing the orphanage for the Open House.

The USA team

The USA team plus all of the local workers

Some of the shots showing various phases of the preparations that needed to be done. Don had brought along a spray gun and the various attachments and was busy painting the buildings.

Don Houger painting one of the buildings

Van installing a sink

One night while Don and I were there we were in bed and heard some commotion, dogs barking, etc., just outside of the orphanage, but we did not bother to investigate what was causing it. The following morning, we learned what it was all about, and it was because a huge green anaconda snake had crawled past the orphanage and went on to town where someone killed it by beating it with a baseball bat. Some interesting facts; Green Anacondas are one of the largest snakes in the world. Females are considerably larger than males. They can reach lengths of 30 feet (9 meters), diameters of 12 inches (30.5 centimeters) and can weigh 550 pounds (250 kilograms). Green anacondas are native to the northern regions of South America, which is where we were. There was a couple that lived in the area that Lucas had be-friended that take snake skins and other animal skins and make billfolds, etc. out of them. Every team that came to work on the orphanage were given the opportunity to buy something made out of some animal skin.

Van with the green anaconda snake

Don Houger holding a large snake skin

Before Gary set off on this particular trip to Bolivia, he had contacted a firm stateside to make the letters for the sign that was to be placed above the front gate. Don and Katy Geddes had volunteered to come to Bolivia to be LIAIM missionaries to Guayaramerin several years earlier. Don is a retired civil engineer and owned a plane back in the states. Here he is renting a plane to take some photos of the orphanage from above.

Hogar de Andrea Esperanza y Alegría

Gary is pleased with the sign

Don Geddes is being checked out

After Don was checked out and everything appeared to be in order, he flew the plane and took a number of photos. The orphanage was getting close to being ready for open house. As you can see 2 Casas were ready, the office and admin building were ready, another classroom building was ready, and the cafeteria and workshop area were also ready.

The Orphanage from above

Hogar de Andrea de Esperanza y Alegría

The June 2008 team at the main gate

Some photos of the "Andrea's Home of Hope and Joy" open house ceremony.

Townspeople arriving on their motorbikes

Taking the tour

Celebrating with good food

Dining hall set up for the meeting

Typical Classroom

Casa one typical bedroom

When Andrea's Home is completed, it should look something similar to the computer rendering below. There will be up to 6 casas as illustrated in the upper part of the computer rendering. The building in the lower center is the Chapel.

In addition to the orphanage complex in Guayaramerin one of the local church members donated a small farm to "Andrea's Home of Hope and Joy" and when completed will have cows and a garden. LIAIM intended to not only supply the orphanage with milk and vegetables, but open a store to sell milk, vegetables, etc. to the town people. Thus, its LIAIM hope that the orphanage will eventually be somewhat self-supportive.

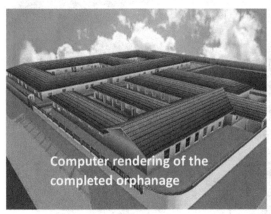
Computer rendering of the completed orphanage

The beginning of the barn

After Don and I returned to Colorado Springs, Gary and Jerri Zimmerman the directors of LIAIM, in their summer addition of the "Love Letter" publication, had a very moving/touching Thank You. It reads as follows:

Dear Van, Big Don, ...

We are writing today to say thank you from two very grateful hearts for your awesome ministry and servant hearts on our June team. God truly put together this special team for the opening of Andrea's Home of Hope and Joy. We are so thankful He was and is in charge.

Van and Don-What a blessing you both were in all your excellent work in electrical, plumbing, and painting for the month you were there. How beautiful all the buildings and walls looked. Van, all your expertise and long hours spent in designing Andrea's Home has come to fruition and this team is just one of many where you have given so generously of your time and talents.

The copy and paste piece below appeared in "The Love Letter" summer of 2009.

I believe the summer of 2009 was the last time I went to Bolivia; however, I continued to convert and fine tune the various drawings to my new software package Autodesk Architectural Desktop 2007.

In the spring of 2009, I had come to the realization that in my design work I was really getting involved. Thus, I took it upon myself to establish a limited liability corporation. I went to a local law firm and on April 21, 2009, I established the firm "Volunteer Design LLC", a Colorado limited liability company.

Urbanes (Van) Van Bemden

Van has been an integral part of Love In Action International Ministries since the year 2000, serving on at least six teams. He and his wife, Brenda, joined a team to Santa Cruz, Bolivia to help build the church in Totaises. During that time, he noticed Gary Zimmerman scratching out a drawing on the wall for the bathrooms of the church and said to him, "Gary, we've got do something better and more professional than this". After that, he purchased software for architectural drawings to begin the design for the remainder of the church and a Sunday School wing When the Love in Action. ministrybegan building the orphanage in Guayaramerin, Van knew what God had in mind for his part in the new ministry. He, together with Gary Zimmerman, designed Andrea's Home of Hope and Joy and is presently working on the design for the barn at the dairy farm. Keep in mind that Van is retired and never before had done anything in the architectural building design field, but he decided to do something significant in his retirement years. Van is now known as Love in Action International Ministries' "**Architectural Design Professional**".

Additionally, I had the lawyer create a boiler plate letter so that for whomever I was doing work for they would fill in the blanks and sign at the bottom.

VOLUNTEER DESIGN llc
URBANES VAN BEMDEN, MANAGER
1835 Sand Rock Point
Colorado Springs, Colorado 80919
Phone (719)528-8489

Date: _____

Dear _____

You have requested that Volunteer Design LLC design blueprints, or plans, for your building project in __(place)_____, known to our company as "_(project)_____".

We design all of our blueprints and plans using commercially available software. To the best of our knowledge structures built following these blueprints or plans will be structurally fit for the use intended. We cannot guarantee, however, and we make no representation that the blueprints or plans will satisfy any level of scrutiny imposed by any governmental or private entity as to any particular standards. We have not and will not perform any research into the particular building requirements of _(place)_____. We are not experts in the area of building design or construction.

In accepting these blueprints by your signature below, you acknowledge that Volunteer Design LLC specifically disclaims any liability for their use, and you hold Volunteer Design LLC harmless for any and all claims arising from the use of these blueprints. Furthermore, you agree to indemnify Volunteer Design LLC for all costs and attorney's fees and settlement costs and award or judgment costs which may be incurred by Volunteer Design LLC due to the use of these plans, whether or not any basis in fact exists for any particular claim, and whether or not a matter is considered for settlement informally or by formal judicial or private dispute resolution processes. Such costs may include, but are not limited to, travel and lodging expenses, expert evaluation and witness fees, costs of settlement, and other foreseeable and unforeseeable costs associated with possible claims arising from the use of these blueprints or plans.

Date: _____

_____
Urbanes Van Bemden, Manager, Volunteer Design LLC

Acknowledged and approved this _____, 20____.

_____
Signature:
Capacity:

On every blueprint/drawing that I created for the various projects I was involved with I had the following disclaimer printed on it:

"PLEASE NOTE these blueprints and plans are intended for informational purposes only. These plans were not designed in accordance with any particular building standards or codes. Volunteer Design LLC makes no representations to their suitability for a particular site or project and specifically disclaims any warranty as to their suitability or adequacy for any particular project. The drafter of these plans has no responsibility or liability for any construction based upon these plans."

I had friends in various fields such as plumbing, electrical, construction, etc. that reviewed and provided guidance to me as I drew up the various plans. I also tried to conform to the local as well as our state building codes. Thus, I believed my plans were more than adequate because these plans/drawings/blueprints were going to such places as Bolivia and India.

I must confess, that on one occasion when I was in India, I pointed out to the general contractor that the column did not live up to what I had on my drawings. However, he did not do anything to fix what I thought and knew was not up to the standard that I wanted.

Global Action–My India mission work.

Global Action. Feb 8, 2006.

During this time when I was doing the drawings for the orphanage for LIAIM, I was also helping our church build houses for **Habitat for Humanity**. It so happened that the person, Earl Bailey from our church, who was heading up our effort at Habitat for Humanity died. So being one of his right-hand men I went to his funeral, Wed, Feb 8, 2006, and at the funeral luncheon I was introduced to **Lars Dunberg**. During the conversation, we had to find out what each of us did for a living. My party line currently was **"As little as possible."** I went on and said, "I **ski** and **hike** a lot and go on **mission trips**. Currently I am working on some drawings for an Orphanage in Bolivia. In fact, I have a model of it out in my car." (The Punch software that I was initially using allowed one to make a **scale model** quite easily). I went to the car and brought it back to the table where we were having lunch and Lars could not believe what he was seeing and hearing because a week or so earlier he sent out an email to some of his contacts and supporters asking if any of them knew of any Christian draftsmen who could put some lines on a piece of paper for the Orphanage that he wanted to build in **Motipur, India.** Now he was sitting across the table from a person doing the very thing he needed to be done. (Lars Dunberg is the president of **Global Action** a worldwide mission organization based in Colorado Springs). He asked me if I was interested and willing to do the same thing for his organization. I told him I would and that was the start of my developing drawings for an Orphanage in Motipur, India. I had the opportunity to travel to India 3 times to review the building site and the drawings/blueprints for the various buildings that were being planned for the Orphanage in Motipur. I also got to visit a half dozen or so of the larger cities such as Delhi, Kolkata, Mumbai, Hyderabad, Bhubaneswar, and Lucknow.

A similar story of how Lars met me is in a book written by Sheeba Subhan and Lars Dunberg named The Road to Motipur. In the book Sheeba and Lars detail what the area around Motipur is like and the obstacles and the difficulties that needed to be overcome to make the India Hope Center a success.

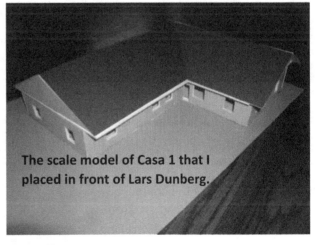

The scale model of Casa 1 that I placed in front of Lars Dunberg.

I believe it was a Wednesday that Brenda and I attended Earl Bailey's funeral. After the funeral luncheon and meeting Lars, we still had some errands to run and so we did and then when we got back home there was a message from Lars on the answering machine where he mentioned that he would like to get together ASAP. Well, I called him and suggested that we meet the next morning. He came over to our house on Sierra Oak and we proceeded to go down to my office, and I cranked up my software and proceeded to rough out an admin building that he had in mind. I have a copy of the original sketch that Lars had drawn up.

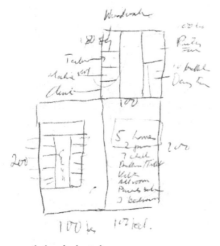

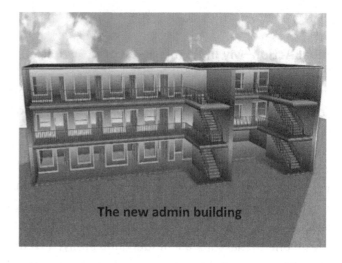

The new admin building

Lars original sketch.

There was a basic church there that had classrooms and bedrooms off to the sides, but it had no roof, no windows, no doors, and no floor. Lars wanted to build a second story on the current structure. Thus, I started to rough out what I envisioned needed to be done to complete the Church building.

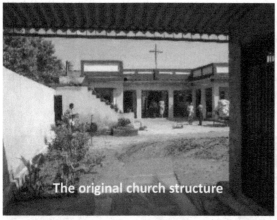

The original church structure

A typical classroom

My first rendering of the additional construction that needed to be done to the church is shown to the right.

Now a combination of the church, administration building, and classrooms was being discussed. I started working on that concept and what you see is my first rendering of this combination.

368

The computer rendering of the combined church, admin building, and classrooms.

Thus, that was what I started out with in the original sketch. But at the end of the first day this is what the first house would look like. 4 small bedrooms, 2 baths, a family room. 1313 Sq. Ft.

House 1313 Sq. Ft.
122 Sq. Meters

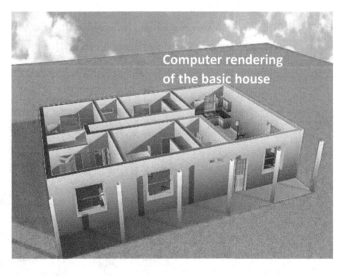

Computer rendering of the basic house

From there I kept massaging the initial design based on input from Lars. The next phase we decided to stack one on top of the other. Now based on the limited size of the property, I started to play around with the concept of a cluster of houses (dormitories) that were like an apartment complex. I now had a house design that Lars and company had bought off on, but it was my job to make it as compact as possible to fit as many into the lot that they were to be built on. Thus, I started working on taking the basic house and flipping it, mirroring it, etc. thus it wound up looking very similar to the computer rendering below.

Cluster of 6 houses

The computer rending is pretty much the way the actual first cluster of houses looks. The exceptions was that the stairways wound up between the set of condos. I spent most of the summer and early fall roughing out various designs for the India Hope Center.

My first trip to India—fall of 2007.

The fall of 2007 Lars wanted me to join him on a trip to India. We would fly into New Delhi and visit the slums where Global Action is serving over 5,000 children weekly in eight different centers. Visiting one of the centers, I can only say I had never seen so many little kids. I had never experienced a slum area like these. Walking down a street (it was what we would call an alley) you saw plastic bags and garbage all over the place and you could not walk anywhere where you did not run into a bunch of holy cows.

Kids at one of Delhi centers

Looking down the alley, waiting for the rest of the team

After visiting one of the Delhi kid's centers we were on our way to Bhubaneswar in the state of Orissa. The state of Orissa is one of the Hindu strongholds in India. Here, Global Action decided to invite young Christians together to what they called a "New Generation Youth Event," where they train young people in living for Jesus Christ and sharing their faith with non-Christian friends. They had planned for 1,000 delegates but people kept coming to register until 2,300 people had done so. Obviously, I did not understand any of the speakers other than Lars and Rick Thompson. But I enjoyed the enthusiasm that the crowd displayed. I could not image how they intended to feed all the people that attended this event.

Lars speaking to the crowd

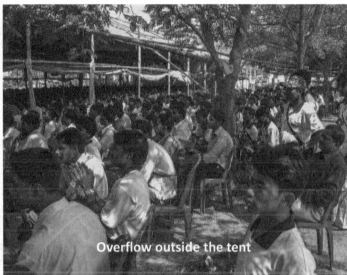
Overflow outside the tent

Watching the volunteers prepare the meals was remarkably interesting. Watching several workers carry the large pots that must have weighed a hundred pounds or more, tipping them on the side and letting the fluid run on the ground was something to behold. I believe the US health department would have shut them down in a minute.

Draining the excess liquid from the hundreds of chicken wings
Preparing the veggies

Luckily, we had a lodge that we could go to and relax. We also did not have to eat with the 2300 delegates in that we had a dining hall apart from the attendees where the event leaders could eat and relax. We did eat what the group in general were eating. But for the Yankees we had knives and forks.

Sheeba Subhan does not need a fork or a knife

Van having lunch

While we were in town, we got to do some sight-seeing and visited some incredibly old buildings and temples.

MUKTESWARA AND SIDHESWARA
THE MUKTESWARA ASSIGNABLE TO THE MIDDLE OF THE 9TH CENTURY A.D IS ONE OF THE MOST REFINED TEMPLES IN ORISSA ON ACCOUNT OF ITS ELEGANT PROPORTIONS AND DELICATE CARVINGS THE TEMPLE OF THE SIDHESWARA, APPROXIMATELY DATABLE TO 10TH CENTURY A.D HAS A TYPICAL ORISSA FORM IN THE DEVELOPED FEATURES OF THE COMPONENT.

Photos of several of the Temples in the state of Orissa built during the 9th-10th century.

We now flew on to Kolkata. The city of Kolkata (Calcutta) was viewed as the armpit of the world, the black hole, the place of despair. It is still all of that for millions of people. But here and there are some bright rays of light, as God takes people who are faithful to Him and uses them to impact the lives of others. Global Action has five outlets doing various activities such as day school, Sunday school for children, etc. We got to see where Mother Teresa lived and worked. Mother Teresa was the founder of the Order of the Missionaries of Charity, a Roman Catholic congregation of women dedicated to helping the poor. I remember walking down the alley to visit her Order, I could not help but notice a sign as well as the flag strung across the alley for the communist party headquarters in the city of Kolkata. We also visited Carey Baptist church in Kolkata.

After visiting Kolkata, we flew on to Lucknow spent the night, and the following morning we got

At Mother Teresa

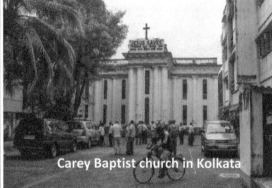
Carey Baptist church in Kolkata

into several vehicles and were on our way to Motipur. I think most people have never heard of the village of Motipur. Most will have a hard time pronouncing it correctly. It is not even on the map. It is a dirty little village about 20 miles from the Nepal border in northern India.

After a 6 hour rib-jolting ride dodging everything from dogs to cows to on-coming (I mean right in your lane kind of on-coming) trucks, we arrived in Motipur. Three times we had to stop to repair the same tire. Though the monsoons were over, it still rained, and the place was filled with mud, sludge, and trash.

On the way there we stopped along the road to eat breakfast, but they really weren't ready for us since they just opened. However, we were hungry so we just waited until they were ready.

Waiting for the Café to cook our breakfast

Looks like they are making progress

Everyone did finally get their breakfast. Once again, we were on our way only to be stopped by one of the water buffalo not wanting to get out of the middle of the road.

Everyone did get breakfast

Please move!

I could not get over the way they overloaded their wagons and had the poor little horses pull them down the road. There were several times when I literally saw those little horses get lifted off of their feet because the balance wasn't quite right. As we got closer to the village of Motipur I noticed some brick layer working on a multi-story building. I could not help but notice the way they build a scaffolding.

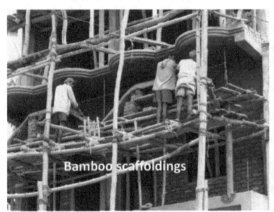
Bamboo scaffoldings

A small horse pulling a big load

The Hope Center – Motipur.
Well, we finally arrived at "The Hope Center" in Motipur. Now I saw for the first time the condition of the complex that I was asked to revise and make livable. It had rained the night before and things were a little damp. There were mud puddles all over the place.

The entrance to the courtyard

Looking into the courtyard. The kitchen and the café in the background

That evening a typical Indian meal was well received by a bunch of hungry team members. The kids had their meal in the cafeteria as you can see. They did not get what we got!

The team having dinner in the church foyer

The kids in the open-air cafeteria

The photo below is a view of INSIDE the church. No roof, dirt floor, etc. Also, the kitchen area.

Inside the church

Looking into the kitchen area

Here are some of the orphans getting ready to sing for us. A photo of most of the staff currently at "The Indian Hope Center." Notice that the kids are all dressed alike. That eliminated a potential problem of jealousy if some kids were better dressed that others. I never did have a long and serious conversation with any of the staff members.

The children in Motipur love singing songs

The staff at Motipur

The rooms off on the side of the church were used by the orphans as sleeping quarters, etc. Also, a photo of the generator that was used for an hour or two in the morning and evening.

Typical orphan's room

The generator

The Hope Center also had a small buggy that they went to town in to get supplies, etc. One night while we were there we had a meeting in a tent in the village square. Lars had a hard time convincing the Village Chief our intentions were authentic and real. Since this was a Muslim area, we Christians were not well received. We had several run-ins with the village chief during my visits to Motipur.

The Hope Center's only means of transportation

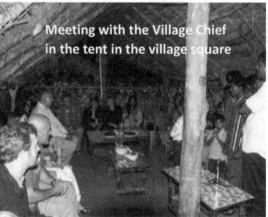

Meeting with the Village Chief in the tent in the village square

Sometimes the locals would dig up the only road leading to the center to keep the traffic from going in and out. Finally, Supratim Dey met with the local forest officials to seek their assistance to prevent this from happening. The locals were somehow impressed by the fact that we never retaliated, but that the staff helped to fill in the ditches dug across the pathway. Each morning the children line up in the courtyard for prayer, singing, etc.

The children in formation in the courtyard

India–2008. I did not go to India in 2008. However, I was busy designing the school and hospital buildings that Lars envisioned being built there in the future when more land became available. As you can see below, the construction of the first housing complex (the 6 plex) had begun.

Starting the first 6 plex

Another view of the 6 plex

My third trip to India, Oct 19, 2009.

On my return trip to India in 2009, Lars and I flew from Denver to New Delhi. Once we checked into the hotel, we were on our own to do some sightseeing. So, I grabbed my camera and hit the streets so to speak. One of the more famous war memorials in Delhi is the India Gate. When I got there, they were just finishing with a ceremony. Nearby is another famous structure called Amar Jawan Jyoti which consist of a marble pedestal with a cenotaph on its top.

India Gate

Finishing a ceremony

Amar Jawan Jyoti

From the India Gate we toured the government of India area. i.e., the Parliament. Parliament is the supreme legislative body of India. The Indian Parliament is comprised of the President and the two Houses - Rajya Sabha (Council of States) and Lok Sabha (House of the People). The President has the power to summon and terminate either House of Parliament or to dissolve Lok Sabha.

A government building in New Delhi

A government bldg.

2009 team

The young lady drawing the attention of the young men

There are many ways of getting around and an extremely popular means is either by a scooter or motorcycle. Sometimes you see an entire family on one scooter or cycle. Other common means of transportation are bike rickshaws.

A family on a scooter

Bike rickshaw (Taxi) and a Freight transport

After lunch we were on our way to visit one of the many Global Action Children Centers. Just like my first trip to India I discovered that most of these Global Action Children Centers are in the slum areas. Going down the alleys one see a terrible sight with all of the junk, plastic bags, garbage, etc.

A half-dozen sacred cows resting in the garbage

Some of the children in one of the centers

Also, until this trip I never witnessed in person a young boy playing his little flute with a cobra snake performing for the onlookers. What a way to make a living. I don't believe I want to pet the snake even if it is in a trance state.

A deadly cobra

The next morning we flew to Lucknow. Then drove on to Motipur. Travelling along the streets and roads on the way to Motipur we passed an India school bus taking a bunch of kids to school. Further down the road we saw a rolled over truck. People were salvaging what they could. The highways in India are extremely dangerous!

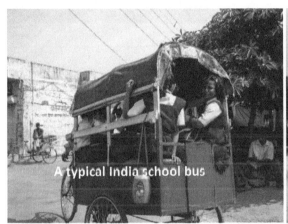
A typical India school bus

A rolled over truck along the highway

All the way along the roadside you find many small stalls selling produce and almost anything that a person needs to support daily life. Well, it was lunch time so now we are looking for a place to eat. We found one that could accommodate our small group. They even had fresh unpasteurized milk in that they had a few cows tied up in the back of the lunchroom.

A typical roadside scene

There were several cows in the back of the restaurant

As I was walking around during a lunch stop, I could not get over the scene of this family living under a tarp. This was not an out of the ordinary scene, it was everywhere. We finally arrived in the village of Motipur. Below is a typical scene along the main street of Motipur.

A family living under a tarp

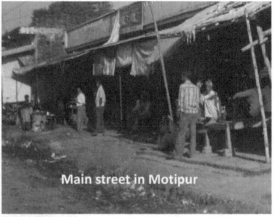

Main street in Motipur

Another couple of views of Main Street in Motipur.

A view of main street in Motipur

Main street in Motipur

When we arrived at the "India Hope Center" Daniel Subhan was in the process of having the children go thru their morning routine. Later that morning, the various leaders took the group to let them look at their future new housing/dormitories.

Going thru their daily routine

Marching over to their future new housing

Their first look at where they will eventually be staying. The workers that the contractor had hired were hard at work building the 6ft high brick wall around the plot of land where the housing complex was being built.

The first 6 plex is looking good

Hard at work building the 6ft high brick wall

All the bricks used are locally hand made at a large furnace and brought to the building site with a tractor and trailer. The reader of this script probably did not know I know how to lay bricks. In my teen-age years I worked several summers for brick layers!

A tractor delivering another load of bricks

Van laying some bricks

A bit later that morning Lars and I met with the village chief to try to get him to see the good that Global Action was trying to do for the community. He brought along many of the village women.

Lar's meeting with the village

Lars meeting with the Village

Van, Rick Thompson and the Village Chief

I believe it was on this trip that we were trying to convince the Village Chief we needed additional land so we could build a hospital so that the women would not have to travel several hours to the nearest hospital to give birth. In the photo below you can see that we are discussing what additional property we would like to purchase to build the hospital. We are looking at a plot map of the surrounding area. It seemed the village chief had complete control as to what happened in the community. I was just amazed that most of the work was very manual labor. Even mixing the cement was done by hand. No portable cement mixer and certainly no cement trucks like you see in the states. Additionally, I could not get over the fact that women were doing most of the heavy lifting at our site. Carry bricks and motor on top of their heads.

Looking over the community plot map

Carrying a heavy load

Boys doing their Algebra assignment

Starting to cook the noon meal

Back at the Hope Center, kids were busy studying, and the women were starting to fix lunch.

One time we went to town to get some more chicken meat. Some of the boys got to go along and see what was happening. We stopped at the local butcher shop and got them to butcher a couple of live chickens for us. I swear that every chicken in the Motipur area must have 4 necks because every time I ate lunch all I got was a piece or two of neck.

The boys are enjoying the ride into town

Working on our order

It appears that they are enjoying butchering the chickens as well as having their picture taken. Riding the bikes along the main street in Motipur. Note all of the filth that is swept into the street.

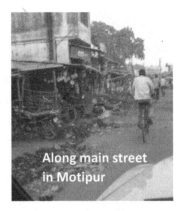
Along main street in Motipur

Here I am discussing with the Village Chief the need for additional property so we could build the Hospital which I had designed and had a scale model of.

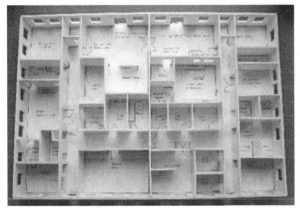
Scale model of the Hospital.

Discussing the Hospital with the Village Chief.

One day during my stay we went to one of the nearby villages and conducted a blanket distribution. In this part of India, it does get cold, and a nice wool blanket is a well-received gift. Daniel Subhan introduced our team and then some of the children from the India Hope Center sang a song or two. I do not recall how many blankets we had with us, but as you can see there were quite a few. Following the introduction and the singing each of the team members got to give a blanket to the people who had a need for one.

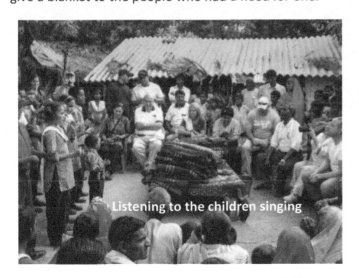
Listening to the children singing

Van giving a blanket to a lady who was very thankful

Trying to get the alligator to show its head

Van has the alligator by its tail

Another exciting thing happened during this trip, the locals had seen a young alligator in a nearby ditch. This was quite unusual in that there supposedly were no alligators in this area. Anyway, we hopped into our vehicle and proceeded to where they had spotted it. They poked around in the water and finally it came out and made a run for it. They slowed it down and trapped it. Then I grabbed it by its tail. Now some of the locals saw me do this and now everybody wanted their picture taken while they were grabbing the alligator tail.

Van holding one of the silkworms

A silkworm spinning a cocoon

Another nearby side trip that I was privileged to make was to see a silkworm enterprise.

The man on the left is cutting up Mulberry leaves to feed to the silkworms. The photo on the right shows Van feeding Mulberry leaves to the silkworms. There are

Van feeding the silkworms

hundreds of silkworms in each wooden tray stacked on the racks.

During my 2 week stay in India, I got the opportunity to also visit Nepal several times. The time we crossed a floating bridge to cross the border we encountered this beautiful lady who was wearing all of her earthly possession in the form of gold. I asked her if I could take her picture and she obliged.

I cannot leave the India Hope Center before I say something about my 4 star accommodations. I had a private room and 2 hr. of electricity daily to recharge my laptop. I had a mosquito net over my bed. Also, I had a bathroom area with a toilet but no running water. However, I had several pails

A beautiful
Nepal woman

that I would fill with water from a hand pump, then I could dump it into the toilet and that is how I flushed it.

My plush bed with a mosquito net

My work area

Sink and countertop

These two photos show what my bathroom facilities looked like. There was no running water and every time I needed to flush the toilet, I simply dumped a pail of water down it. Thus, every day I would use the hand pump and pump several pails full of water so I would be ready to flush the toilet if needed.

The toilet and pails

Leaving the India Hope Center we were off to Lucknow. On the way back to Lucknow we encountered several bad accidents along the road as well as getting a flat tire which we had to change. However, we found out that our driver really did not have the proper tools to change a flat tire. We had to make do with what he had which was a small tool pouch which contained a couple of screwdrivers and a couple of open-end wrenches. As Lars said on every trip that I took to India, India is a dangerous place to drive!

Van helping to fix a flat tire

A wrecked SUV

A truck hauling wood did not make it

Once we were on the road again, we saw several teams of water buffalo pulling a large wagon loaded with sugar cane on the way to the sugar cane processing plant. In Lucknow I got a photo of a man powered rickshaw.

Water buffalo pulling a wagon loaded with sugar cane

A man powered rickshaw

From Lucknow a couple of us from the team flew on to New Delhi. The following morning we were taken to Agra where the Taj Mahal is located and which we all wanted to see before we left India.

My visit to Taj Mahal, Oct 28, 2009.

This is what Wikipedia has to say about Taj Mahal. The **Taj Mahal** (/ˌtɑːdʒ məˈhɑːl, ˌtɑːʒ-/; lit. 'Crown of the Palace')[4][5][6] is an Islamic ivory-white marble mausoleum on the right bank of the river Yamuna in Agra, Uttar Pradesh, India. It was commissioned in 1631 by the fifth Mughal emperor, Shah Jahan (r. 1628–1658) to house the tomb of his favourite wife, Mumtaz Mahal; it also houses the tomb of Shah Jahan himself. The tomb is the centrepiece of a 17-hectare (42-acre) complex, which includes a mosque and a guest house, and is set in formal gardens bounded on three sides by a crenellated wall.

Construction of the mausoleum was essentially completed in 1643, but work continued on other phases of the project for another 10 years. The Taj Mahal complex is believed to have been completed in its entirety in 1653 at a cost estimated at the time to be around ₹32 million, which in 2020 would be approximately ₹70 billion (about US $1 billion). The construction project employed some 20,000 artisans under the guidance of a board of architects led by Ustad Ahmad Lahauri, the emperor's court architect. Various types of symbolism have been employed in the Taj to reflect natural beauty and divinity.

The Taj Mahal was designated as a UNESCO World Heritage Site in 1983 for being "the jewel of Muslim art in India and one of the universally admired masterpieces of the world's heritage". It is regarded by many as the best example of Mughal architecture and a symbol of India's rich history. The Taj Mahal attracts more than 6 million visitors a year[3] and in 2007, it was declared a winner of the New 7 Wonders of the World (2000–2007) initiative.

When we got to Agra we had to take a camel ride. After the camel ride we toured some of the other temples and monuments like Jama Masjid Mosque, Fatehpur Sikri, and Jama Masjid before we went to Taj Mahal. It is hard to comprehend some of the detail in these mosque/temples, etc. It must have taken hours and hours.

Our camel ride

Jama Masjid Mosque

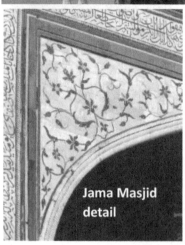
Jama Masjid detail

Now on to the one and only Taj Mahal which is perhaps like no other building in the world.

The one and only Taj Mahal

The hand carved detail in the Taj Mahal marble is incredible as seen above.

After visiting Taj Mahal, it was back to New Delhi for a good night's sleep before I boarded the plane to fly back to the good old USA. This trip to India was my 3rd and last trip there. Although I continued to design other buildings, such as a high school, dining hall, welding shop, staff housing, etc. I eventually stopped doing design work for Global Action because Lars Dunberg left the organization that he started, and I was never contacted by the new management. Thus, I do not know whether the project continued or not.

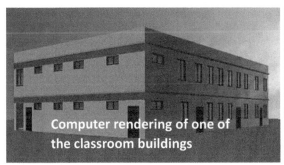

Computer rendering of one of the classroom buildings

Computer rendering of the staff housing unit

Below is a section out of the India Hope Center report giving the readers an idea what is happening at the Motipur "India Hope Center".

Building Update

On March 9th we had the privilege of having Urbanes Van Bemden, also known as Van, come and help with some of the pre-building plans for the children's homes at the India Hope Center! Van lives in Colorado and is no novice when

Urbanes Van Bemden

it comes to building orphanages. He is not only helping with our center but is also helping build an orphanage in Bolivia! This was his second trip to India. Even though Van is retired, you won't see him just sitting around at home. When he is not climbing mountains, he loves to be involved in missions work as well! For two weeks, Van was able to stay here at the Hope Center to work out the drawings he has made for the

Construction Work

housing project, and was also able to spend time with the kids and encourage them. We were very blessed by his humble heart and willingness to serve. His passion and zeal were an inspiration to us all! The two week trip was overall successful, and has given us a good place to start for building, as well as what steps we need to take next!

This concludes the Volume 1 of 2 of Van's Memories.

Volume 2 from a time line is a continuation of Volume 1.

Made in the USA
Monee, IL
31 July 2024

63023275R00223